JEWS IN
LATIN AMERICA

Jews in

Latin America

Jacob Beller

JONATHAN DAVID PUBLISHERS • New York

To My Dear Wife

R A C H E L

With Love

CONTENTS

CONTENTS—continued

Preface

My knowledge of South America is of long standing. I resided there for many years and after a long absence, re-visited the continent several times. The first of these visits took place in 1946. Starting from Mexico I traversed the continent as far as Bolivia, using all modes of transportation, from jet planes, modern boats, trains and busses to primitive canoes and donkeys. Four times I crossed the mighty snow-capped Andes and Cordillera mountains at a height of more than 30,000 feet, and traveled by train with the Transandino from Chile to Argentina, through one of the longest mountain tunnels in the world. On another occasion I traveled the same route by car, from Santiago to Mendoza. With a plane from Buenos Aires, I landed in the airport of La Paz at an altitude of 14,500 feet, the highest city of this hemisphere; from there I went to the waste districts of Bolivia which might be called the end of the world.

"One cannot travel any further," is the inscription on a post in the out-of-the-way town of Cochabamba. There, not far from a range of mountains which seem, indeed, to mark the end of the world, one finds a small Jewish community of several hundred souls who lead a Jewish life and have their own synagogue.

As one travels through the deserts of Ecuador, Peru and Venezuela for thousands of miles one sees only sandy rocks, extensive wastelands without any sign of human life. Then pueblos (villages) suddenly emerge out of the desert—and one finds Jews living there. Widely scattered as they are, the Jews of these isolated places meet periodically and maintain communicable bonds. They have built Jewish homes on whose walls hang pictures of the Gaon of Vilna or of Theodor Herzl, and each of them has a blue and white Jewish National Fund box.

I once had the honor of serving as *sandek* at the *b'rit milah* of a child in such a distant town. The *mohel* flew a distance of 1,000 miles from a larger Jewish community. The boy was named Israel, in honor of the Jewish State.

In Arequipa, a small town near the Cordillera mountains on the boundary between Peru and Chile, not far from Cuzco—the most beautiful spot in the world—live ten Jews. One Friday night I was the guest of this remarkable *minyan* in their synagogue. I came across the same kind of *minyan* in Callao, the university city of Peru, and in dozens of other places in Latin America.

In order to reacquaint myself thoroughly with the conditions of life in Latin American countries since the time I had left them, I did not limit my visits to short stays and superficial observations. My first post-war visit lasted more than one year and the second more than two years.

It is difficult to follow the political developments in many of these countries because of the rapid changes of government. But irrespective of the specific changes, the basic causes which are responsible for them remain the same. I endeavored, therefore, to concentrate my observations and studies upon the fundamental problems of the countries, and to relate the political developments to these problems.

I had interviews with heads of states, political leaders, and spokesmen of the Catholic Church, seeking in particular their views on Jewish questions. Jewish life, too, is subject to changes in response to changing political conditions. For example, Jews exposed to anti-Semitic pressures in one country will migrate to a neighboring land and then, once conditions have improved, return to their home country. I had long talks with Jewish leaders, attended Jewish communal meetings and spoke to innumerable individual Jews, accumulating an enormous amount of information.

In South America there are more than 800,000 Jews. About half of them live in Argentina, 160,000 in Brazil, 50,000 in Uruguay, 40,000 in Chile, 12,000 in Venezuela, 8,000 in Colombia, 5,000 in Peru, 3,000 in Bolivia, and about the same number in Ecuador. The remainder is scattered throughout Paraguay, the

Central American states of Panama, Costa Rica, San Salvador
and Nicaragua, as well as the West Indies.

In 1953, my book, *Across Twenty Latin American Countries,*
was published in Yiddish in Buenos Aires. In 1955 the Jewish
Cultural Congress in New York awarded it the Surovitch Prize.

In 1960 I revisited South America as correspondent of *The
Globe and Mail of Toronto,* and the *Jewish Daily Forward* of
New York. In 1968 I again visited some of these countries and
brought my material on general and Jewish life up to date.

This volume provides historical background information about
the Jews in South America. There were three periods of Jewish
settlement in Latin America, beginning with the Spanish Conquistadores in the 15th and 16th centuries, among whom were
many Marranos. They came to the New World, primarily, with
the hope of practicing the religion of their fathers freely. But
the cruel arm of the Inquisition reached across the ocean, with the
result that today only a few, obscure traces of this migration remain. The second wave of Jewish settlement, which dates from
the 18th century, faced a similar fate of assimilation and extinc-
tion.

The historians who have dealt with this subject in the past are
referred to in this volume, and those seeking additional information of a historical nature may turn to these sources. It is difficult,
however, to produce an accurate and coherent picture of early
Jewish life in Latin America, for the conclusions reached and
even the source material used by various historians are often
contradictory. Undoubtedly, this is due to the fact that despite the
wealth of material originally available, many of the documents
and records gathered dust in museums and archives for hundreds
of years, and were subjected to the ravages of time. Often dates
and names are illegible. Other documents were willfully distorted
at the hands of men who wished to hide unpleasant facts.

I wish to conclude by expressing my heartfelt thanks to my
friends who helped in the translation of this book. I am particularly grateful to Mr. B. G. Kayfetz of the Canadian Jewish

Congress, to the well-known writer Joseph Leftvich, and to my dear wife, to whom this book is dedicated, and who spared no time or effort to make its publication a reality and a success.

This book has been published with the help of a grant from the Social Science Research Council of Canada, using funds provided by the Canada Council and the Canadian Jewish Congress, to whom I am truly thankful.

JACOB BELLER

JEWS IN
LATIN AMERICA

CHAPTER I.

The Marranos of Spain, Portugal and South America: Yesterday and Today

It is understandable why so many Marranos came to the New World. The discovery of new continents took place at the very time when Spain and Portugal were persecuting the Jews and "New Christians" (outward Christians who, in private, observed Judaism). In the same month in which the Spanish King and Queen ordered all professing Jews to be expelled from their dominions, Columbus wrote in his journal, "They gave me the order to prepare an expedition of suitable men to seek new territories."

A substantial number of those involved in the New World explorations were Marranos. Indeed, there is some (disputed) evidence pointing to a Marrano origin for Columbus. There is no doubt, however, that there were many Marranos in his expeditions. It was due to the persuasion of two influential Marranos, Luis de Santagel, the royal treasurer, and Gabriel Sanchez, treasurer of Aragon, that the Queen took Columbus' plan seriously. One of the few "authentic' Christians involved in the plans was the royal secretary, Juan de Coloma, whose wife was of Marrano origin. Both the expedition's physician and the interpreter, Luis de Torres, were Marranos or of Marrano parentage, and the first crew member who sighted land was a Marrano, Rodrigo de Triago.

The Marranos, on their part, feeling that they had much to gain by gambling for a new-found freedom, were ready for any risk. Their hope was that in the territories of the New World they would be far from the ever-present eye of the Inquisition, and would be free to practice their faith. Moreover, both the Spanish and Portuguese monarchs gave certain concessions to those Marranos willing to settle in the New World, and even negotiated franchises with those who would battle with the Indians and annex new territories for the Crown. In the year 1509, in the city of Seville, an agreement was completed between the New Christians and the Spanish Crown by which, in payment of the sum of 20,000 ducats, they were free to travel to the newly discovered colonies and to carry on trade for two years. There were many such contracts entered into.

The Marrano, Fernando Noronha negotiated with the King of Portugal on behalf of a group of Marranos in 1506. These chose to go to Brazil where, for one year, they would be freed from taxation on a territory of a thousand quintales which they would cultivate. In the second year they would pay one sixth of the normal tax. The Marranos actually were the first to cultivate sugar plantations in the New World. An island 300 miles from Belem, in Brazil, today bears the name of its founder, Fernando Noronha.

But in the New World, too, the Marranos were disappointed in their hope that there they would be far from the watchful eyes of the Inquisition; that they would find peace and refuge and be able to practise their religion. The fury of the Inquisition pursued them to the New World. Spain set up its tribunal in the Viceroy's capital of Lima, in Mexico City, and in Cartagena in Colombia, with Inquisitorial commissioners or commissars in all neighboring countries. These agents began their hunt for all Marranos suspected of the illegal practice of Judaism.

Whereas the Spanish Inquisition tribunals carried out trials against the accused on-the-spot, and burned the victims at *auto da fe,* the Brazilian Inquisition sent the accused to Portugal where they were put on trial and condemned.

Despite the persecution and the tortures, to this day, four hundred years later, one can find traces of that martyrology not only in the museums and archives, but even in living vestiges of their culture in many South American countries. Jewish prayers, and knowledge of Jewish festivals, have been handed down from one generation to the next, and have been retained over the years in garbled form. To this day, it is possible to find in the distant corners of Latin America groups, which have their own houses of prayer, and proclaim that they are descendants of the Marranos of old.

Before World War II large numbers of laborers used to come from Portugal to Brazil to help bring in the coffee harvest. The Brazilian government allowed these workers to accumulate money, up to a certain sum, and take it back to Portugal. This would be repeated each season, year in and year out.

In 1927, when I was in a remote section of Brazil, Jewish *clientel'chiks,* as they are called, i.e. peddlers who sell their wares among the workers, told me that there were among the workers some whom the others called *Judeus,* and that these had even asked the peddlers if they knew the whereabouts of a synagogue. Filled with curiosity, I arranged to meet some of these workers, who said they came from Braganca, Portugal. They said they observed the Jewish laws and even recited a prayer in Portuguese mixed with half-recognizable Hebrew words. Instead of *k'vodo,* they said *kebrado.* They told me that there were such groups in a number of provinces which observe Jewish festivals and Jewish laws.

From that point my curiosity grew, and I decided to visit Portugal to become acquainted with these descendants of the Marranos whom the Portuguese still call, "Cristaos Novos" (New Christians). Arriving in Lisbon I met Samuel Schwartz, an engineer, the discoverer of these Marranos. He wrote a book about them in Portuguese, *Los Cristaos Novos em Portugal no Secolo 20,* which, translated into English is, *New Christians in Portugal in the Twentieth Century.*

At that time, an effort was being made to restore the Marranos to the Jewish people by a captain, Arturo Carlos de Barros Basto, of the Portuguese army. Basto's parents were Marranos who secretly practiced Jewish rituals. Even as a youth, he felt the urge to return to his source, Judaism.

During the First World War, while stationed with a Portuguese army unit in France, he became acquainted with Jews.

3

Upon his return to Portugal, he began to study Hebrew, and then turned to the Jewish community of Lisbon and asked to be circumcized and converted to Judaism. He was turned down. But he persevered, and eventually went to Tangier, in North Africa, where he was converted. He adopted the name Abraham ben Rosh, married a girl of a rabbinic family, Azankut, and wrote a series of books and articles, some in Hebrew.

Abraham ben Rosh returned to Oporto, and there established a center for the full return of the Marranos to the religion and people of their fathers. He published a journal for the Marranos named, *HaLapid,*—The Torch. In our conversation, he told me that there were some thirty thousand Marranos in Portugal, many of them living in the area of Tras-os-Montes, and that he had taken upon himself the mission of organizing them. Before the expulsion of the Jews from Portugal, Tras-os-Montes was a spiritual Jewish center. Baruch Spinoza was born there. In the year 1388 it had a flourishing synagogue.

The news about the mass return of the Marranos spread quickly throughout the Jewish world. A pro-Marrano committee, under the leadership of the well-known philanthropists, Lucien Wolf and Wilfred Samuel, was established in London. Similar committees began to function in America and in other countries. The noted philanthropist, Eliya Kadoory of India, built a synagogue for the Marranos in Oporto. It is called Mekor Chaim Kadoory, and still exists.

The rabbi of Lisbon, at that time, Dr. Menahem Disendruck, who is now rabbi of Sao Paulo, Brazil, conducted the dedication ceremonies. He offered a memorial prayer for all the martyred victims of the Inquisition who had died for the sanctification of God's name. At a poignant moment in the ceremony, a Scroll of the Torah which originally had belonged to the pre-Marrano congregation of Oporto, was placed in the Holy Ark. It had been saved some four hundred years earlier by a Jewish family that fled Portugal and settled in London. They had kept this scroll as an heirloom throughout the centuries. Captain Arturo de Barros Basto Abraham ben Rosh became the first president of the new congregation of former Marranos.

Additional congregations were soon established in Belmonte, Beira-Baixa, Braganza, Covilhao and Villa Real. For the first time these descendants of Marranos observed Yom Kippur on the correct date, the tenth of Tishri, and not on the eleventh as they had done for so long out of fear of the Inquisition.

Soon, a school was established in Oporto. It was named Rosh Pina. Its purpose was to train religious functionaries to serve the needs of the new Jews. The pro-Marrano committee of Holland sent a Cantor-*Shochet* by the name of Jacob Shababa. The English committee sponsored a spiritual leader, Rabbi Shalom Treistman of Poland, and the Turkish committee also sent a Cantor-*Shochet* by the name of Rabbi Baruch ben Jacob.

Yet, when I revisited Lisbon recently, I found the local Jews as uninformed about the Marranos as they were during my first visit. I was told that even today, on the High Holy Days, some Marranos visit the synagogue and leave immediately after the service, without any attempt at communication being made between them and other Jews.

The synagogues of Belmonte, Braganza, Beira-Baixa and Covilhao no longer exist. All that remains is the Mekor Chaim Kadoory synagogue in Oporto, which is now a tourist attraction. The Portuguese guide takes the visitor through the synagogue and library, just as his Spanish counterpart in Cordova does, and lets you touch the scrolls of the Torah and look at the books in the library.

Why did this movement end in such failure? From the Jews of Lisbon no answer is forthcoming. But in speaking to various individuals who were active in the movement years ago, I was given various, often conflcting, interpretations. Some think that the Jews abroad did not do enough to sustain the fledgling project, while others suggest the very opposite—because too much attention and publicity was given by the Jews of the world, the movement suffered irreparable damage. It is interesting to note that when Samuel Schwartz published his book on the Marranos, some objected. They felt that the publicity would be harmful to their cause.

But the truth of the matter lies along other lines: The truth is that the Catholic Church resented the movement. When the Marrano's return to Judaism began to involve military officers, bankers, and high municipal officials, the Church found itself in an increasingly awkward position. Not only would this return to their ancient religion highlight the cruel religious persecution of the Jews in the past, but it would also reflect upon the holding power of the Church which, despite all the centuries of Christian indoctrination, could not draw in the Marranos.

But the movement is not dead. There are still groups of Marranos in remote corners of Portugal that celebrate Jewish festivals and ceremonies. One such group is in Belmonte. A number of their members still observe such rituals as lighting candles on Friday night, and refraining from eating pork.

Despite the fact that the great earthquake that hit Lisbon in the year 1755 destroyed most of the documents of the Inquisition, material relating to this chapter of Jewish martyrology is preserved in the Ethnological Museum, the National Museum and the Museum Torre de Tombo. The church, de la Carmo, is a significant storehouse of information. In these archives the student of history will find minutes of inquisitional proceedings against Jews and Marranos, accusations and sentences. It also has relics of synagogues, torn sheets of Torah scrolls and hundreds of prayers written by the tortured victims in which they express their tribulations and consolations. These prayers, listed by number, are part of the "evidence" the Inquisition used in its accusations to prove the stubborness of the Jews. Some of them were deliberately smuggled out of the prison cells by spies in order to trap the suspected Jews.

In Plaza Rossio, in the center of the city, not far from the royal palace, there took place in the year 1506 a slaughter of Jews that lasted three full days. Two thousand Jews perished at the sword in the presence of many noblemen.

A reminder of the Inquisition tribunal was destroyed in the famous earthquake of 1755, then replaced by a theatre, and now the site of a monument to the Portuguese playwright, Vincenty Bill, considered the father of the Portuguese drama. He was so popular that King Joao (John) of the sixteenth century offered to perform in one of his plays.

Libraries and museums have preserved thousands of documents from the archives of the Inquisition telling of Marranos who were brought from Brazil to appear before the Portuguese Inquisition where they were to face trial for adherence to Jewish practices. Two of these protocols are quite interesting. They tell the story of a trial against two men which provoked wide public reaction in Portugal and abroad.

One of these two men was Duarte Silva, the king's financial adviser. He was sent abroad by the king in order to purchase boats for an expedition to Brazil for the purpose of dislodging the Dutch. His arrest by the Inquisition on the ninth of December, 1647, caused a panic in international financial circles, and depressed the value of the Portuguese currency. Silva was kept in prison and tortured for five years, and only after he admitted his "mistakes" and asked for forgiveness was he set free. When the king sent him to England to obtain a loan he decided to stay in England. He used his great prestige and influence and offered money and boats to the Portuguese Government for its colonial expeditions in India, provided it would cease the persecution of the Marranos. But to no avail. The church remained adamant, and it prevailed.

The second trial raised a great stir in Portugal itself. The victim was the famous dramatist, Antonio Jose da Silva. Da Silva was born in Brazil into a family of Marranos originally of the city of Covilhao, Portugal. In his writings, da Silva advocated liberalism, and sharply criticised the fanatics of the Catholic Church. The Inquisition struck back in its usual way. He was shadowed for some time, until enough "evidence" was gathered to prove his secret adherence to the Jewish faith. Da Silva was arrested, and under terrible tortures he broke down and "confessed" his sins. He was eventually released from prison, but his later writings bore the scars of his experiences. His dramas were tragedies, and their characters and heroes were full of melancholy and sorrow. However, he could not repress his true self, and gradually his sharp pen, through the mouths of his

7

created characters, again heaped scorn upon the bigots and fanatics of the church.

A domestic in his household informed that he was secretly practicing the Jewish religion. Once more he was arrested, and the intervention of many important personalities in his behalf was to no avail. This time the Inquisition would not release him from its clutches. Spying on him in prison, they fabricated new "evidence" of his heresy, and charged him with reciting Hebrew prayers. This time da Silva did not confess to anything and, heroically, faced martyrdom. On the first of October, 1739, in the city of Lisbon, da Silva was publicly garroted, and then burned at an *auto da fe*.

Public resentment of his cruel treatment was so vociferous that even the Inquisition had to reckon with it. Henceforth, it reduced the enthusiasm with which it persecuted its victims. In 1925, as an act of atonement, Portugal erected a monument in honor of the martyred Da Silva on the spot of his execution. Camil de Castelo Branco, a well known Portuguese writer, wrote a book in his memory and called it, *O Judeu* (The Jew).

A characteristic document is numbered, 4427. It is about a Jewish girl, named Brites Henriques, who, while courageously facing the Inquisition, recited by heart all the Jewish prayers she knew. These prayers are inscribed verbatim in the proceedings. The girl, not yet eighteen, had been arrested with her family for secretly observing Judaism. Her father and an older sister were burned at the stake. An elder brother was sentenced to life imprisonment. The persuasive words of the Inquisition were to no avail; they tried to convince Brites of the truth of Christianity and assure her that all would be forgiven if she would confess and repent her sin. The girl remained obstinate. Vexed by her determination and obduracy, the Inquisition condemned Brites and a younger brother to life in a nunnery and monastery.

Among her prayers in the Inquisition Tribunal, that were later published by the historian Maria da Saa, is included also a Passover song, "Canta da Pascua." It begins as folows:

Adonai, Adonai!
Adonai, my Lord,
Let us sing today to the Lord,
Of that singular hour,
The horse and the rider
He threw into the deep sea.

In remote corners of Portugal where descendants of Marranos still live today—especially in Belmonte—this song and other prayers are recited.

The prayers and blessings to be found among the documents consisted of prayers recited daily and on festivals, prayers for various ceremonies and occasions including marriage, death, and the advent of the new moon. Prayers recited by travellers were also found, as were *Techinoth,* prayers recited by women. Among the documents were also blessings of various types: the blessing over bread, over the salting of meat, etc. On the eve of Yom Kippur when the Marranos lit their oil lamp called, *candela da Senhor* (the Lord's candelabrum), they pronounced a prayer before and after the fast which they observed from early in the morning until sunset.

It is understandable that many errors are found in the prayers and blessings which they recited. Originally, and for obvious reasons, these were not written down. They were transmitted orally, and in the course of time became distorted.

Only a limited number of the protocols of the Inquisition have been made use of by Portuguese historians. More than forty thousand such documents are known to exist, and are located in various parts of the country. The attitude of Spanish and Portuguese historians to the Inquisition and Expulsion is far from uniform. Such historians as Alexander Herculano, Salvador de Madariaga, Dominguez Ortiz, Amador de los Rios and Dr. Mendes de Ramirez are generally objective. The historian Morejon, in his *History of Medieval Spain,* expresses sympathy with the victims, and criticizes the persecution of the Marranos. He states that the banishment of the Jews "must be considered a crime." Even the secretary of the Inquisition Tribunal, Bartolome de los

Casas, in his book, *Historia del Santo Oficio,* has no great sympathy for the Inquisition. But others, like Mario Saa, in his book *Invasao dos Judeus em Portugal,* Lucio J. D'azevedo, in *Cristaos Novos Portuguesos* and Antonio Baiao, in *A Inqisicao em Portugal e no Brasil,* have tried to defend the Inquisition. Mario Saa, in particular goes so far as to express his hatred of the Marranos and of the Jewish people. Indeed, there is a strong resemblance between his book and the anti-Semitic, *Les Juifs,* by the Frenchman, Roger Peyrefitte. The Jews, claims Mario Saa, have ruined the land. They destroyed the monarchy, weakened religion, and are to be blamed for all the ills of Portugal. He presents a long list of Portuguese personalities, amongst them high government officials (together with their pictures), and points to their Jewish ancestry. All Portuguese, he maintains, who were not born in villages, are of Jewish descent. In the year 1673, out of a population of one million people, there were, according to Saa, two hundred thousand New Christians (Marranos). Indeed, he says, Portugal was known as a "Jewish Kingdom."

Lucio D'Azevedo defends the Inquisition on the grounds that it had no other choice but to use extreme measures. The influence of the Marranos was so great, he says, that they constituted a people within a people. In the year 1497, when Portugal had less than a million inhabitants, there were some one hundred and ninety five thousand Marranos in the land. He has no qualms about re-stating some of the old, absurd accusations against the Marranos, charging them with cruel customs. One wild charge was that they would choke their dying relatives in order to prevent them from professing Christianity in the presence of the summoned priest.

In a similar vein does Antonio Baiao present the case for the Inquisition. He points to the alleged domination of the Marranos over Portuguese trade and commerce, science and free professions. These historians were undoubtedly under the influence of the Catholic Church. The church in republican Portugal was attempting to regain its power.

✓   ✓   ✓

The Marranos of Spain, Portugal and South America

Much more research on the Marranos has been carried out in Spain, and that country continues to study and explore the tragic history of its Jews, using all available records and evidence. The difference of attitude may be explained by the fact that the Jews of Spain, expelled from their homeland in 1492, became, whether they wanted to or not, ambassadors of the Spanish language and, to a lesser degree, of Spanish culture. The liberal senator, Angel Pudillo called them, *Españoles sin Patria*—Spaniards without a Fatherland. When Portugal, too, expelled its Jews, most of them were actually of Spanish extraction, having come to Portugal in the wake of the expulsion from Spain. Marranos from Portugal, who later succeeded in escaping found refuge in places like Amsterdam, London, Italy, Salonica, Morocco, and Tunisia. In these places they found well-established, fellow-Jews of Spanish origin with whom they quickly became integrated.

On my most recent trip to Spain, it was quite simple to obtain access to the vital documents of the Jewish past or to obtain information on the newest developments with respect to Jews in Spain, about which much is now being written. The word "Inquisition" did not provoke any distress or suspicion as in my previous visit in 1927, and I did not find it necessary to spend long hours poring over dusty files in libraries or glass cases in museums. All the details of Jewish history in Spain are easily available in a centralized documentation center named, *Arias Montano*, which was founded in Madrid in 1941, and has a branch in Barcelona. Anything that possesses any relationship to the story of the Jews in Spain is concentrated there. It has been collected and classified with great effort and care.

The first person I met at the documentation center was Padre Peral, a friendly young man who greeted me with *"shalom,"* and who spoke a fluent Hebrew in the Sephardic pronunciation. He had studied in an *ulpan* in Israel. He showed me through various departments containing documents reflecting the Jewish past in Spain. There were long massive shelves with books in many languages, and periodicals from various countries, no matter how remote, where anything at all has been written about the Jews of Spain.

11

In order to acquaint me with the functions of the center, Padre Peral introduced me to the director of the Institute, Professor Francisco Cantera Burgos, who holds the chair of Hebrew at Madrid University and is one of the most important historians of Spanish Jewry. He received me in a most friendly manner, and instead of an interview our meeting took the form of an instructive lecture. Not waiting for my questions, he immediately plunged into an explanation of the program and goals of the Montano Institute:

> It was in the year 1941, in the darkest period of our times, when the world was convulsed with war and the distresses of war that we founded this Institute. In the beginning it was a difficult task to instruct our type-setters and to familiarize them with the Hebrew letters. Now we have our own Hebrew linotypist, Mr. Hattan, a Sephardic Jew from Morocco. Our wish is that this work should not merely remain romantic sentiment. We realize there are two million Sephardim dispersed all over the world at the present time who have conserved the Spanish language, culture and customs. . . . Take as an example the Jews of Salonica who for generations spread and popularized Spanish speech and culture, first among the Turks and later among the Greeks.

He went on to say:

> We realize the great injustice done to the Jews in 1492 and now we want to rectify. it. We do not wish to maintain contact merely from a distance; but we want to have the Sephardim among us . . .

> In order to demonstrate our intentions to our own public and to the world abroad, in 1959 we arranged an imposing exhibition of important documents relating to the Golden Age of Jewry in Spain. The display was held at the University of Madrid, was attended by the country's most important personalities, and was opened by the Minister of Education."

I asked if this exhibit of Judeo-Spanish history was to be shown in America. He replied:

> Our government had promised to loan the *Geniza* (he used the Hebrew word) to an important American Jewish organization (he referred here to B'nai B'rith whose former president, Label Katz, had discussed this with General Franco) . . . We put great emphasis on acquiring every possible document that pertains to the former period of Jewish settlement in Spain and whenever archeological discoveries of this kind are made, we immediately despatch our experts to study them. As for the shipment of these to New York, I believe we shall see that this is done on a large and appropriate scale.

One gets the feeling in this Institute of being inside an endless labyrinth, swimming in a sea of books, journals and learned periodicals from all corners of the earth, all having to do with Jewish interests. The Institute also publishes its own scholarly journal called, *Sefarad.* In it is noted any piece of news that appears on Sephardic Jewry or on Hebrew. It carries reviews of books on Jewish revival and reconstruction in Europe, written with understanding and sympathy. There are reviews of the publications of practically all Jewish publishing houses throughout the world, and no item of Jewish scholarly research goes unmentioned. References are found to the *Shulhan Aruch,* the *Midrash Rabba* and the latest Hebrew book appearing in Israel.

The most important archives of the Inquisition are available there: judgments, proceedings, facsimiles of the Hebrew inscriptions of hundreds of synagogues (now churches), epitaphs on tombstones, Hebrew wills and marriage contracts, and the writings of Spanish and Jewish historians on the rich and productive past of the Jews in Spain. The documentation goes beyond what was actually produced in Spain, and includes material from many countries and languages dealing with the subject of Jews in Spain.

Torah scrolls and Bibles of the Middle Ages, scores of volumes

13

of encyclopedias, critical treatises by biblical researchers—all of these are to be found here, carefully assembled for the purpose of providing a complete picture of the Jews of Spain and their contribution to its civilization and culture.

Professor Francisco Cantera Burgos is the author of ten vital books on Jews and Spain, among which is, *Synagogas Españolas,* that tells of 350 Jewish houses of worship which were either destroyed by fire or transformed into churches. This volume is dedicated to "Maimonides of Cordova," on the 750th anniversary of his death. Burgos collected the various Hebrew inscriptions which appeared on the walls of these buildings, both inside and out, and, in many cases, he restored the correct wording which had become illegible. He has also written the history of the *Juderias,* the Jewish quarters of the various cities of Spain. He is editor of a Hebrew anthology starting with the prophets and the Mishna, and embracing the Hispanic Jewish poets, scholars, and statesmen of the Middle Ages such as, Solomon Ibn Gabirol, Maimonides, Yehuda Halevy, Abraham Ibn Ezra, Abraham ben David of Toledo, Nachmanides (Moses ben Nachman), Shem Tov ben Joseph, Joshua Halorky, Joseph Alba, Ibn Tibbon, Solomon ben Meshulam La Piera, Solomon Verga, Abraham Zacuto, S. M. Luzzatti, and many other poets, writers, philosophers and scholars. The anthology concludes with Mendele Mocher-Seforim, Ahad Ha'am and Haim Nachman Bialik.

An exhaustive study by Professor Gonzalez Maesa on Ibn Ganas; an encyclopedic work on the book, *Yesodei Ha'tvuna v'Migdal Emuna* by Rabbi Abraham bar Hiyya Ha-Bargeloni (*bar* means "son of"); a detailed study on the two apostates: Shlomo Halevy, the rabbi of Burgos who later became bishop Pablo de Santa Maria, and Alfonso de Cartagena by Luciano Serrano—the discussion carried on with them by Jewish scholars; Migdal Oz, an important manuscript found in the Royal Library of Madrid; the writings of Rabbi Yom-Tov Ha-Sepharadi, the son of Rabbi Abraham Ha-Sebilli (called El Sevillano) who was highly praised by his contemporaries for having published in 1380 a defence of Maimonides' *Yad Hazaka* which Rabbi Yom-Tov, a disciple of Shlomo Adret, defended against

14

the attacks of Abraham ben David—all these are but a few of the important works in the abundant collection available in this Genizah, as it is termed by Professor Burgos.

Other vital and historic documents to be seen and studied in these depositories include the translation of *Sefer Hokhmath Elohim,* an important manuscript relating to the religious disputations which were carried on between Christianity and Judaism in Spain, written by Alonzo de Zamora and translated by Professor Federico Perez Castro; a study of Yehuda Halevy's poetry of apologetics by Dr. Jose Millas; also by the same author, a study of the religious Hebrew poetry of Spain, and of Solomon Ibn Gabirol's philosophic poems; Antonio Vinayo Gonsalez' book on the anti-Jewish polemics of San Martin of Leon; Miguel de la Pinta Llorento's *History of Religious Ideas,* and his history of the Jews in Medieval Spain, with a special chapter on the criminal trial against the Salamancan Hebraist, Martin Martinez Cantalapiedra; Michael Molho's *Peculiarities and Customs of the Sephardim in Salonica; the first edition of the poems of* Rabbi Is'haq Israeli, *Las Fiebres;* and Alejandro Diez Macho's examination of the poet Moses Ibn Ezra.

Works of science are also represented in the collection: studies by the Salamanca astronomer, Abraham Zacut and Abraham Ibn Ezra's vital work in this field called, *Reshit Hokhma* (The Beginning of Wisdom). Drs. José Millas and D. Romano completed a *Cosmography of a Roman Jew in the Seventeenth Century,* and Dr. Millas also edited Abraham Ibn Ezra's study of astronomic calculations. In the Universities of Madrid and Barcelona there are special sections on Semitic studies within the faculties of philology. In Spain, a "Bible Week" is held annually for the promotion of Old Testament study, and there is a publication called, *Estudios Biblicos.*

In June, 1961, a congress of Spanish language organizations was held in Madrid, in which there was participation of representatives of Sephardic *kehillot* from various countries. A commission was named to work towards rapprochement with the Sephardic Jews. Among the resolutions passed was one asking the Spanish Government to send Spanish teachers to Sephardic centers, especially to those which are training rabbis who will eventually be assigned to Sephardic communities; and to award scholarships to Sephardic Jewish students to enable them to study at Spanish universities.

The interest shown by Spanish liberals and intellectual circles in the Sephardim, symbolized in the phrase *Españoles sin Patria* (Spaniards without a fatherland), has undergone a change because of the holocaust. Such important Sephardi communities as Salonica were destroyed by the Nazis. The Sephardic centers of Morocco, Tunisia, and other Arabic states, have been greatly depleted because the changed conditions caused both by independence from France and the rise of Israel. The main Sephardic communities are now located in the Latin American countries, where the old centers have grown because of increased immigration in recent times.

It is estimated that the number of Sephardic Jews in Latin America is about 150,000. Though they have their own *kehillot,* they are also affiliated with the central Jewish communal bodies, and play an important role in the life of the local Jewish communities. In many South American countries the Sephardim were the first to set up Jewish communal organizations. There was no language barrier for them, and they found it easy to communicate with the indigenous population.

The Sephardic communities are integrated into the Spanish culture. Even many of the prayers in their synagogues are recited in Spanish. Whereas, the first and, to an extent, the second generation keep to themselves—even establishing a separate Zionist group—between the second and third generation a noticeable change takes place, and there is a trend towards integration with the Ashkenazim of a similar generation.

CHAPTER II.

Mexico: The Land of the Aztecs

The story of Mexico's emancipation is one of bloodshed, civil war and internecine strife, a story of successive revolutions and constant invasions by foreign armies. In the years 1519-21, when Hernando Cortes conquered Mexico and proclaimed it a province of Spain, he found there a highly developed Aztec civilization which extended as far as Lake Nicaragua. The ruler of this kingdom received him as a friend, but was later cast into prison and subjected to torture. The native population was pillaged and enslaved.

Spain ruled Mexico with an iron hand for three centuries, and it was not until 1810 that a revolt against the Spanish yoke broke out. The fighting lasted ten years until, in 1821, Mexico was finally freed of its Spanish bondage and obtained full independence. But then, internal strife, civil war and revolution arose in earnest. By 1877, Mexico had gone through two kings, several dictators, and a number of presidents. At most, a president would retain his position for nine months.

This was the aftermath of 300 years of Spanish misrule. The liberated people were not yet competent to handle self-government because of Spain's brutal suppression which had robbed them of their spirit of nobility and initiative. Their lack of political sophistication was exploited by demagogues who advanced to power by means of devious and diverse machinations. This phenomenon was by no means purely a Mexican problem. The identical exploitation and extortion has been repeated in almost all the liberated countries in Latin America, and in many it is still going on.

Simon Bolivar, the liberator of South America foresaw this shortly before his death, when he said: "Democracy is a long way off. The constitutions of these countries are merely ink and paper, their elections, wars and bloodshed." But he saw a ray of hope when two years after his last victory over the Spanish conquerors he called a conference in Panama of all the new republics and said: "Neither we nor the generation after us will enjoy the fruits of our great victory, but I am sure of this—the same language, race, and culture will bind us together in the end."

Two heroes are inscribed in letters of gold in the history of Mexico's liberation. Both were men who fought and died. One was Benito Juarez, the Abraham Lincoln of Mexico; the other was Father Miguel Hidalgo, the George Washington who courageously fought the exploitation of the Indians by the Spaniards, and was shot for his efforts. Benito Juarez first appears on the political scene in 1855 with a firm decision to introduce democratic reform. As Minister of Justice he was successful in 1857 in introducing a number of changes: he confiscated the great land estates of the Church which had survided from the Spanish conquest, and he introduced freedom of speech, freedom of the press and religious tolerance. This provoked the opposition both of the Church and of the conservative elements who were closely attached to the Church. The liberals won out, however, and in 1861 Benito Juarez was elected President of Mexico.

Napoleon III intruded at this point, coming to the aid of the Church and the conservatives. With the help of French troops the Austrian Duke Maximilian was imposed upon Mexico as a monarch. Benito Juarez was forced to flee to the mountains where he organized a war against the foreign impostor. After Maximilian was abandoned by the French troops, he capitulated and was sentenced to be shot. Benito Juarez returned to resume the presidency.

Today friendship reigns between Mexico and her neighbor to the north, but it was not always so. It was certainly not so in 1938 when Mexico confiscated all foreign-owned oil wells, among them many which were United States-owned. But, by then, times had changed. War was not declared. Mexico paid compensation, and the matter was disposed of in a peaceful way. A similar peaceful solution was found when the Rio Grande River washed out a stretch of territory on the border between Ciudad Juarez and El Paso, Texas. At first the U.S. claimed and took the territory, but after diplomatic negotiations the late President John F. Kennedy recognized Mexico's claim and handed back the territory.

Mexico thrills you with her scenic panoramas and beautiful buildings. But side by side, on the same streets with a beautiful park and attractive plants and flowers, are nestled, sandy streets of collapsed houses. Poverty and wealth live side by side. The same scenes may be witnessed in other Latin American countries.

The main streets of Mexico: Madero, San Juan de Letran, Juarez, Paseo de la Reforma and Bucareli need not be ashamed of their appearance. They compare well to the main streets of the largest cities of the world.

Tourism is the most profitable business in Mexico, and is one of the main sources of income for the country. Millions of dollars are spent by tourists annually.

Mexico has many points of similarity with European cities. Here are a combination of Latin American and European houses. This is an attraction for the American tourist who seldom sees such architecture in America. There are many cafes, and each cafe has its own clientele. The meeting-place for Americans is the Sanborn Cafes, a combination of restaurant and cafe. The inside atmosphere is appealing to those who seek Mexican color and are interested in exotic furniture of colonial days.

JEWS IN MEXICO

Mexican Jewish history starts with the Spanish Conquest. One of the men in the expedition of Cortes was the Marrano Hernando Alonso. Because of the persecution waged by the Inquisition against the "New Christians' who were suspected of observing Jewish rites in secret, many Marranos emigrated to the lands of the New World in the hope that it would be easier for them to practice Judaism there. But the Inquisition pursued them relentlessly. Inquisitorial tribunals were established in Mexico City, Lima and later in Cartagena, with commissars in the adjoining provinces.

According to the American Jewish historian Dr. Seymour B. Liebman, who has thoroughly studied the subject, Jews first came secretly to Mexico from Portugal via Campeche. Mexico's first victim of the Inquisition was Hernando Alonso, the man who accompanied Cortes. He was put on trial in 1528 for adhering to Judaism in secret, and was burned alive at an *auto da fe*. In 1596 Luis de Carvajal, founder and later governor of the province of Nuevo Leon and its capital Monterey, was sentenced to be burned, undergoing much physical torture.

In the *Yivo Annual* of 1938, Meyer Berger published twenty letters which this martyr wrote from prison inscribed on the dessicated peel of various Mexican fruits. A second martyr, Tomas Trevino de Sobremonte, was also sentenced to death in 1649 for practicing Judaism. An American historian, Dr. Shalem, in his book *Troubled Times in Mexico*, reminds us of a second governor of a Mexican province, Bernardo Lopez Mendizabal, who in 1659 was sentenced jointly with his wife for this offense.

Mexican archives are full of orders, protocols, and verdicts of the tortures and trials of the accused, of accusations and charges based on the word of informers. It also contains some cases of confessions and pardons. Many Marranos were trapped by informers in that tragic period. Dr. Liebman writes of martyrs burned at the stake over 200 years ago for their loyalty to Judaism, and feels that we should honor these martyrs just as we honor the martyrs of the Warsaw Ghetto.

Not until 1862 do we again hear anything about Jews in Mexico. A report of the *Allgemeine Zeitung des Judentums* relates that there were 100 Jews in Mexico, for the most part agents of Danish, Belgian and French firms. In the course of time, however, they were absorbed into the surrounding population. Twenty years later, the Austrian Chief Rabbi, Jellinek, published a letter in the *London Jewish Chronicle*, proposing Jewish migration to Mexico. Whatever became of this is not known. John W. DeKay, president of the Mexico-Peking Co., made a similar proposal to President Porfirio Diaz.

An opinion exists that Francisco Madero was a descendant of Marranos. There is a hint of this in the anti-Jewish book *America Peligra* (The Danger of America), in which the author, Salvador Borrego, comforts himself with the fact that Madero was born a Catholic.

Eduardo Weinfeld emphasizes in one of his works that according to the National Archives in Mexico half of the Spanish population in the city of Mexico, in the 16th century, was suspected by the Inquisition of being of Jewish origin. The composer of the first Mexican national anthem was a Viennese Jew, Henry Hertz; and one of the initiators of statistical science in the country was a Jew named Isidor Epstein. Also, the first theatrical performance in Mexico (and perhaps in all of Latin America) was the work of a Jewish author named Corvero, a native of Toledo, Spain, who was later put on trial by the Inquisition in Guadalajara for certain sonnets of which the Inquisitors did not approve.

At the beginning of the nineteenth century, however, a number of Sephardic Jewish families from Turkey and Syria had settled in Mexico. As in all other countries of the New World they started as peddlers with packs on their backs, knocking at doors and offering various goods. Soon they began to be concerned about their Jewishness. A *minyan* would gather in a private home for prayers. A group of Jews from the Arabic countries bought a piece of land from a Spanish cemetery and consecrated it as a Jewish burial ground. At the time of the Mexican Revolution (1910-12) Francisco Madero gave the Jews, who had originally come from Damascus, permission to build a synagogue. This is the Mount Sinai synagogue which still stands and is in use.

During the first World War a number of American Jews came to Mexico, some as agents of U.S. firms. These were men with organizational and communal experience, and they founded a Young Men's Hebrew Association on the model of the American synagogue-centre, i.e. a place not only for worship but for numerous other activities. In the year 1921-22, when the United States started to restrict its immigration, many Jewish immigrants from Eastern Europe came to Mexico in the hope that it would enable them to obtain easier admission to the States. They were soon persuaded, however, that it was possible to settle in Mexico just as well. Despite the difficulties of becoming established commercially, they soon began to organize a communal and cultural structure. They established a synagogue in 1922 with the appropriate name of Nid'chei Israel (The "Castaways" of Israel). In the same year the secularists among the Jews founded the I.L. Peretz Cultural Association.

With the rise of Hitler, Jews from Czechoslovakia and Hungary came to Mexico. This might be considered the "third migration."

In 1967 there were 30,000 Jews in Mexico, possessing a model organizational structure. In the capital alone there are seven communities. The former peddlers, or as they are called in Mexico *aboneros,* are now factory owners, financiers, or importers. They began with packs, then opened *puestos* (open-air stalls) in the marketplace. Because of pressure from non-Jewish merchants who feared their competition, the *puestos* were abolished, whereupon the Jewish merchants opened workshops. These eventually expanded into large-scale factories. Now Mexicans who sell in the market are supplied with their merchandise by these Jewish manufacturers.

Jews contributed considerably with their vitality, experience and energy to the rise of Mexico's economy, the nearness of the United States was helpful in this respect, for they were able to establish contact with the world of American commerce. Today, Jews play an important role in many of the country's industries: textiles, knitted wear, furniture manufacture, chemicals, the film industry, and import and export in general.

The Jewish community in Mexico no longer lives in the narrow streets and dark and dingy lodgings of their early days. They are now to be found in the ultra-modern, spacious homes in the most comfortable parts of the city, such as Hipodromo and Chapultepec (where King Maximilian once lived), and Polanco.

The growth and improvement in the economic status of Mexico's Jews has given them the opportunity to build their cultural and community life on a broad and generous scale. The Nid'chei Israel *kehilla*, once so tiny, has become a modern community with a departmentalized apparatus embracing an entire range of activities and program. Now known officially as the Askenazic Kehilla Nid'chei Israel, it recently opened its new headquarters, a splendid new building at 70 Acapulco Street, equipped and provided with the ultimate in conveniences and facilities. There is a hall for meetings and entertainment, a museum of European Jewry, a religious department which is devoted to all questions of religious life, a department for social assistance which provides aid for yeshivot abroad, an education department, a youth department, and a teachers seminary. The *kehilla* provides 30% of the budget for the schools.

The other communal groupings have also expanded their programs. Some have their own synagogues, some their own rabbis. The Ashkenazic *kehilla,* Nid'chei Israel, and other communal groupings are affiliated with the Central Jewish Committee—the roof organization of the Mexican Jewish community.

A few years ago, a Conservative temple, Beth El, was erected, and is the largest in Latin America. Its structure and beauty resemble the famous Conservative synagogue, Shaarei Tzedek, in Toronto. Two facsimiles of Marc Chagall's windows are on either side of the Holy Ark.

A second Conservative synagogue, called the American Synagogue, was the first Conservative temple in Mexico. Beth Israel, the Community Center where services are conducted in English, has (in 1968) Rabbi Samuel S. Lerer as its spiritual leader.

Mexico City possesses a Jewish sport center for the youth called *El Centro Deportivo Israelita* with a membership of 14,000. This institution fulfills the same function as the YMHAs do in the United States and Canada, and the *Hebraica* in Buenos Aires. It is an institution in the North American style which far-seeing communal planners transplanted to Latin American soil. In addition to athletic and cultural programs it has another important function—it erases the differences between children of

Ashkenazim and Sephardim, German and Hungarian Jews. Proof that this experiment has succeeded is that in the last few years similar youth centers have been established in Chile, Peru, Venezuela, Colombia, and other countries.

The Jewish schools in Mexico are integral schools—what we call all-day schools. They begin at kindergarten level and reach as far as high school, preparatory for university. Those who complete it can be admitted to a faculty at the National University. The schools are of various types: a secular school based on Yiddish, another called the I.L. Peretz School, a Hebrew Tarbut school, a religious Yavne school, and even a yeshiva. According to statistics, 80% of Mexican-Jewish children attend these schools.

Mexico was fortunate in her first Jewish immigrants. A group of idealists of various ideologies came in the early stream of immigration. They brought with them a faith and an ideal, they built the community and were careful to transplant the Jewishness they knew to the soil of Mexico. Mexican Jewry has travelled a great distance since the first Jewish teacher, Meyer Berger, visited the nearest North American cities to seek aid to establish and maintain a Jewish school in Mexico. Today Mexican Jews do not have to seek aid abroad. They maintain their own schools quite generously. They erect excellent buildings, with the most up-to-date equipment, and use the very latest educational techniques.

Here we must quote the folk saying: "If things are so good, why are they so bad?" And things are bad with Mexico's Jewish youth, for despite all the efforts, the results are negative. After forty years of Jewish schools, the youth, with small exception, speaks very little Yiddish or Hebrew, and is remote from Jewish interests.

This is not only a Mexican phenomenon; it is a problem with which Latin American Jewry in general is wrestling. The Mexican Jewish community has grown in numbers, but it has not grown in depth. On the surface all looks well, but the legacy of the Jewish tradition has not been handed over to the younger generation, and a community without a youth, like a nation without youth, is condemned to hopeless prospects. Many of the former

24

idealists and champions are no longer alive; others have remained obdurate and stiff-necked, unwilling to understand that times have changed, and unwilling to cope with the day by day changes that compel one to talk to the youth in its own vernacular, and unwilling to recognize that Yiddish without *Yiddishkeit* has no basis for existence, and that secularist Yiddishism is bankrupt and cannot divert the current of assimilation.

When the visitor to Mexico and other Latin American countries is shown such magnificent buildings and statistics he is, at first blush, astonished, but when he studies the facts a little more closely they appear differently. I know quite well that Latin American Jews are very sensitive to criticism (this they have acquired from their non-Jewish neighbors) so I will cite the words of a Mexican Jewish writer, the late Salomon Kahan, one of the veterans of Yiddish letters in Mexico and a pioneer builder of the Jewish Community there. Writing of this distressing problem in his book *Mexikaner Reflexn* (1954) he said: "Sometimes it can occur that a visitor . . . sees no further than his nose. Usually a visitor arrives and is shown hospitality, banquets and friendship by a special group. He is shown the finest and the best, to make the best possible impression—but he doesn't get a chance to see the other side of the coin."

The Mexican Jew, like his non-Jewish neighbor, suffers from an inferiority complex with respect to the United States, and is involved in an ongoing effort to outstrip the United States in the comforts and luxuries he acquires. Mexican luxuries, generally speaking, are inflated, without a secure foundation of all-around prosperity. Not only does indescribable poverty and destitution prevail less than one-half an hour from the capital, but one comes across it in the capital itself, face to face with magnificent palaces and lavish villas.

Most Mexican Jews entered the country years ago in the hope of using it as a means of facilitating their admission to the United States. Because of the immigration restrictions, this was not possible. Now they want to show the American Jew that they have surpassed them in the magnificence and luxuries of their community buildings and institutions—a luxury built on a shallow, unsure foundation.

The Mexican Jews have acquired the mentality of their neighbors and have adopted "Mañana" and "Abrazo" as their philosophy of life. Their homes are barred and locked to strangers. They would rather arrange a banquet for you at which they can make a speech than invite you into their home for tea.

Among the negative elements mentioned by Kahan is the Jewish estrangement of the youth that goes through the Jewish schools! Their absence from local community life creates a serious problem for Jewish education and the community's future. The former pupils of the schools are never seen at any of the community undertakings. On the third anniversary of the uprising in the Warsaw Ghetto not even a few pupils of the high school were to be seen.

In a "Letter to Parents" Salomon Kahn wrote: "Even though your children may attend the Yiddish school, they get no stimulation to use the language in their own home and, listening to their parents painfully straining in some masochistic way to speak a fractured Spanish, in time they acquire a disdain for Yiddish as something inferior. Their Jewish studies become mechanical rote, with no connection to the inner expression of their life."

The younger generation's indifference to Yiddish is not their fault alone—nor is this phenomenon confined to Mexico. People who have improved their social and economic status often develop a complex about Yiddish. The language seems to remind them of the poverty and the mudstrewn street they would rather forget. Since these people would rather use faulty Spanish than Yiddish that they know, needless to say, they set up a wall between parent and child. The children become estranged from Jewish content, and they grow up without any cultural heritage. Yiddish to them is a language of ignoramuses. In time the chasm widens.

An article which appeared in the *Shtimme* on February 23, 1944, by "one of the youth"—a leader writes of the "East European Jewish tailors and cobblers who came to the shores of Mexico and rose to fairly impressive heights, but are people totally devoid of culture. They do not understand the life around them and cannot bear being told."

This article appeared more than 20 years ago, when the first traces of a second generation of Jews was appearing in Mexico. Today these young people are grown; they have become engineers, doctors, architects, mathematicians and members of other professions. However, they lack Jewish spiritual or cultural baggage, and look upon their parents with disdain.

Eliahu Chinich, one of the veterans of Jewish education in Mexico, in an article in *Hadoar* came to the conclusion that between kindergarten and the university preparatory class the knowledge obtained in Jewish culture and history is quite limited. "It does not even reach the level of the ability to read a Hebrew or Yiddish book," he writes. This after 40 years of Jewish education in Mexico!

In September, 1967, K. Landau wrote in his column in *La Voz Israelita de Mexico*: "Our education system was admired all over the world including Israel. For years we invested sweat, blood and millions of dollars. Now, it is going from bad to worse. Yiddish is deteriorating in such a degree that it is impossible to stamp it."

Years ago, the editor of the *Shtimme* in Mexico wrote that among the notices he received in his office was one written in Spanish; an invitation to a youth conference arranged by Israel *shlichim* (emissaries) which was to deal with problems of Jewish education. Such Spanish-language releases, the editor stated, are not published on principle, since using Spanish promotes assimilation!

One of the *shlichim* replied: "Simply because the invitation is not in Yiddish, is this a reason to ignore a conference of Jewish youth? Must Zionist training be scuttled because the only way to reach the youth is via the Spanish language? Are you aware," he asked the editor, "that the great majority of the younger people who had spent years in the Yiddish schools do not even use the language at home with their parents?"

In fact, the tragedy goes further and deeper. Menachem Gelehrter, an emissary of the Jewish Agency, writes in his book,

Yahadut B'Yabeshet M'Soeret (Jews in a Restless Land) that during a visit he made to Monterrey's small Jewish community of 120 families, he found that the first contributor to the fund-raising drive had a daughter who had intermarried; the second contributor had himself married out of the fold; and in the home of the third the mother was ill because her daughter had just married a non-Jewish butcher.

Paradoxically, the younger generation of Jewish professionals, though fully Mexicanized and having dissociated themselves from the Jewish community, have not succeeded in integrating themselves into the non-Jewish environment. They are not at ease with the lower levels of the Mexican population, and the upper strata will not accept them. The danger, therefore, is that they will be suspended in a limbo, lacking even the background and knowledge of Jewish values to fortify themselves. Rather than drawing nourishment from their Jewish roots, they are embarrassed by them. And this situation is not unique to Mexican Jewry. The same militant Jewish editor who years ago refused to publish a report of a Zionist youth conference only because it was not written in Yiddish, and who complained that the weeds must be eradicated from the Jewish garden in Mexico, has since written in his column in the *Shtimme* a piece entitled, "Short and Sharp," complaining that the youth does not want to become involved in Jewish communal life. "Come, we tell them, and you will take over the leadership—but with little exception they do not come. We have erected structures, established schools and institutions of all kinds, and nothing moves them."

How can he now expect them to come, when years ago he and others blindly resisted approaching the youth and bringing them closer to Jewish interests in the language they understood? In the battle of Yiddish or nothing—nothing won.

Even when the struggle for Yiddish was going on there were Jewish writers who were far-sighted enough to foresee the inevitable reality. These were men whom no one would suspect of not being attached to Yiddish. In *Mexikaner Reflexn,* Salomon Kahan wrote:

Of course there is among youth a minority element which experiences a cultural and intellectual hunger. We meet them at symposiums, at concerts, at the better-type of Mexican theatre. Insofar as our Jewish organizations have succeeded in interesting these young people in Jewish matters, they are interested in hearing about Jewish authors and artists, but on the condition that these talks be given in Spanish.

The same author expressed his satisfaction with two books of religious Jewish content which appeared in Spanish some years back—the Passover Haggadah and the Book of Esther, published for children by the Mexican Mizrachi. "The fact is that Spanish is submerging all Jewish life. In the home Spanish dominates, in business life its intrusion is more and more a concrete reality. The best barometer in this respect is the youth: almost all the youth groupings use Spanish exclusively—even those involved in *hachshara,* including the Orthodox youth group, B'nai Akiva."

Now that the danger has been perceived, and courageous critics point to the unpalatable truths, there is still time to save the third generation by a new approach which does not concentrate on language alone. Pressure has come from various quarters for a reassessment and revision of Jewish education.

A recent occurrence gives indication of this. A former leader of the Hashomer Hatzair, and a former director of the Tarbut School; a writer who had been a teacher for many years, has come out with the demand that Jewish studies commence with group prayer in the kindergarten class. "Instead of teaching the Yiddish word for a flower or other dry words, the children should begin with, *Mah tovu oholecha Yaacov* (How goodly are thy tents O Jacob)."

ANTI-SEMITISM IN MEXICO

Yet another problem in Mexico involves the distribution of anti-Semitic books which contain the ugliest of libels about Jews. Mexican bookshops display copies of *The Protocols of Zion.* Not long ago, two vitriolic anti-Jewish books appeared; one by a priest who regretted that the Inquisition had been abolished, and the second, *America Peligra* (The Danger to America), by Salvador Borrego. The latter became a best-seller, and was also read in other Latin American countries. It is replete with the ugliest vilification of Jews, modeled after the hate-filled statements of the late Julius Streicher.

Mexico has become the center for the publication and distribution of such books. Most are published by Editorial Jus Publishing Co. I counted a list of 20 such books. They are exported throughout Latin and Central American countries. The Union Nacional Sinarquista actively promotes this material, and its brother organization, the Partido de Accion Nacional is regarded as sympathetic to neo-Nazi elements. A student group, Movimiento Universitario de Renovadora Orientacion (Muro), as well as conservative Catholic Church elements expound anti-Semitic views. The Arab League disseminates anti-Jewish propaganda, and anti-Semitic incidents occur occasionally.

In December 1966, for the first time in the history of the Jewish community, the Mexico City cemetery was desecrated and synagogues were smeared with swastikas and anti-Semitic slogans. Leaders of the Comite Israelita, together with the American Jewish Committee and the B'nai B'rith, spoke to the Mayor and requested a police investigation. Shortly thereafter the press published a statement by the Mayor declaring that Mexico upholds human rights and justice, and will not permit destructive acts against any group in its society, and that the police would investigate the swastika daubings.

Jewish community leaders expressed interest in assistance from the AJC, which had been functioning in Latin America since 1948. A plan was designed to help Jewish communities to function effectively in matters of common concern: to combat anti-Semitism, to conduct investigations into anti-Jewish activities, to encourage better understanding between Jews and the general community, and to create educational and cultural projects aimed at maintaining traditional Jewish values and strengthening Jewish identity, especially among the youth.

A Consultation Committee of outstanding leaders from a variety of Jewish organizations was formed to serve as a continuing link between the AJC office in Mexico and the Jewish community, and to provide advice and counsel. A demographic study of the Mexican Jewish community was initiated in order to have a clear picture of its composition, background, interests, affiliations, relationship with the general community, etc.

A monthly bulletin, "Par Su Informacion," is published by the AJC, containing news of Jewish life on the Latin American continent and in other parts in the world, and is widely distributed in Mexico and Central America. Its aim is to provide the Spanish press and the Jewish community leaders with information often not obtainable elsewhere.

The first issue of *Cuadernos,* a community service publication containing the text of "From Kishinev to Hitler," a paper by the distinguished English sociologist Dr. Norman Cohn, appeared. This activity will be extended.

The Instituto Cultural Mexicano Israeli is conducting a series of lectures on "Religion as the Crux of the Cultural Tradition," in which prominent Jewish and non-Jewish scholars are participating.

In the realm of Catholic-Jewish relations, an AJC study group which visited Mexico laid the groundwork for subsequent contact and cooperation with influential Church figures, and recommended inviting liberal Church leaders to speak at a leading Mexican synagogue.

On the first anniversary of the promulgation of the Vatican Council's Declaration on non-Christian Religions, Father de Ertze Garamendi, President of the Mexican Theological Society, Canon of the Metropolitan Cathedral and professor at the National University, spoke on, "Christians and Jews in the Post Council Perriod," at a meeting co-sponsored by the AJC and the Centro Deportivo Israelita.

First steps toward improved understanding between Arabs and Jews in Mexico came with the creation of a committee of interested Jews, and efforts by Salvador Abdo, prominent Catholic journalist of Arab descent, to involve Arab leaders in this project.

IN VERACRUZ

After an entire day of travelling through sandy, parched fields, among which one catches sight of small *pueblos* with narrow little streets, rows of vari-colored *casitas* and primitive churches, the express train from Mexico City arrived at Veracruz. A crowd of porters flung themselves at my baggage as soon as the compartment door opened. There were also women with babies on their backs, made secure in cunningly tied and knotted shawls. Before I could say a word, two of my suitcases were slung over the shoulders of a strong young Mexican porter. A woman with a baby carried in a knotted shawl on her back seized my briefcase. Both of them escorted me to the taxi.

I took a room in a modern hotel on the water-front, where the sea breezes made the blazing heat a little more tolerable. As the day wore on the air grew more humid and stifling, and this was midwinter. I watched the people in the street, utter weariness was in their walk.

Veracruz is the largest port in Mexico, the country's chief communication center with the outside world. It is an impressive town, with its old, Spanish-style, massive houses and churches. The houses are joined to each other through long passage-ways, like tunnels, that provide good protection from the rain. It's reminiscent of Seville or Granada.

How does one find a Jew in Veracruz? The name itself, "the true cross," is enough to put any Jew off. It reeks with the smell of the Inquisition. Four hundred years ago the Marranos who fled from Spain lived here in considerable numbers—it is quite possible that they founded the town. As with so much else about the Marranos, the name of the town must have been chosen deliberately, to mislead the Inquisition into thinking of them all as devout Christians.

To-day, I was told, there are few Jews in Veracruz. I looked in vain through the telephone directory seeking a Jewish name among the thousands of Domingos and Juarez. So I resorted to my old method of discovering Jews in a remote out-of-the-way place—I took a walk through the main street and read the names over the shop-fronts. I stopped at two shops—Casa Jose and Casa Barata (House of Bargains)—where huge signs, painted in red on the windows, announced a *Remate Grande* (Grand Sale).

I walked in. The shopkeeper eyed me curiously. Then he smiled —a broad, friendly smile.

"Sholom aleichem!" and he extended his hand in greeting.

A few minutes later he closed the shop for the *siesta*, which lasts about three hours, and I sat talking with him in his comfortable home which had an open patio. The breezes from the sea cooled the hot stifling air in the house. He told me about the small Jewish community in Veracruz.

Many recent Jewish immigrants who had settled there had managed to establish themselves quite well. Yet, the number of new arrivals keeps decreasing. Everybody wants his children to get a good Jewish education, so they leave for the bigger Jewish centers. Years ago, he said, there was a Jewish school in Veracruz, but now many Jews have gone to Mexico City, and others have grown old and tired, and haven't the energy.

The next day the papers carried a report that several Nazi prisoners being held in the Perote fortress in Veracruz would be released that afternoon. I went to the prison in time for the "ceremony," to watch it with my own eyes. Two local Jews came with me.

Hundreds of curious Mexicans had made their way there in the baking heat. The "heroes" walked out, not reflecting Hitler's defeat and overthrow, but as though he had triumphed. With a band playing, they held their heads high, and arrogantly sang the Mexican anthem, "La Glanderino." The crowd cheered them. I counted 174 German Nazis. I could hardly restrain myself when the two Jews with me told me how, at the height of the European Jewish extermination, two hundred Jewish refugees, fleeing from the massacres, had arrived on a boat at Veracruz—and were not allowed to land. When one of the refugees, in desperation, attempted suicide, they took him off, half-dead, to hospital.

A second ship arrived from Spain with hundreds of Spanish political refugees on board and also 120 Jewish refugees who had escaped the Nazi slaughter. The Spanish refugees were welcomed with flowers and music. The Jewish refugees were not allowed to land. "All our interventions," these local Jews told me, "were of no avail—not even the intervention of the big American Jewish relief organizations." The Jewish refugees on the boat were sent out again onto the open sea.

The Mexican Government issued an expulsion order against an American Jew, Lionel Dalkovitch, from San Antonio, Texas, who had lived in Mexico for years, on the charge that he had helped Jewish refugees enter the country. Dalkovitch had to seek the protection of the United States Embassy. Another expulsion order was issued against the correspondent of the Associated Press.

I made my way through the crowd with my American Press Card, and presented it to a high Mexican official seated at a table by the prison gate. Several men in military uniform were with him, handing each prisoner a sealed envelope as he came out.

"Señor," I said, "I am an American journalist. Will you tell me what's going on here? What sort of a celebration is this? Didn't thousands of Mexican soldiers fight with the American army? Many of them were killed by the German Nazis. The Nazis burned millions of Jews in their crematoria. And here you make a celebration for them!"

The soldiers looked at me silently. They dropped their eyes. The high official said: "It's an order, Señor!"

The following day the newspapers carried a report that each of the Nazis had been handed a thousand *pesos*, as a gift from the Mexican Government; and if they wished they could stay in Mexico and be given Mexican citizenship.

There was a picture on the front page of one paper, showing the Minister of the Interior handing out the gifts, with the Mexican Nazi leader, Willi Jurgens, smiling happily at his side.

CHAPTER III.

Jewish Communities in Central America

The Jewish communities in Central America comprise six tiny *kehillot*: Panama, Guatemala, El Salvador, Costa Rica, Nicaragua and Honduras. Their total Jewish population is just over 5,000, distributed as follows: Panama 2,000, Guatemala 1,000, Costa Rica 1,500, El Salvador around 300, Nicaragua 250 and a small number in Honduras. These farflung communities have lately begun to show a positive interest in Jewish identity and in preserving Jewish values. Jewish educational institutions, youth organizations and summer camps have been created, and a Spanish language Jewish publication called *Baderej* appears in Costa Rica.

The unforgettable Jewish leader, the late Moshe Sharett, visited these communities in 1962, and encouraged the establishment of a Central Committee with the name: Comunidades Judias de Centro America y Panama (FEDECO). Its first convention was held in Guatemala, the second in Panama, the third in El Salvador, and the last in San Jose, Costa Rica. The current president of this organization is Jacobo Grynszpan of Costa Rica. A Central American and Panamanian Jewish Youth Federation was established lately.

From a reading of the addresses delivered at these conferences one can tell that the participants are the intellectuals. These are the second generation—the sons and daughters of the Jewish immigrants—who have now taken over community leadership, and who feel solidarity with Jewish people and with Israel. They feel pride in Jewishness and Jewish identity, and are concerned with Jewish problems abroad.

The communities of Central America and Panama are affiliated with the World Jewish Congress.

GUATEMALA: THE SWISS OF CENTRAL AMERICA

Guatemala City makes a wonderful impression on the visitor. It is clean and tidy, with splendid buildings submerged in a sea of trees. In the heart of the city, facing the beautiful park, where the trees grow close together and the branches intertwine forming and archway that shields the strollers from the blazing sun, stands the Palacio Nacional and various Ministries.

A few steps from the Plaza and you are on Fifth Avenue, the city's main shopping center. Here are the best and biggest stores.

The great display windows show the most modern equipment and the latest styles from abroad, as well as native products. Here are the theatres and cinemas, the hotels, cafes and the fashionable restaurants, all in modern architecture and most up-to-date style. No wonder Guatemala is renowned as the Switzerland of Central America.

When the Spaniards conquered Guatemala in 1554, they found an ancient Mayan culture in the country, and for over three centuries it was the central seat of the Spanish rulers of all the Central American territories. In an area of about 40,000 square miles Guatemala has a population of four million people, the most densely populated country in Central America. Over 53 per cent of the population are Indians who still live under primitive conditions, segregated from the other inhabitants not only by their language—for they know no Spanish and speak only their native Indian tongues: Quichua and Aymara—but also by their way of life. Some towns have two municipalities, one for the Indians who form the majority, and the other for the remaining population.

Guatemala, like the other Central American lands that were part of the viceroyalty of Mexico, became independent in 1821 after liberation from Spanish rule. The five Central American States afterwards formed a Federation under the leadership of

Francisco Morazan. But the newly-liberated countries were not yet ripe for his liberal reforms, and the conservative elements, especially the Church, which viewed his reforms as imperiling its position, opposed him. In the struggle Morazan was killed, and in 1838 the Federation collapsed and was dissolved.

A succession of uprisings, revolutions and despotic dictatorships followed. The people of Guatemala were ruled with an iron fist; every attempt at liberation was drowned in blood. The last of the dictators, Jorge Ubico, was a ruthless ruler. Stories are still told of his cruelty and brutality.

The Jewish community in Guatemala, officially, goes back about one hundred years. The first Jews came from the Caribbean islands. Afterwards, Sephardic Jews arrived from Aleppo and Salonica, and built a synagogue named Magen Abraham, which still stands. They were followed, in the late 19th century, by German Jews, mostly from Posen. Jews from Posen also settled in Peru at the same period, but that community has completely assimilated. Those who settled in Guatemala, however, have children and granchildren who are now active in the leadership of Jewish life.

The shop fronts on the principal streets bear Sephardic names like Zadok, Askalay, Mizrachi, as well as names which indicate a German-Jewish origin. On Fifth Avenue one may also find East European names, borne by Jews who arrived in Guatemala between the two world wars. Some also came from other Latin American countries where they had not been able to adjust themselves. Each of these sectors, Sephardic, German and East European has its own communal life, but are all represented in a central committee.

Jews in Guatemala started, as in other countries, as pack-peddlers, and went on to better things. Julio Seidler, one of the first East European arrivals, told me the story of an edict decreed by dictator Jorge Ubico who, during the second World War, was openly in sympathy with Nazism, and had Hitler's *Mein Kampf* translated into Spanish. When the Nazis won their big military victories in Europe, the dictator issued a decree forbidding the Jews in Guatemala to be peddlers, ordering them to leave the country within 48 hours. Julio Seidler sent a cable to the World Jewish Congress in New York, asking for help. The censor intercepted the cable, and Seidler was arrested. But a traveller who passed through Guatemala carried the message to the World Jewish Congress, and the Congress intervened. When Seidler was brought before the dictator, the latter received him amicably, and the decree was modified. It still provided that Jews must not engage in peddling, but it did not mention expulsion. So the Jews opened small shops instead, and the shops prospered and grew, and are today the leading stores in the shopping center of the capital.

The Jews in Guatemala lead an active Jewish life. They number about 1000, have their communal machinery, a Zionist Organization, a WIZO, a Jewish Sports Club, a Jewish school—Colegio Guatemalteco Israelita—and B'nai B'rith. Recently, the Guatemala City Council named one of its schools, "Estado de Israel." The opening ceremony was attended by the Minister of Education and the Israeli Consul. The Minister of Education said in his address that the school would be a symbol of Guatemala's friendship with the State of Israel.

This much for the official material concerning the lively little Jewish community in Guatemala. The unofficial material goes back to the days of the Inquisition, which was active in Guatemala, and had its commissars throughout the country.

There is a book by Chinchilla Aguilar Ernesto, called *La Inquisicion en Guatemala,* dealing with this period. The Inquisition was abolished by the Cortes of Cadiz, but it was restored when Ferdinand V came to the throne, and was not completely abolished until the liberation of the Latin American countries.

There are still traces of that period to be found to-day. Julio Seidler, told me that the Procurador-General had once come to him, removed his jacket, rolled up his sleeves, asked him to do the same, and said: "We are both descendants of the same race, with the same blood flowing in our veins." Seidler told me that Indians sometimes bring him old menorahs with half-obliterated Hebrew words. One of the streets in Guatemala City is named Calle de los Judios, Jews' Street.

After the assassination of the strongest candidate for the Presidency of Guatemala, in 1951, election posters and slogans cluttered the walls of buildings. Among the names of the candidates was that of the well-known liberal Garcia Granados. My eye was caught by a big poster for Jacobo Arbenz, who was also running for President, and which referred, in derogatory fashion, to Garcia Granados as "El Mesias Judio" ("The Messiah of the Jews"). He was accused of being more concerned with securing Israel as the land of the Jews, than with the welfare of his own country. And the Jews of the world, it said, hailed him as their Messiah.

Conditions at the time were tense and strained, and the Palacio Nacional looked like a military fortress. Armed soldiers were patrolling the streets, and it was impossible to get through to any government office. Yet, I felt that I could not leave Guatemala without trying to see Garcia Granados.

Through the intervention of Eric Heinerman, then Israeli Consul in Guatemala, I asked for an interview. And Garcia Granados, hearing that there was a Jewish journalist visiting the country who wanted to speak to him, agreed immediately. The interview was arranged at his Party headquarters.

We were not the only ones in the waiting room, wanting to see Granados. Many people sat there, including a peasant from a remote region, an Indian in his primitive dress, and several young students. They had all come to lay their complaints and grievances before Garcia Granados, Heinerman explained, or to thank him for some favor he had done. Through his intervention, one student had received a grant to study abroad; another sought a grant to continue his studies.

The walls were hung with portraits of Latin American heroes and celebrities. The massive bookcases were full of works of literature, philosophy and science. There were also some books in Spanish about Jewish problems.

A secretary said that Garcia Granados was awaiting us in his study. When we came in, a pleasant man of average height greeted us with the Hebrew salutation, *"Shalom."* Without waiting for my questions he began to talk about his visit to Israel. He

spoke with admiration about the young people in the *kibbutzim*.
"I have rarely seen such fine young people anywhere," he said. "I
wish our Guatemalan youth had the same idealism."

"When your State was still a State-on-the-way," he continued,
"I already saw that you had everything a State needs: an idealistic youth, ready to give their lives for their land, good statesmen and diplomats and scientists who have done much for the
progress of the world. When I visited Palestine—Israel—I soon
realized that there was only one solution to the tormenting problem of a persecuted and wronged people against whom the world
has committed an injustice: to give them their own land. That is
when I began to interest myself seriously in the fate of the Jew."

At this point I found an opportunity to put my first question:

"Had you any previous contact with the Jewish problem before you visited the Jewish homeland as a member of the United
Nations Inquiry Commission?"

"No! Previously I had almost no interest in Jewish problems.
I knew no more about Zionism than anyone who is at all acquainted with world politics. I knew about Dr. Herzl, the founder
of the Zionist movement, and I knew about the Balfour Declaration. But I didn't know about the Jewish problem as a whole."

"When," I asked, "did the Jewish problem and Jewish de-
mands come to be closer to you?"

"In the last World War, at the time of the terrible Jewish holocaust, when six million Jews were exterminated by the Nazis in
the ghettoes and the crematoria. I felt that something must be
done for the Jewish people whose tragedy was so great because
they had no land of their own. I believe that if the Jewish people
had their own State before the last war—no matter how small—
Hitler would never have dared carry out his plan of extermination. When the Jewish question was under discussion at the sessions of the United Nations I was my country's representative,
and later I was appointed a member of the United Nations Inquiry Commission that went to Palestine.

"When I was in Beer Sheba I spoke with the American news-
paperman, Gerold Frank, who had a year before accompanied
Bartley Crum, and supplied him with information which Crum

afterwards used in his book *The Silken Cord.* He gave me the book. I was so moved by it that I sat down and wrote my own book, *The Birth of Israel,* and I became an avowed supporter of the aims of the Jewish people.

"While I was in Palestine," he continued, "I met some of the commanders of the Jewish underground, the Haganah, and I was left in no doubt that if it came to open war, the Jewish army would be able to deal effectively with the Arab countries. I said at that time at a press conference in New York that the Haganah would win, and I am glad that my prophecy came true."

"What is your feeling," I asked, "about the strained political situation between Israel and her Arab neighbors?"

"I said years ago, when I was in Israel, that Israel can live in peace with her Arab neighbors, and even play a great part in the development of the Near East. I want to repeat this now."

"And what is your feeling," I put my third question, "about our other war—the war on the Israeli economic front?"

"That is the right word," Garcia Granados answered. "I am sure that the young State will win this war as well. The only difference is that the economic war calls for cold, sober calculation, not passionate idealism. I trust the strategy of the Israeli diplomats and statesmen, just as I trusted the strategy of her military commanders. I have confidence in the Jews all over the world that they can build their own land."

Not long after, Garcia Granados was appointed Guatemalian Consul to the State of Israel.

Guatemala still suffers from political convulsions and economic difficulties. The regimes change frequently, punctuated by uprisings and military *putsches.* As usual, the Jews are a target and scapegoat. Vice President Clemente Marroquin Rojas led a campaign of anti-Semitic propaganda in his newspaper *La Hora.* He published vilifying articles and long quotations from the Protocols of the Elders of Zion.

Upon the request of Guatemalan Jewish community leaders who had conferred with a representative of the American Jewish Committee, the latter's representative in Washington discussed the problem with State Department experts and the Ambassador of Guatemala to the U.S.A.

The Ambassador described the respect and esteem in which the Jewish community is held in Guatemala, the country's friendly relations with Israel, his own friendship with prominent Guatemalan Jews, and said that the Vice President's views do not influence thoughtful citizens. There is no evidence of rising anti-Semitism, and the *La Hora* articles do not represent a campaign against the Jews. The Ambassador agreed to bring the situation to the attention of the President, and recommend that he issue a statement referring to the equal rights and responsibilities of all Guatemalan citizens.

Vice President Rojas probably received payment for publishing the anti-Semitic articles—possibly from Arab League or German elements—although there is no concrete evidence to this effect. There is a large Arab population in the country and a number of German coffee planters have lived in Guatemala for many years. During the last World War they were faithful followers of Hitler, and some of their sons volunteered to fight in the Nazi ranks.

EL SALVADOR: A TINY JEWISH COMMUNITY

El Salvador has one of the smallest Jewish communities in Central America, numbering around 300 souls, all living in the capital city, San Salvador. The official history of the Jews of El Salvador dates back to 1875, when a number of German Jews, mainly from the province of Posen, arrived in El Salvador, Guatemala and Peru. (In Spanish colonial days, El Salvador was part of Guatemala and shared the same commissar of the Holy Inquisition. Unofficial Jewish history dates back to that era.) The next small infusion consisted of Alsatian Jews from France, joined by a smaller number of East Europeans.

Among the Jewish pioneers was the Sephardic family of de Sola, whose head, Herbert de Sola, succeeded in establishing a prosperous business. He reached the venerable age of 100. Two of his sons carry on the business. A third son is a physician, and a fourth is one of the Republic's leading architects. (For a while,

Dr. Orlando de Sola was the country's Minister of Health.)

Another leadership role belongs to the Liebes family. Their enterprise, Goldtree, Liebes and Co., is one of the country's largest businesses. It was founded in 1888 by the brothers Leon and Carlos Liebes (who had come from Germany), in partnership with the Goldtree brothers (who had been in business in California). Later, the families were linked more closely through marriage. As their import business expanded, they became exporters of domestic products, such as coffee.

The Liebes family is well-known throughout Central America. The father left a substantial sum for the Hebrew University in Jerusalem. One son, Ernesto, is the Consul for Israel in El Salvador. Another son, Gerhard, was Vice President of the Hebrew University and is now a professor there. He is also the Consul General for El Salvador in Israel.

In 1950 the Jews of San Salvador built their own synagogue. Before this time they met for services in a private home. The community supports numerous functions and activities: there is a cemetery, a WIZO group, a Zionist association, and a Jewish National Fund committee whose chairman was Ernesto Liebes. The community has no needy members. Though a relief committee exists, there are no recipients of its assistance.

During the rise of Nazism in Europe the number of East European Jews in El Salvador increased. These Polish and Rumanian Jews now work together with the earlier arrivals—the Sephardim and the German Jews—in a central *kehilla,* and all live in harmony. The central community body is affiliated with the Federation of Central American Jewish Communities.

El Salvador's Jews take pride in pointing out that 60% of them have paid a visit to Israel. To maintain further contact, they are visited by *madrichim* who carry out leadership programs and other activities among the youth.

The great problem affecting the younger generation is: where to obtain brides. Some have sought them in Israel, others in Brazil. Others go to the United States to study. They remain there because it is so much easier to find a life's partner.

On my first visit to San Salvador I came across a hotel called,

Nuevo Mundo (the New World), a massive modern building in the European style. Noticing a Star of David design in the very middle of the lobby, I asked the proprietress why she placed this design in the largest hotel in town. Her reply was: "What would you expect me to put up—a crucifix?"

I was told of a moving incident characteristic of Jewish solidarity. Several hundred refugees from the European holocaust had managed to board a ship going to Costa Rica. All had obtained visas from Costa Rican consulates abroad, but despite this they were forbidden to land in Costa Rica. Fortunately, the manager of the Italian travel service in San Salvador was Jewish, and he immediately informed the local Jewish community of their compatriots' plight. Who knows what would happen to them if they were returned to Europe which was still in the throes of the war? The San Salvador Jews sought and received permission for them to land in El Salvador, on condition that they would not be a burden on the State, and that they would be supported by the Jewish community until some other destination could be found for them. The group was maintained in San Salvador until the war ended.

A second story sheds some light on the Jewish past of El Salvador. The community had ordered a Torah scroll which had been salvaged from one of the German communities destroyed by the Nazis. When the scroll arrived, it was explained to the customs officials that this was not a piece of merchandise, but a religious object which was free of duty. In the presence of the customs inspectors the scroll was unrolled in order to reveal its contents. Having done this the synagogue president who had come to claim the Torah scroll proceeded to re-wind the scroll—rather hastily. The customs official interrupted saying: "Not so fast! If this is a sacred object we must be more careful with it and re-roll it properly." When the Jew had completed the re-winding the customs inspector pressed his lips to the *Sefer Torah* before handing it back to the astonished Jew. The official said: "I am descended from Jews, and I know that this is the Holy Bible that God gave the Jews through Moses on Mount Sinai."

Although the Jewish community numbers only about 300 persons in a total population of nearly three million, the Jews became a target of anti-Semitic propaganda during a presidential election campaign, when the newspaper *Diario de Hoy* attacked two community leaders, both of whom are involved with large business interprises. They were Francisco de Sola and Ernesto Liebes, honorary Consul General of Israel in El Salvador, and the brother of the President of the Jewish Community. Pamphlets signed by the military committee, Al-Roce, attacking "International Judaism," were widely circulated at the same time.

The German coffee planters sympathized with Hitler during the second World War, and organized a clandestine spy network, furnishing the Nazis with frequent reports on U.S. shipping in Central American ports. U.S. intelligence succeeded in tracking down the spy ring.

NICARAGUA: A BESSARABIAN JEWISH SHTETL

Nicaragua was discovered in 1502 by one of Columbus' lieutenants. He found a peaceful tribe dwelling between two oceans and living mainly from fishing. The head of the Spanish expedition presented the tribal chief (his name was Nicaragua) with a shirt, a red hat, and a silk cloak. The chieftain reciprocated with the drink of a fruit called coco. When the Spanish leader tried to convert the Indian chief to Catholicism, the latter asked if the king of Spain was also immortal.

Until 1821, Nicaragua and part of Guatemala belonged to the Viceroy of Mexico, and were under Spanish rule. In that year, when many of the Latin American lands were freed from Spain, a federation of the provinces of Central America was formed to which Nicaragua adhered. When this was dissolved in 1838, Nicaragua became independent.

The country consists of a narrow, serpentine belt winding between the seas and the mountains.

The history of the tiny community of some 250 Jews is similar to that of many other Jewish communities in Central and South America. It has passed through three periods of development.

During the Spanish period, Nicaragua was part of Guatemala, and was under the Sacred Tribunal of the Inquisition whose headquarters were in Mexico and whose commissars were dispersed, and later, when the Portuguese regained Brazil, the Jews fled in terror scattering throughout the Caribbean islands; some coming to Nicaragua. All that has remained of this period are various family names that perversely attest to Jewish ancestry because of their Christological form. They include, Santos, Espinoza, Santamaria and similar names which Jews had adopted as a protective device to shield themselves against the suspicion of the Inquisition.

Some vestigial evidences of the second period have remained to this day. In the nineteenth century Jews from Germany and France (Alsace) came to Nicaragua. Many of them mixed with the local population, and their descendants were so submerged that all consciousness of their Jewish origin was lost. There are, however, some highly placed families who recall with pride their Jewish beginnings. These include families such as Huek, Salomon and Teple.

A Señor Raczkiewski who for a while was the mayor of Managua, and Carlos Huek who was Minister of Finance, are both of Jewish descent. The latter regards himself as a "Catholic Jew." The late President of Nicaragua Dr. Rene Schick, formerly Foreign Minister, was of Jewish origin. Vice-President Chakowski is the son of a Jewish immigrant, though he seems to take no special pride in this. The wife of former President Anastasio Somoza, Isabel, had a Jewish great-grandfather named Manuel Gross who came to Central America in 1848. In Granada there are graves belonging to a Jewish cemetery of that period.

When President Schick visited Israel a short time before he died, the President of Israel, Zalman Shazar, told him at a reception given in his honor that Schick is an aristocratic Jewish name and is an abbreviation of the Hebrew quotation, *"S'eu yedeichem kodesh"* (hold your hands in holiness). Mr. Shazar stressed that Nicaragua was the first country to recognize Israel's struggle for freedom in 1948, at the time of the United Nations decision.

Nicaragua's present Jewish commuity dates back to 1935 when the first *minyan* (quorum of ten men for a religious service) was assembled on the occasion of the circumcision of the first Jewish child to be born in that period. The child was Saul Retelny, a former Consul for Israel in Nicaragua. His father was the late Jose Retelny, one of the pioneers of Nicaragua Jewry today. Retelny had many plans for the Jewish settlements in Central America; he even had in mind a yeshiva in Managua to serve the whole area, and brought in a rabbi who was to be the spiritual leader for the communities of Central America.

Before the great European Jewish catastrophe many of the Jews in the Central American countries considered themselves as temporary visitors, looking forward to returning to their homes in Central and Eastern Europe. Some had arrived from other parts of Latin America and were hoping to earn some money before returning to Europe. The disaster of 1939-45 exploded their dreams. They then began to adjust to reality, and reconciled themselves to establishing a permanent community. Most Nicaraguan Jews are from Bessarabia—simple, unpretentious folk, as described by the Yiddish writer, Isaac Raboy, in his *Bessarabian Soil:* "Jews who extend a hearty *sholom aleichem,* full of respect and deep warmth."

When I first visited Nicaragua the Jews had a club which bore the straightforward name of *Club Judio* (the Jewish Club). It was divided into two sections: on one side the library, and on the other the house of prayer with the holy ark and scrolls. One Friday night after prayers, I was the guest of Managuan Jews, and spoke to them of the Jewish world beyond Central America. When I ended my talk the President slapped his hand down on the table and announced firmly: "Jews, you have heard what our guest has told us about Jewish troubles and sorrows. Let's begin the campaign now!" After I had persuaded them that I was not there for any fund-raising cause, they all asked, "If not, why on earth did you come to Nicaragua?"

Recently this tiny community has become more active. In 1963 a synagogue and center, Beth-El, was built. Prayer services are held weekly and a cantor is engaged for the High Holidays. The community has been given legal status by the government. The WIZO is active, and a Jewish National Fund committee, a Zionist association, and a B'nai B'rith lodge exist. There is also a school for children and a voluntary burial committee *(chevra kadisha)*. The Israel Ambassador to Costa Rica frequently visits Nicaragua where he addresses the Jewish community. As in most other similar communities, the youth that is reaching maturity faces problems of education and of finding mates. Some youths are sent to North American *yeshivot*. At the Yeshiva Torah Vadaat in Brooklyn I met a group of boys from Nicaragua. In most cases, once the young people leave to study, they remain abroad and do not return. As a result, the problem of finding husbands for the Jewish girls is a very real one.

COSTA RICA: A BASTION OF POLISH JEWS

Costa Rica calls herself, "The Pearl of Central America." She is proud of her long tradition of democracy, religious liberty and freedom of the press. The people will tell you with pride how in 1840, when the Church wanted to have all heretical books burned, the President, Juan Moro, put a stop to it, and ordered more such books to be brought into the country.

Costa Rica is also proud of the fact that her education budget is a fifth of the total budget. Costa Rica is the most educated country in Central America. She has practically no army—only a Civil Guard—and is the most stable state in Central America. In contrast to her neighbors in all her long history she has had only one dictator—a rarity in that part of the world. And he too didn't last long!

After she had won her independence from Spain, Costa Rica belonged, for a time, to the federation of the Central American countries. Apart from some minor conflicts with her neighbors, Nicaragua and Panama, her history has been a peaceful one.

The country was discovered in 1502 by Columbus, who named it Costa Rica, the rich coast. An area of nearly 20,000 square miles supports a population of about 1,300,000 of which less than 1,500 are Jews, mostly of Polish origin. They have established a model social and cultural community.

Officially Costa Rican Jewry began a hundred years ago, when Jews from Curacao and the Caribbean islands settled there. With few exceptions, they mingled and merged with the surrounding population. Unofficially, Costa Rica, like other Central and South American countries, has a much longer Jewish history, going back to the days of the Inquisition. The Inquisition Tribunal in Mexico City exercised jurisdiction over all the Provinces north of Panama, and had its commissars in each of these countries, though no exact trace of their activity (as in Guatemala) has remained.

The present Costa Rican Jewish community is less than 50 years old, about the youngest on the continent. Its founder, I was told in San Jose, the country's capital, was a Jewish shoemaker from Zelichow, who made his way to Costa Rica. He did not know one word of the language when he came. Seeing a shoemaker's shop, he walked in, and with sign language made himself understood: he was a shoemaker, and he wanted work. He was given a job, but soon found the pay was not enough to live on, so he turned to the usual occupation of new Jewish settlers— he became a peddler, going from house to house selling all kinds of goods. Next, he opened a shoe shop, and brought over his sweetheart from Poland.

That was the beginning of the Jewish settlement. Most of the Jews in Costa Rica came from the same Polish town, Zelichov. First they established a synagogue, a cemetery and a Zionist Center. Gradually the community grew and developed. Its members took an increasingly large part in the life of the country, in its trade and industry. They established connections with the United States, where many of them had relatives. They started small workshops in their homes, making leather goods, men's and women's clothing, and furniture. The workshops grew and became factories, and the immigrants became important manufacturers, leaders of the country's industry, and exporters. Costa Rica is a small country, but the influence of its Jews is considerable. They provide employment for large numbers of the native-born population, and contribute considerably to the national economy.

There is now a Jewish intelligentsia in Costa Rica, the sons and daughters of the former immigrants: doctors, lawyers, technicians. The community has created a strong social and cultural organization for its work. It has built a fine communal Jewish-Zionist Center, which has a big library, a restaurant, a modern swimming pool, and an active Young Zionist Club.

Costa Rica has a Jewish Day School, named after Dr. Chaim Weizmann, the first Hebrew-Spanish day school in the Central American countries. There are now plans for building a Jewish boarding school to take children from neighboring countries which have no Jewish schools. At the opening of the Weizmann School, the Minister of Education, Ismael Antonio Vergas, said that the new school would create closer contact between Costa Rica and Israel, and would make a valuable contribution "to the cultural life of our country." The Minister's address was printed in the Spanish-Jewish magazine *Baderej*. The magazine, published by the Federation of the Central American Jewish Communities, reflects the life of the Jewish communities in the five Central American countries.

Among the Jewish organizations are a Zionist Federation, Wizo, B'nai B'rith, a Zionist youth organization (Hanoar Hazioni) and a youth group with the Hebrew name *atid* (Future), consisting of young Jews of the third-generation born in the country. This group has produced Sholom Aleichem plays in Spanish, has arranged an exhibition of books on Jewish subjects in Spanish by Jewish and non-Jewish writers, and has sponsored lectures and round-table discussions on Jewish problems.

For some years, Costa Rica has had a branch of the Confraternidad Judio Cristiana and Instituto Cultural Costarricense Israeli, which seek to promote friendly understanding between Jews and Christians. One of the leaders of the Confraternidad, Padre Benjamin Nunes, spoke about the suppression of Jewish life in the Soviet Union at a conference of 50 Latin American intellectuals which was held in Rio de Janeiro. A resolution was adopted calling on the Soviet Union to restore religious and cultural freedom to Soviet Jewry.

The Jewish youth in Costa Rica is free from the sense of inferiority that was characteristic of their immigrant parents and grandparents, who were unsure of their place and their future in this new country. They identify themselves proudly with Jewish life and Jewish interests, and their unapologetic attitude has won them general esteem. The establishment of the Jewish State of Israel, and the heroic fighting of the Jewish Army there, has also had the effect of winning greater respect for Jews generally. Both former presidents, Francisco Jose Orlich and Jose Figueres, had visited Israel and came back with glowing reports of the Jewish State.

✓   ✓   ✓

In the district just off the *mercado* (market) there used to be a cafe where Jews would meet every day for a chat, to exchange news, or simply to hear each other talk in their own familiar mother-tongue. The eating-house was named after its owner, Cafe Race, and served traditional old country dishes, foods with the taste of the *shtetl* about them—gefilte fish, onion rolls, *kreplach* and even *knishes*. All day long the cafe resounded with the energy and verve of Polish Jewry. It was as though a living cross-section of the Nalewki quarter of Old Warsaw had survived and had been transplanted to this faraway spot, retaining that special color, initiative and mobility peculiar to the Polish Jew, which identifies him immediately wherever he may be.

The first person I met in Cafe Race was a man named Flicker. He traded in a very special item, in which he had no competitors. He would buy from Jews their share of the World To Come. He insisted on purchasing mine despite my insistence that I was not assured of much of a portion in Paradise. Nonetheless he wanted to make a deal with me.

At night, the restaurant was packed and noisy, with everyone recounting the events of the day's rat-race. Notes were compared about deadbeats who don't pay, and views exchanged on how to collect the debts owed.

Late at night, when the coffee house began to empty, those who had families to go home to could be easily distinguished from those who had nothing more than a cold bed in a room, and were all alone in a strange country. During the day, amidst all the talk and tumult, one was not aware of their loneliness. But now that night had come, their loneliness surfaced. They would recall their dear ones who were burned in the crematoria. They had slaved

51

their youthful days away in these tropical streets upon which they were now gazing, and they would remember the wife and child left behind in Poland. They had hoped to earn enough money to bring them over. But the Nazi beasts crushed their loved ones before they could complete the task. These thoughts ran through their minds before trudging off for a nights' sleep in their dismal, solitary rooms.

One of these men approached my table and asked if he could speak to me. "I understand that you are a writer and a man of the world . . . so you may be able to give me some advice," he began in an apologetic manner. "I just couldn't waste my younger years, and since there were no Jewish girls here, I married a local girl, a quiet and good woman. We have two fine children. All would be well—true, she raised them as Catholics—that didn't bother me. I never was much of a saint and wasn't observant or religious. But now that the Nazis have burnt my father and mother in the crematoria, and all I have of them are their pictures, my wife has put on the wall, between their portraits, an image of the Virgin Mary. "They are all holy martyrs," she says. When I awoke once in the middle of the night, I saw my wife on her knees, praying before the image of the Virgin and my parents. Tell me," he asked in desperation, "you are a modern person. Give me some counsel. Should I leave my wife and children for this?"

PANAMA: THE GATES TO THE WORLD

The first impression that a visitor receives in Panama is the striking contrast between the Panama Republic and the American Canal Zone. The American Zone has the appearance of a provincial town in New England—modern villas fenced around with little vegetable gardens, paved streets lined with palms, modern hotels and spotlessly clean restaurants, even a cafeteria where the Panamanian can satisfy his hunger with appetizing *gringo* meals. (In Panama the North Americans are called *gringos*, not *Yanquis* as in the other Latin American lands.)

Panama itself is a typical Latin American city with all its advantages and drawbacks. In the center are splendid, modern structures, comfortable cafes, parks abloom with flowers, and fine government structures built in a mixed architectural style.

Only a few blocks from the city center, however, the picture changes rapidly: narrow, closely-pressed alleyways, old-fashioned buildings resembling fortresses, windows encased in iron bars, antiquated balconies. An encrusted, long-neglected poverty cries out from every side.

Further along is a district which is strikingly similar to a port area anywhere in the Middle East. Business goes on in the open air, the wares spread out on the street: colorful rags from Iran, Japanese kimonas, silk umbrellas from the Phillipines, Mexican ponchos, straw hats (they are called Panama hats, though made in Ecuador), French perfumes, and bargains from Hong Kong. Ships from the seven seas come and go through the Panama Canal bringing goods from everywhere.

Panama was discovered by Columbus on his fourth voyage in 1502, and became the center from whence the *conquistadores* sent their plunker back to Spain. Its population is 1,800,000, on an area of somewhat more than 28,000 square miles. Until 1903 it was a province of Colombia. At that time Colombia, being unwilling to accept the conditions set by the U.S.A. for the building of the Panama Canal, Panama declared its independence and signed an agreement with the United States to construct the canal which Simon Bolivar, the liberator of Latin America, called "the bridge of the world."

After they had conquered the New World the Spaniards had planned a canal to connect the Atlantic and the Pacific Oceans. In 1776 Charles the Great took certain steps towards implementing this, but it was not until a century later that the French engineer De Lesseps began to construct it, and in 1914 it was finally completed by the United States.

Panama is no exception to the rule that applies to all other Latin American countries, where most of the land is in the hands of a small, privileged class—a legacy of the Spanish conquerors which has been handed down through the generations. The average Panamanian feels envy when looking at the wealth of his next door neighbors, and this feeling is strengthened when he sees the wealth of the foreigner in the nearby Canal Zone—foreigners who control *his* Panama Canal.

This sentiment is often exploited by political demagogues who seek to build their careers on this appeal, and incite the masses under the banner of patriotism. It takes little time or effort to agitate masses who see others living much more comfortably than they. The man on the street is certain that if the Canal belonged to Panama all his problems would be solved. But there are also political leaders in Panama who are sober and farsighted and who can see the other side of the coin. They realize that if the United States should cease its support of the Canal even for a short while, the country would be bankrupt. They also are aware that the United States has a concession to build a canal in nearby Nicaragua which could be just as useful to her as the Panama Canal.

Panama's Jewish community, numbering 2,000, is the oldest and the largest in Central America. The official date of its beginning is 1876, when Jews arrived from the West Indies, though evidence exists that English Jews had lived there earlier, and certainly Marrano Jews practiced their faith there when the area was still part of Colombia and was under the jurisdiction of the Inquisitorial Tribunal of Cartagena. It was in 1876 that the first synagogue was founded in Colon: *Kol She'erith Israel*—which is today the Reform Temple. These first settlers came from Barbados, Curacao and the Virgin Islands, after they had been ravaged by an earthquake and floods. Later, Sephardic Jews from Syria came and set up a strictly traditional *kehilla* called *Shevet Achim,* which has its own Orthodox rabbi.

When Panama assumed independence and the Canal was built, the Jewish colony grew in numbers. Russian Jews, fleeing the Czarist pogroms, were the first East Europeans to come, and were followed by others. The most recent influx was in the 1930's. German Jews, seeking a haven of refuge to escape Nazism, discovered that Panama put no difficulties in the way of "tourists" and dispensed with the guarantees that other states required. At that time, several thousand Jews arrived in the U.S. Canal Zone, where they were provided with further opportunities to emigrate elsewhere.

With the growth of Jewish immigration, the economic opportunities for newcomers increased commensurately. Thanks to
Panama's position as a free port and its trade connections, Jews
soon began to assume some importance in the country's economic
life. The newcomers organized their own communal structure. Together with those German Jews who remained in Panama, the
East European Jewish immigrants built a center which embraces
a synagogue, a library, and a recreation hall. It is known as *Beth
El,* and is Panama's third Jewish congregation.

A fourth community group is the Esther Witkin Center in the
Canal Zone, erected by the National Jewish Welfare Board for
the Jewish soldiers serving there, and dedicated to the memory of
the wife of Rabbi Nathan Witkin, the center's spiritual leader.
She was tragically killed when a military plane crashed on the
community center, and set it ablaze. All these *kehillot* are linked
together in a central committee—the Consejo Central Comunita-
rio Hebreo de Panama—though each maintains its own building
and carries on its autonomous program.

The six Central American communities recently held a symposium on Torah and community affairs. The themes included:
The Jew Faces the Twentieth Century; Social Justice in Jewish
Tradition; and The Meaning of Galut. Rabbis Simeon F. Maslin
of Curacao and Dr. Herschel Klepfisch of Panama were the discussion leaders.

Panama has an important educational center for the younger
generation: the Albert Einstein Institute, popularly called the
Instituto. It is a handsome, well-equipped structure, utilizing
modern educational methods, with a staff of teachers under the
direction of Dr. Herschel Klepfisch. In an all-day-school program
a general curriculum of studies is followed along with Hebrew
language and Jewish studies. It is attended by 80% of the Jewish
children of Panama and even non-Jewish pupils are registered.

Panama also has a Zionist organization, a WIZO and a B'nai
B'rith lodge. From time to time youth conferences have taken
place under the leadership of *madrichim* from Israel. Seminars
for Central America's Jewish youth—Seminario Campamento—
are held in a camp near Panama. The larger Central American

Jewish settlements share the same problems as the smaller ones, but because of their numbers, the Jews do not face a great risk of being submerged in the surrounding milieu.

Faithful to its tradition of tolerance and freedom for all, without distinction of race or religion, Panama has had no anti-Semitism. Jews enjoy all civil freedoms, and the country acknowledges their contribution to its growth and development. Proof of this is that the Republic's first vice-president, Max Delvalle was a Jew and a leading member of the *Shevet Achim* synagogue. A second Jew, Moises Kahn, was a member of the National Assembly for the Christian Democratic Party. The government issued a special postage stamp on the anniversary of the historic *Kol She'erith Israel* synagogue. A special postage stamp was also issued displaying the synagogue in the U.S. Zone, bearing the imprint *Libertad de Cultos* (Freedom of religion).

The Archbishop of Panama is associated with the Confraternidad Judio Cristiana.

ᐟ   ᐟ   ᐟ

The Jewish visitor who stays for an extended period of time and examines the life of the Jews there, begins to sense the sadness and longing that pervades the communities of Central America. All day long the Jews are engaged in their shops or factories. In the evening, when the hot sea-breezes subside, and the rustle of the palm trees is heard in the quiet boulevards where the Jews have erected their homes—when you come across one of these Jews in the evening, you get a strange feeling. He gives the impression of still being on board a ship, cutting through the billows. This is especially true of those who come from the East European towns and townlets where there existed a well-rooted, full-sapped and vibrant Jewish life. Though they have more or less made their adjustment it does not take long before they speak their mind and tell what is bothering them.

Isaiah Wischnitzer (a brother of the noted historian, Arnold Wischnitzer) has assumed the duty of bringing the Jewish dead to burial, and providing them with proper tombstones. On many of these stones the inscription reads only (in Hebrew) : Here lies.... (followed by a name and a date). Here lie the unfortunate remnants of the great Jewish tragedy; the holocaust erased all traces of the relatives of these dead who might be informed of their passing.

One Saturday night in Colon, a night of intense heat, of raucous jazz music, of many uniformed men seeking a few hours of pleasure to assuage their loneliness, a Jewish wanderer, stranded in Colon, confided in me: "I've got more than enough for a living, but what's the good of it when not a living soul has remained from my town back home, and when I'm the only one in my family who has survived." A severed limb of what was a widespread family, he pours out his feelings to me in this dance-hall saloon of which he, incongruously enough, is the proprietor. In the background the jazz band keeps blaring louder, and through the paltry open door drifts the laughter of dancing couples, the clinking glasses borne by waiters hustling about with their trays, the metallic sound of cashiers counting the take. Amidst the tumult the owner stands thinking only of his loneliness and his dear ones who perished in the crematoria.

Years ago, he told me, he left home as a stowaway aboard a freighter, without passport, visa or money. When he was caught he had to work on the boat for three months without pay. He was given the hardest tasks, shovelling coal and working in the kitchen. When the freighter approached the port they wanted to hand him over to the Panamanian police. "So," he said, "I became a runaway again, and, as you see, worked my way up rather well. But what's the good of it if loneliness eats me up?" He looked at me sadly. "I can't marry a local girl as others have done. My father was the *dayan* in our town—I've disgraced his memory enough as it is. A decent Jewish girl won't have me when she learns what my business is. I can't leave the country—I have no documents whatsoever! He is reluctant to apply to the police for anything, for fear of being punished for entering the country without a passport. He would like to get out and get aboard a ship and leave all this behind. If he stays, he will choke with loneliness. He looks at me and asks: "As a world traveller, perhaps *you* can advise me of a country I can enter without a passport?"

CHAPTER IV.

Colombia: The Land of Contrasts

Colombia is a land of contrast and contradictions. There is such variance between one town and another that you might think you were in two different countries. Cali and Medellin for example, are sun-drenched and alive with laughing, carefree people; Bogota, the capital, rarely sees the sun, and is cool and rainy. Soon you discover how much people's character depends on climate!

Clouds hang over the surrounding mountains of Bogota and the rain keeps lashing at your face. The town is more than 8,000 feet above the sea, and one soon tires from walking the streets. The wind tears at the ponchos, and the sound of cars whistling by is deafening. But the Bogotanos seem to enjoy it. In the late hours of the night you can hear serenades being sung in the streets.

Bogota is called the Athens of Latin America; it has more bookshops than all the other towns in Colombia. Colombia takes pride in its literary tradition. A great number of its presidents and statesmen have been writers or members of literary families. President Dr. Carlos Lleras Restrepo, is the great-grandson of Lorenzo Maria Lleras, a well-known journalist and poet.

When you read the Colombian newspapers you are struck by the number of open letters to the editor which contain, in between the grievances and complaints, texts written in poetic form. The natural surroundings evoke poetic feeling; the clouded skies, mist-covered mountains, sun-drenched landscape and wonderful panoramas have molded the Colombian mentality, which is often unashamedly sentimental and romantic.

Like all large Latin American cities, Bogota has modern

buildings and paved streets. But walk further down those streets, away from the center, you blunder into a world of poverty and misery. Huts are made of clay or wooden boards knocked together, and the roofs are made of tin which any strong wind can blow away. In these mouse-holes whole families live without electricity, and without water installations. There is a primitive communal well, and people wait their turn to draw enough water for their daily needs.

In Colombia, as in other Latin American countries, one can find evidence of secret Jews who arrived here with the first explorers from Spain. There is even an opinion that Rodrigo Bastidos, the discoverer of Colombia, was himself of Marrano stock. There are places in Colombia which bear biblical names like Jericho, Bethlehem, Lebanon.

In 1609 the head of the Inquisition Tribunal in New Granada, as Colombia was known at that time, wrote to the Grand Inquisitor in Spain that an Inquisition Tribunal must also be set up at Cartagena, which was a free port, because large numbers of Marranos, refugees from Spain, were entering there and spreading throughout the neighboring lands. By 1881, 800 Jewish victims were condemned and burned at the stake by the Tribunal in Cartagena. Then, Simon Bolivar, the Liberator of Latin America threw off the Spanish yoke and abolished the Inquisition.

In the Museum of Cartagena, kept under glass, there are scores of yellowing, semi-legible records of the Cartagena Inquisition Tribunal. The building which housed the Tribunal is in the center of the town, facing the Plaza Bolivar. It is a squat, massive, fortress-like structure which is used today as a girls school.

The wheel of Jewish history turns strangely. Not far from this former Inquisition Tribunal the small Jewish community of Cartagena has established its synagogue, and on Friday night, after the Sabbath service, I conveyed to them the greetings of the Jews from the outside world.

Later that night, I returned to my hotel whose doors and windows opened upon a spacious patio, overlooking a sea of flowers and tropical plants. But there was no relief from the heat, and the sweat poured down my face. Suddenly, I heard Yiddish words coming from the patio. I followed the sound of the voices and found myself at a table where two Jews sat, broad *sombreros* shading their faces, and scarves around their necks to absorb the perspiration. They spoke a rich Bessarabian Yiddish.

"*Shalom* Jews!" I said. They both rose and looked at me in surprise.

"Where have you come from? What are you doing here in Cartagena?"

I took a seat at their table and they eyed me strangely. After a long silence, one of them said:

"I'm sorry you made such a long journey! Pity! You won't do much here with your pack."

Then I understood. They were afraid I was a business competitor. They thought I had come with a pack of merchandise to sell, going like them from door to door. I reassured them. I told them who and what I was. And then they became quite friendly. This was their second week in Cartagena, and they had been doing well. The local Jews had prospered, and now owned their own shops, so that the towns people appreciated having goods brought to their own doors. They were waiting now for a bit of cool air, before going into the streets again with their packs.

✓   ✓   ✓

It was past midnight, but people were about in the streets, for the heat all day had been stifling, and everybody wanted fresh air. Wandering, I found myself in the center of Barranquilla, near the radio station Emisora Atlantica. Two young Jewish boys and a Jewish girl were preparing a broadcast about a blood libel which had been circulated. It was a real medieval story. A Christian boy had disappeared and had then turned up and said that Jews had kidnapped him; that they had shut him up in a synagogue and sought to draw off his blood. Things were looking ugly. But the police cross-examined the boy, and in the end he confessed that he had been put up to it by people who wanted to stir up anti-Jewish feelings.

"Colombianos! We are addressing ourselves to you and to your feelings of humanity," the Jewish broadcast began. "Don't believe the malicious stories that are being spread about us Jews. We are telling you the true facts now—what actually happened."

Then the girl recited the poem "El Judio" (The Jew), by Gabriela Mistral, the Nobel Prize Chilean poetess. This was followed by a record of Cantor Hershman singing "Habait" from the synagogue liturgy. The plaintive notes of the prayer poured out over the loud speakers outside the radio studio. Under a line of palm trees stood a group of Jews singing softly in tune with the Cantor's recorded voice, word by word. And in the light of the street lamp I saw tears in their eyes.

✓   ✓   ✓

Medellin, the capital of the province of Antioquia, is in the most beautiful part of Colombia. All the rest of the country is envious of Medellin. Everybody knows that if any new and original idea is put forward, it must have been born in an Antioquian brain.

Jews have a big stake in this province, for it was founded by Marranos who had fled from the Spanish Inquisition. To the present day Antioquian will tell you that they are descended from Spanish Jews who had accepted Christianity. The New Christians found an Indian tribe there more civilized than the others. They came to an understanding, and instead of fighting and conquering, they succeeded in living together as friends.

For years they had been isolated, ringed round by their high mountains. They had large families, often as many as eighteen or more children. They continued to increase, and over the years grew to be a distinct race called the Paisas, a mixture of Jews and Basques. Nowhere else in Latin America have I seen such Jewish features as among the people you come across in the streets of Medellin. The tall handsome young women with black burning eyes might easily be Jewish. In addition to their faces, which reflect a Jewish origin, their whole way of moving, the very gestures of the Antioquians, mark them as distinct from all other people of the Latin American continent.

The founding families of Colombia were laid to rest in the

aristocratic, Catholic cemetery of San Pedro. Long rows of gleaming white monuments bear names like Perez, Messias (one of the most famous families in Colombia, from the Hebrew *Meshiach*— Messiah), and Santa Maria, all names indicating a Jewish origin, for Marranos often adopted religious Christian names (like Santa Maria) as a cover against the Inquisition.

Another grave that stands out in the San Pedro cemetery is that of Jorge Isaacs, Colombia's national poet, the author of the great novel *Maria*, one of the acknowledged masterpieces of Spanish-American literature. It was published in Colombia, and when it appeared in English translation in the U.S., it was acclaimed as "one of the first, and one of the few novels of Spanish America to transcend the bounds of merely local interest, and to be regarded as a part of world literature." The heroine is a Jewish girl named Esther, modeled after the author's own cousin.

According to Jorge Isaac's daughter, the two brothers, Solomon and Enrique Isaacs, had come to Colombia around 1880 with Simon Bolivar's English Legion. Solomon later settled in Jamaica, but when his young wife died, he brought their daughter to Colombia, to his brother Enrique, who had married a Spanish captain's daughter. Solomon's daughter was brought up together with Enrique's son, Jorge, who became the novelist. Young Jorge was passionately in love with his cousin, and when she died at the age of fifteen, his deep sense of loss fathered the novel, *Maria*.

Jorge Isaacs had been born and raised a Catholic. But when he died he left a will asking to be buried in the San Pedro Cemetery, "with the people of my race, a people that is creative like the bees." The story is told that when he was dying the priest asked him if he believed in Jesus, and he answered, "Of course! He is of my race!"

Recently the Yiddish press reported that the greatgranddaughter of Jorge Isaacs, Maria Gloria Isaacs of Bogota (herself a published poet), had expressed her desire to convert to Judaism. The reason she gave was that she had read the book *Mila 18* in which the brutal killings and murders of the Jews by the Nazis are described. "This moved me very deeply. Then, I read *Exodus* and I found a longing and nearness to the Jewish people. I was inspired and wrote a poem, 'A Song to Israel,' which was published in several magazines in Latin America.

"When I read that Argentinian Nazis carved a swastika on the body of a Jewish girl, I felt that I belonged to the race of my grandparents, and I am now certain that I want to become a Jewish daughter. I began to study the Bible and I know why my greatgrandfather's name is Isaac—it is the name of one of the Fathers."

It is very hard for Catholics to convert to Judaism in Colombia. The Catholic Church has an agreement with the representatives of the Jewish community: They cannot convert Jews, and Jews cannot convert Catholics. This case is particularly difficult in that it involves the great-granchild of a national writer. Maria Gloria Isaacs and her mother approached the Jewish government about the possibility of going to Israel, studying Hebrew in an *ulpan* and sending the children to a *kibbutz*. Her husband is not opposed to this decision, despite the difficulties involved.

In 1894, two brothers named Eder purchased the coffee plantations which had been owned by Jorge Isaac's father. One of the brothers, James Eder, married a Colombian girl, and his children were, therefore, not Jews. His son was at one time the Colombian Minister of Agriculture. The other brother returned to England where he was involved with a shipping company doing business between England and Colombia. His son, Dr. Eder, was active in Jewish affairs, and a cousin of (on his mother's side) Israel Zangwill. After the Balfour Declaration he became head of the Zionist Executive in Jerusalem.

Another leading Catholic family, which goes back to an early period, is descended from a German Jew named Leopoldo Kapp, who came from the traditional Jewish community of Frankfurt am Main. He married into the Castello family, who were relatives of the Montefiores. The Castellos are also believed to have come to Colombia from England with Simon Bolivar's English Legion more than a century ago. Leopoldo Kapp founded what is today Colombia's biggest brewery. Despite his traditional Jewish background Kapp's children had him buried in the Christian cemetery.

It is typical of the fate of many Jewish families who came to

Colombia in the '80's, often with Bolivar, to fight for the liberation of Latin America, to be absorbed into the general population.
All that remains of these Jewish immigrants are tombstones, with
Hebrew inscriptions and symbols, some of them in Catholic cemeteries. Among them are the graves of Bernardo Elbert, the pioneer navigator of the River Magdalena, and Ernesto Cortesos,
who founded the Colombian Airline Scota, which is now the
Avianca. He was killed on an experimental flight with a new
model, and was buried in the old Jewish cemetery, which is over
a hundred years old. Among the Marranos buried there is Jules
Abraham, one of whose grandsons, Zacharia Abraham, was a
General in the Colombian army. Another grandson was Fuentes
Lopez, a distinguished Colombian author. It is not unusual when
the father in a leading Colombian family dies, for his Christian
children to call the *Chevra Kadisha*. At the funeral the non-Jewish children and grandchildren, often high-ranking officers in the
Colombian forces, follow him to the Jewish cemetery.

The present Jewish community in Colombia, which numbers
about 8,000, is a new community, not quite fifty years old. East
European Jews started coming to Colombia in 1921-22, when immigration restrictions tightened in the United States. When they
arrived they found a few Sephardic Jewish families from Syria.
These East European Jews still speak with awe of the way in
which they reached the Colombian shores. There were no modern
harbor installations in Colombia at that time. Passengers were
lowered in baskets on a rope, like cargo, into primitive boats that
took them ashore. And there, the new arrivals, without family or
friends, felt lost and lonely.

But their Jewish vitality and hopefulness pulled them through.
They shouldered packs, and went knocking from door to door,
peddling their wares. Things went well with them; they prospered, and established large textile and furniture concerns, and
became important factors in the growing economic life of the
country.

After the Sephardim and the East European immigrants,
came the refugees from Hitler's Germany in 1933. They brought
with them business training and international connections. The

Second World War opened new economic opportunities to all the Latin American countries, including Colombia. Thanks to their contacts with the United States, Jews in Colombia began to play an important role in industry and commerce. They stopped thinking of Colombia as a way-station. They put down roots and began to build a religious, social and cultural life in Colombia. The immigrants at that period were mostly young men, either unmarried or with wives waiting back home until they could sent for. After their day's work they would meet on the stone seats of the public square in the cool of the evening. Later, they rented a room for a synagogue and got a Sefer Torah from America. And the little synagogue became the meeting place where they sat and talked about their affairs.

These were the initial steps in the development of the new Jewish communities. The small prayer-rooms have grown to be splendid structures, built in the latest architectural styles. Land was bought and Jewish cemeteries were laid out. Sometimes the town council gave the land free. Some Jews who were buried in Christian cemeteries were transferred to the Jewish cemeteries.

The Sephardim, the German Jews and the East European Jews generally maintained a separate life. Even today four Jewish communities can be found in Bogota: Sephardic, German, Eastern European and Hungarian. The German Jews have their own institutions, centering round the Montefiore Club. The Sephardim have their Carmel Club, and synagogue, Magen Ovadiah, named after the Sephardic philanthropist Shaya Ovadiah. The Sephardim and Ashkenazim have their own rabbis. Lately, a central organization has been built in Bogota—a "Beth Am" —a people's house for all the Jewish organizations.

Until 1948 Jewish education in Colombia was on a very low level. Private teachers were from the "old-school," and they taught the children in their homes. However, in 1948, the Colombian Hebrew school was established. About fifty percent of the Jewish children study in the school which consists of classes from kindergarten to high-school. A larger building is now being planned in order to be able to take in more children. Jewish laws and traditions and Jewish history are taught in the language of

65

the country. Traditional Jewish holidays as well as Israel's Independence Day and the Warsaw Ghetto Uprising are commemorated. Hebrew is taught one hour a week. Many Jewish youngsters who finish high-school leave to study in the United States. This creates a problem since many of them remain there, and there are fewer and fewer Jewish youngsters remaining in Colombia.

The Jewish communities in Cali, Barranquilla and Medellin have similar Jewish schools. In Cali, the school is named after the Colombian National writer, Jorge Isaacs. Half of the community is Sephardic and the other half is mainly Eastern European. The percentage of attendance of the Jewish children is much higher here than in the capital city of Bogota. The same holds true in Barranquilla, which now has one of the most modern Jewish schools, the Colegio Union Hebreo.

The Jewish school in Medellin is called Theodor Herzl and is situated outside the town, on a farm. As you walk through the streets of Medellin, you see the blue and white buses with the name Theodor Herzl on them taking children to and from the school, along the same streets where the first Jewish settlers in Colombia walked furtively as Marranos, in order to avoid the terrors of the Inquisition. All the schools have Israeli teachers on their faculties, and Yiddish is not taught at all.

On the whole the Colombians, and Latin Americans in general, are not anti-Semites. Anti-Semitism is imported mostly from outside. Many Germans living in Colombia volunteered to fight in Hitler's armies when they marched as conquerors over Europe. After the Nazi defeat they returned to Colombia, where many had left Colombian wives, and began spreading anti-Semitism.

The seed has borne fruit. I was a witness in Colombia when Jewish shops were smashed. I heard the mob shout *"Matar Polacos"* (Kill the Poles!), by which they meant Jews. At the time of the Nuremburg Trials slogans which read, "The dead will be resurrected," were chalked on walls. One church even held a service for the executed Nazi murderers. But in recent years we have not heard of any anti-Semitic outbursts. The Colombians are generally friendly people, and are anxious to dwell amicably with those who have come to settle peacefully in their country. Anti-Semitism in Colombia, as in the other Latin American countries, depends on the economic health of the country and, more importantly, on the leader of the government at a particular time.

CHAPTER V.

Venezuela: The Land of Black Gold

I visited Venezuela twice. On my first visit the country was ruled by a liberal democratic regime of the Junta Revolucionario, which Romulo Betancourt, a former journalist, headed as President. His official title then was "Citizen President." Throughout the American hemisphere the regime was considered so radical as to be almost Communist.

I had applied for a visa to Venezuela while visiting Bogota, the capital of Colombia. There, the Venezuelan Consul had asked me what my religion was. When I replied, he told me he would send a wire to the Immigration Department in Caracas. For weeks no answer came. During my visit in the town of Barranquilla, also in Colombia, I went to see the Venezuelan consul there. "You're a Catholic, aren't you?" he asked, he tried to forestall my answer to the prescribed question. "You're wrong," I corrected him. "I happen to be a *Judio*."

"In that case," his face shed its amiable expression, "we will have to wire to Caracas."

"And the reply, of course," I said, "will come *mañana*" (tomorrow, that is, *never*). Then I went on: "Aren't you ashamed? Your country which is a revolutionary government is discriminating against people of other races and faiths. How does racism square with revolution?"

The consul became more serious, obviously stung by my words: "Well ... you understand," he stammered, "the Jews ... your people ... are a different, unproductive element ..."

"Those were Hitler's arguments!" I interrupted him, feeling that I was losing control of myself.

He became angry: "I am not issuing any visas for you, and you can do as you like about it!"

"In that case, Mr. Consul," I retorted, "I will get to Caracas without your visa and lodge a complaint before the *Junta Revolucionario.*"

There happened to take place in Bogota at that time a Conference of the Pan-American Press (Prensa Pan-Americana), which was attended by a large Venezuelan delegation. The latter naturally, took up the cudgels for the freedom of the press. With the help of an influential American journalist I made the acquaintance of a member of the Venezuelan delegation, and confronted him with my case. Eight days later I received my visa on a special recommendation. When I arrived in Caracas two days thereafter, one of the local papers ran a streamer across the front page: "Is it true that Venezuela does not admit Jews?"

In dealing with a country which has undergone so many changes in government, and so many revolutions, it is probably wise to refrain from mentioning the names of my benefactors. Who knows where they are today?

The first thing I sought to ascertain, upon my arrival in Venezuela, was the position of the liberal revolutionary regime on the question of Jewish immigration. It was possible, I thought, that the anti-Jewish policy might only represent the individual caprice of an official in the department, or of a consul in a certain country.

I spoke to a high official in the Department of Immigration and was told that very few Jews had been admitted to Venezuela because they were not given visas. Homeless Jewish survivors of the camps, one official frankly said to me, were not a desirable element because they did not make good workers. Besides, he stammered, he was not making the regulations.

Anywhere in Latin America, a press card from the United States opens all doors. But in Venezuela I found it difficult to arrange a personal meeting with "Citizen" Romulo Betancourt, President of the liberal government, who permitted racial discrimination in his country. When I became insistent, the Chief of the Press Bureau at the President's office advised me to leave with him the name of the newspaper I represented. Subsequently, I received an answer that the President was busy with special meetings and that I was to put my questions in writing. I then realized my blunder in showing my press card which had Hebrew letters on it, but it was too late to repair this. I wrote out a question asking why the President, who was a liberal democrat, and the head of the revolutionary regime, tolerated immigration legislation which discriminated against Jews. The Chief of the Press Bureau assured me that I would receive a written reply within two days. Three days later I did receive an answer couched in saccharine tones: The legislation barring Jewish immigrants, the letter said, was a survival from the reactionary regime of Dictator Vicente Gomez. In time, the Citizen-President assured me, the question would be studied.

The legislation was not altered.

There is a piquant episode to report on the ban against Jewish immigration to Venezuela. Once my colleague, the late Dr. Chaim Shoshkes, a world traveller and correspondent, was returning to the United States after an interview with Dictator Perez Jimenez of Venezuela. On the plane he met the democratically-oriented Romulo Betancourt, an ex-President, and asked him why Venezuela does not admit Jews. The reply was: "Look at me! I'm not a Jew! I'm the former president and I'm not permitted to enter either!"

The name Venezuela, which means "Little Venice," is derived from the resemblance of the first hamlet discovered by the Europeans at the Maracaibo River to the Italian city. Out of a population of just under five million souls, 65% are *mestizos* (half white, half Indian), 20% are white, and the rest are a mixture of Negros and Indians.

Venezuela is the most expensive country in Latin America, with a hard currency tied to the dollar. Prices for hotel accommodations, food, and other articles are at least twice those of New York. Most of the goods consumed in the country, including much of its food, is imported from abroad.

Caracas is being built at a feverishly rapid pace. Luxurious villas and beautiful new modern structures rise overnight, some resembling Swiss villas, others New York-skyscrapers.

The poverty-stricken slums of Caracas face the luxurious villas and skyscrapers on the hills surrounding the city with an envy that may easily be turned into an abiding hatred. It is a panorama of disharmony and striking contrasts. The rows of small huts, the so-called *ranchos,* are made of boards and tin and are occupied by families with dozens of children who live in the greatest discomfort and under the most unhygienic conditions. These *ranchos* sway with the wind, and when the rains come they are totally inundated.

There are more than 80,000 such *ranchos* in Caracas, and the government, aware that the constant political turmoil has a direct relationship to their existence, is making an effort to build decent housing projects. The shocking contrast between the extremes of wealth and the most abysmal poverty is apparently not only true of the capital city of Venezuela, but is a universal problem in Latin America. The dream of the libertador Simon Bolivar was to share the great acreages of idle soil among the landless peasants of Greater Colombia, which comprises present-day Venezuela, Colombia, Panama and Ecuador. His dream was not realized. The lands belong, in the main, to a select group which controls the nation's weath. Bolivar himself had to flee to the island of Jamaica. Each time the governments of these countries make an attempt to introduce land reforms and to divide the land among the peasants, they come up against the iron wall of the rich *latifundistas* (land owners). In Venezuela there is an additional difficulty: because of the discovery of "black gold," agriculture has been totally neglected.

Foreign capital keeps flowing in and out of Venezuela. World-famous oil companies, which have concessions in the country, do not even dream that their days may be numbered. They consolidate their positions, building offices and homes marked by the latest comforts and luxuries. They feel that there will always be new oil wells to be discovered when these run out . . .

Situated on a high elevation, Caracas enjoys a mild climate. It is only twenty seven miles from Venezuela's main port of La

Guayra, but the difference in the climate is such that it is hard to believe you are in the same country. La Guayra is as hot as a furnace.

Maracaibo is the country's leading oil center. Its climate is even more torrid than La Guayra's. The moist heat is made even more unbearable by the fumes of the oil wells rising to the sky and overhanging the city. The soil is soaked with oil, which makes it even hotter. In the vicinity of the city are burning oil wells whose fires have not been put out for twenty-five years; Maracaibo is too busy for that, as it has to supply oil to the machines of the whole world. The hot glowing sun and the smoking clouds give the newcomer the impression he has fallen into an inferno. But this place is like paradise to the foreign investors. Today Venezuela is third in the world in the production of petroleum, and first in the capacity of its oil wells. The latter belong, for the most part, to foreign businessmen, and the country gets royalties.

As you step out of the cool air-conditioned hotel, you are suddenly overwhelmed by suffocating heat, and as you walk along the streets of Maracaibo you feel the heat issuing not only from the sun above, but from the earth below as well. Before you have gone very far a scrawny woman's arms are thrust at you, begging for alms. The woman is dressed in rags; she holds one or two children also stretching out their hands to beg. Another few steps and you imagine yourself in the *Villa Miserias* of Buenos Aires, in the *favelas* of Rio de Janeiro, or in the slums of Peru. The slums of New York are palatial dwellings in comparison. You begin to realize why the Venezuelans are always so nervous and restless. They have not found a way of distributing with some degree of fairness the fat checks they get from the foreign oil companies.

✓   ✓   ✓

Unofficially, the Jewish history of Venezuela dates as far back as 1610, when a third Inquisition Tribunal was established in Cartagena, Colombia, with jurisdictions in the neighboring countries of Panama, Santa Marta, Venezuela, Puerto Rico, and Santiago de Cuba. A commissar was appointed in each country.

Following the destruction of the Jewish communities in Brazil

72

after the Portuguese conquest, many Jews escaped to Surinam, Cayenne and Curaçao. Venezuela lay at the junction of these countries. Many Jews remained in Venezuela. The family of Rabbi Choumsaya, whose grave lies in the historic cemetery in Curacao, still lived in Maracaibo a short time ago. The daughter of the household never married, for lack of Jewish menfolk. As in other Latin-American countries, many scions of aristocratic families have Jewish blood in their veins.

It is known that General Antonio Sucre, the friend of Simon Bolivar, was of Marrano descent; also, that the Jew Luis Byron, helped Bolivar in his struggle. Dr. David Lobo, a Jew, served as professor and as Rector of the National University in Caracas, and played a large part in the scientific development of the country. The first railway in Venezuela was built by the Jewish engineer, Jacob Boaz. Isaac Seligmann organized the banking system of Venezuela. In Core, where a few recently arrived Jewish families are still to be found, there is an old cemetery with Hebrew inscriptions going back one hundred and thirty years.

Official government records show that a large group of Sephardic Jews in Venezuela, in 1873, were joined as one community with the *El Porvenir* community in Curacao. In 1891 the Sephardic Jews founded a communal organization called *Armonia* and published a paper by that name. There is still a Sephardic community in Venezuela known by the name of *Asociacion Israelita.*

Modern organized Jewish life in Venezuela begins after World War I, when Jews came from European countries and from other countries in Latin America to seek their fortune in this land of promise. By the end of 1917 there were about five hundred Jewish families in Venezuela, and the number increased during the years between the two world wars.

Following the great tragedy in Europe, and despite the increasingly severe restrictions on Jewish immigration, Jews did manage to find their way into Venezuela. Many entered by using baptismal certificates, for which there was a thriving trade in Europe. The conversion certificates were necessary not only in Venezuela, but in many other Latin American countries. Immediately after disembarking, many tore up the documents. It is said that in one Latin American country some kept these certificates, for who could tell what the future might bring.

We may assume that the Jewish population of Venezuela has by far exceeded the 10,000 mark. The greater part of these Jews live in the capital city of Caracas. Smaller Jewish settlements are found in Valencia, Maracay, Barcelona and Maracaibo, and some three or four Jewish families live in the farthest part of the country. At first, these immigrants utilized their contacts and experience in a very limited way. For the most part, they became importers, and in a country so dependent on imported goods, the Jewish importers contributed much to the economic welfare. The former peddlers followed the general pattern of opening small stores, and later larger ones. Now, over 300 Jewish-owned factories employ over two thousand local workers, producing furniture, leather goods and textiles.

The government recently gave citations to several Jews who distinguished themselves by contributing to the growth and industry of the country.

The pride of the Jews of Caracas is the Herzl-Bialik School, which 90% of the local Jewish children attend. The school also has 120 non-Jewish pupils, including the children of the Minister of Education. The staff consists of 100 teachers, among whom are a conspicuous number of Hebrew teachers. The school starts with kindergarten and runs through high school. The founder and director of the school is Dr. David A. Gross, a well-known pedagogue from the United States. Every year at vacation time a group of students visits Israel under the supervision of their Hebrew teachers.

The children of the early immigrants, who had difficulty entering the country, are now occupying important positions in the professions as well as in the field of literature.

The Orthodox community has its own synagogue, *Shomrei Shabbat,* and rabbi. The Sephardic Jews also have their own community and synagogue. The Union Israelita de Caracas, of which all the organizations are constituents, built a one-million dollar center for the benefit of the whole community. It houses a synagogue and a sports center. Recently, they engaged a young rabbi, Pinchas Brener, who was born in Lima, Peru, and was ordained by the Isaac Elchanan Theological Seminary in New York City.

The Venezuelan Jewish community has won the respect of the non-Jewish population, and particularly the intelligentsia. This is, in great part, related to the formation of the State of Israel. Venezuelan intellectuals have established a committee of "Friends of Israel" which has often made known its admiration and sympathy for the State of Israel and the Jewish people. On Israel Independence Day a special program was performed on television. In commemoration of the Warsaw Ghetto uprising, a representative of the Ministry of Culture lauded the ghetto heroes and condemned the Nazi mass murders. An Israeli exhibition was held in the civic theatre to which the press gave considerable attention. Illustrated pamphlets, graphically depicting the growth of the Jewish state were distributed.

In honor of the publication in Israel of the novel *Doña Barbara*, by Romulo Gallegos, a former Venezuelan president, the Jewish community arranged a festive evening which was attended by three presidents: the author, Romulo Gallegos; Romulo Betancourt, and Raul Leoni, the former Presidents.

Despite all these efforts, one cannot be a complete optimist about the future of Venezuela's Jewry, anymore than one can be overly confident of the future of the other small Jewish communities in Latin America. The threat of assimilation causes real anxiety among the responsible Jewish leaders though, as it happens, Venezuela does not have as large a proportion of mixed marriages as some other Latin American states. This, however, is explained by the fact that a large part of its youth has left to study abroad (mainly in the U.S.A.). Often, they do not return.

It is noteworthy to report the words of a representative of the Jewish Agency, Eliahu Dobkin, when he spoke at a session of the Central Committee of Ichud Olami after a visit to Venezuela:

Jews in the smaller countries of South America, especially those with a population of less than 10,000, are in a situation of national attrition. They will stop being Jews, despite their having Jewish schools and even Hebrew teachers. Assimilation dominates the youth. The Jewish school is a supplementary one only. In the morning the child attends the general public school and, as far as its influence is concerned, let me tell you this story: In a certain town in a Latin American country I was told that a Jewish child asked at home that the bread be sliced by the Christian maid and not by his father, as his father's hands were 'soaked in the blood of Jesus.' In Venezuela there is a Jewish school with 600 children enrolled. I wanted to find two children who could read a Hebrew book. I was directed to one child who happened to be the son of an Israeli emigrant. The teacher, himself an Israeli, expressed his disappointment and concluded: 'This is what Jewish education looks like in these remote communities.' He saw no other solution than 'complete evacuation.'

Though, as I mentioned, I am not a great optimist, I am, nevertheless, not too great a pessimist. This speech of Eliahu Dobkin was delivered in 1960. Since then certain changes have taken place. The schools which he described as "supplementary," are now full all-day schools. Not only Venezuela, but Chile, Colombia and Peru have Jewish Day Schools attended by the majority of the Jewish children. Jewish youth is beginning to find its way back to its source. There are various motives for this, the basic one being that they have received a hint from the non-Jewish side that they are unwelcome.

Their parents, the former immigrants, brought with them lamentably poor spiritual and cultural equipment, and threw themselves entirely into the race for the *peso.* It is due to their pattern of living that the younger generation have become estranged from Jewish values. Now that economic position and security have been attained, they suddenly are aware that something is missing. Serious attention is being given to this. During my last trip to Latin America I had conversations with Jewish professional men who react with indignation to anti-Jewish manifestations. They react with courage and pride and are more agressive than their parents were.

The "total evacuation" prognosis is, in my view, an overstatement.

✓   ✓   ✓

LATTER DAY MARRANOS

The scene of a ship leaving port is the same everywhere. The only difference is in the identity and make-up of the travellers. The boats leaving Italian ports for South America are generally laden with emigrants leaving their beautiful, but poor *"patria"* to seek a living in a new home.

Italians, like all "Latinos," are sentimental by nature, and the scenes at parting are touching and emotional—fathers and mothers break into sobs, kissing, huge bouquets of flowers getting confused with the baggage. The shouts of the crew drown out the farewell melodies played by a band of musicians with guitars, and a covey of white handkerchiefs flutter from the deck-railing as the ship shoves off to the open sea accompanied by shouts of *mama mia.*

Standing in the beautiful port of Naples, as I watched parents bidding farewell to children, I searched among the faces for a Jewish face, and listened in vain for a Yiddish word. Was I really to take such a long sea voyage without meeting any Jews on board?

I thought I recognized a few Jewish faces among the passengers streaming up the gangplank. In particular, I noticed one young couple with two small children who seemed to be nervous, looking back periodically though no one had come to see them off. However, Italian faces can be very deceptive, as some of them often resemble Jews. This couple, however, did have a look about them. . . .

On the second day aboard, I observed that the majority of the passengers on the second class deck were wearing crucifixes. In the very center of the promenade deck stood a chapel with a large portrait of the Virgin Mary and other saints; also on board were many priests and nuns. Some were going on various missions into the remote parts of South America to save souls; others were busy at their work right on the ship.

When I again saw the couple who had boarded the ship, I approached the woman. She spoke to me in a "German" that had sounded like a camouflaged Yiddish, but as I looked at the crucifix hanging prominently from her neck I thought that I must be in error. Nonetheless, I forged ahead and asked directly: "Are you Jews?" She immediately cried out nervously: "No, no, no." Then she shrank from me as though I were a poisonous snake. This, of course, aroused my suspicion even more.

On the fourth day, I had a chat with her husband on the deck quite early in the morning, and I had better luck. He told me they were fleeing from Czechoslovakia where he was a cloth manufacturer. We soon ranged into the field of politics, and I could sense that he was burning to say something, but was careful to make sure with whom he spoke before expressing himself freely.

We had just finished lunch when the bells called the travellers into the chapel. The deck was soon deserted, as I was the only one who had not gone to mass. I sat on a comfortable deck chair, and took it easy reading a Yiddish book. Thus, several days passed. After a while the priests started to check why their attendance at mass was dropping off, and why people were staying in their cabins. One of them came up to me as I sat lounging in my deck chair. In a tone of piety and friendliness he asked why I was not going to mass.

"Padre," I replied directly, "I am a Jew; that's why I don't attend mass." But this reply did not inhibit him in the least, and he went on to admonish me. "Because you are a Jew is the very reason you should attend mass, to cleanse and purify your soul. That is what happened to Rabbino Zolli of Rome ... his soul is now purified and exalted."

He then delivered a lengthy sermon on how the Jews have suffered because they have sinned in not acknowledging the Holy Spirit. I answered rather abruptly that every nation is entitled to its quota of renegades, and Rabbi Zolli was one of them. We had no further conversation for the rest of the trip. He avoided me completely after this.

When our ship docked at Dakar, many of the passengers went ashore to buy souvenirs. Returning to the boat late in the evening, I suddenly heard Yiddish being spoken quite softly. It was an elderly couple among the passengers conversing in a broad Bessarabian dialect.

I came up to them like someone who has made a great discovery, and asked. "Are you Jews?" "Hush-sh," was the man's request, "Take pity, be silent. We're Catholics, don't you understand?" He took me to his cabin on the first class deck and there he told me his story. The country he and the other emigrants were heading for did not admit Jews. He, therefore, carried Catholic identity papers. Later, he said, he would destroy the papers. "And we're not the only ones on the ship," he assured me.

After this, all the crucifixes looked suspicious to me. The larger the crucifix that hung on the woman's bosom, the greater my suspicion! My table-mates in the dining room were a young Hungarian couple, a German (i.e. a "real" German), and a Dutchman. The young woman wore a heavy silver cross. I drew the conversation to the subject of the Hitler massacres. The German grew uncomfortable and protested that not all Germans were responsible for Hitler's deeds. The woman wearing the cross blushed, but said nothing. When the German left the table she smiled at me in gratitude.

"Sie sind von Palestina?"—(Are you from Palestine?)—she asked in Hungarian-accented German, looking around to see that no one should overhear. However, she said nothing further, for she felt she was being observed from the next table.

By now the Czech manufacturer was my good friend. I had his fullest confidence, and he told me how he succeeded in obtaining Catholic papers. He pointed out someone walking on the first class deck. "Do you see that fat man? He is the former director of the 'Joint' in Genoa, and he too is now travelling with the same kind of papers as I."

"I know no one else aboard this ship personally," he assured me, "but I am certain there are several dozen like us aboard."

As the ship approached the Equator we got ready for the immersion ceremony that is traditional for those who are crossing it for the first time. The "dunking" ritual is normally a harmless bit of fun. But this time, because of the large numbers of clergy present, it was transformed into a virtual baptismal ceremony. All those undergoing it were sprinkled with holy water while the priests inclined their heads and hands heavenwards, pronouncing a benediction.

A day before the ship was to stop at a Brazilian port I got up quite early to read the daily telegraphic news bulletin. I noticed a news item emanating from Tel Aviv. Another passenger noticed me reading it, looked at me closely with a smile, and then asked, *"Yehudi?"*

When I answered with a positive *"ken," he replied, "Gam ani Yehudi,"* and put a finger to his lips. Later he told me that the godfather and baptizer at the immersion proceedings were also Jews! Only as he left the ship did he wave to me and shout: *"Shalom, Shalom."*

Later I learned that the leader of the "baptism" ceremony was Dr. Breda of Vienna, who now has a travel bureau in Montevideo.

By the time we landed, I had counted 50 Jews (Marranos) among the total of 80 passengers in the second class—all, of course, wearing crucifixes. When the ship landed several hours later and the immigrants had passed the passport screening, the crucifixes suddenly vanished.

On my second day on land, I stepped into a currency exchange office, and met a "confirmed anti-Semite" who used to flee from the deck the moment I unfolded a Yiddish newspaper. He smiled at me amiably, extended his hand with a warm *sholem aleichem* saying: "It seems to me we've met somewhere before. . . ."

CHAPTER VI.

Curacao and Aruba: Islands with a Jewish Past

After a one hour flight from Barranquilla, the Flying Dutchman of the Royal Dutch Airlines drops down at the Curacao airport. The traveller's first impression after travelling through other Latin American countries (all so much alike), is that he is in quite another world. A bit of Holland is revealed before one's eyes. The pontoon bridge which links the two parts of the city resembles a huge boat. Whenever a large ship passes through, the bridge separates, traffic across it is halted, and little ferriers transport the traveller to the other part of the city. The brightly painted houses, the roofs covered with red tile, resemble a Dutch fishing village. The waters are crowded with craft of all kinds, and in each boat is the owner, his family and all his wordly goods.

Yet the two main streets of Curacao, Heernstraat and Breedestraat, give the island the appearance of a big city. Here are shops with first class goods from all over the world, to be bought more cheaply than anywhere else, for Curacao is a free port.

The island is 370 square miles in area, and its 120,000 inhabitants, made up of over thirty six nationalities, with Negroes predominating, speak four languages: Spanish, Dutch, English and Papiamento, the native dialect, a jargon of these first three languages plus Portuguese. The liberal spirit of the Netherlands, which does not discriminate because of race or religion, prevails on the island. The economy is based on oil refineries and highly developed trade relations.

Curacao was discovered in 1499 by the Spanish navigator de

Ojeda, a colleague of Columbus, and as far as can be ascertained, the first Jew, Samuel Coheno, arrived in Curacao in 1634 with the first expedition of the Dutch "West Indische Campagnie." In 1651 Joao Ilhao, a Portuguese Jew, established the first Jewish agricultural settlement in Curacao. The first charter, by which freedom of religion was granted the Jews in the Western hemisphere, was given to Joseph Nunes da Fonseca. In 1654, after the Portuguese recaptured Pernambuco, Brazil, a group of Portuguese Jews fled the Inquisition in Brazil, arrived in Curacao, and formed Congregation Mikve Israel. The first Chief Rabbi of Curacao was Jacob Lopez da Fonseca, the only rabbi ever born on the island. A second Chief Rabbi Aharon Mendes Chumaceiro, arrived from Holland.

The news that Curacao gave full freedom to Jews soon spread to the many settlements of Marranos scattered throughout the New World, who lived in constant dread of discovery by the ever present Inquisition. Many Marranos poured into Curacao and a large Jewish community soon developed. The agents of the Spanish Crown, whose mission was to extract as much gold as possible from the colonies, to spread Catholicism and to pursue those who were practicing Judaism in secret, began to send alarming reports to the head of the Inquisition Tribunal. A letter written in 1672 by the Archbishop of Cartagena (which was the seat of the Inquisition for many of the South American colonies) complains that the detection of Jews and enforcement of the laws against them is rendered quite difficult by the existence of the island of Curacao which has become a center for the "accursed infields" and a source of contamination and heresy to the Catholic faith.

The Inquisitorial agents also complained that many Negro slaves were brought from Africa on ships owned by Jewish infidels, and this had an evil effect on them. They became infected with the views of the ship-owners and later, when they were purchased by Spaniards, it was difficult to convert them to Catholicism.

The Jews of Curacao were understandably anxious to repay the Spaniards for the many martyrs who died in autos-da-fe, and in Curacao they had the opportunity to do so. It is likely that they had a part, indirectly, in the liberation of the colonies from the yoke of Spain. Though there is no clear data, it would appear that they provided money for the rebel armies and even took part in the actions themselves.

Among the early Jewish families who settled in Curacao, were such prominent Sephardic names as Aboab, De Messa, Perera, Cardoza, Fonseca, Fernandez, De Castro, Namias De Crasto, Jesurun. These are names that one still meets quite commonly in the various lands of Latin America, but their bearers are now devout Catholics.

There are many interesting tombstones in Curacao's historic over 300 year-old graveyard. The historian Dr. I. S. Emmanuel, a former rabbi of Curacao, wrote a book about this historic cemetery. It is titled *Precious Stones of Jews of Curacao*. Many of the stones are broken, others lie flat on the graves instead of being upright. Only a few massive stones have withstood the onslaught of the Caribbean hurricanes and have remained intact, with fully legible inscriptions from which one may learn the names of the dead. Most of the writing is in Spanish and Dutch, some in English. Only a small percentage of stones bear a Hebrew inscription. There are also family vaults of granite with graven likenesses of the dead. Baron Abraham de Lopez, who died in 1721, has such a portrait. Replicas have been made of a number of the finest monuments, as it is feared that exposure to the destructive forces of the weather, and the acid fumes from the adjacent refinery, will cause them to be lost within a few years.

Until recently, I was told, adjacent to the graveyard, stood the walls that encircled the Jewish quarter. At one point in the island's history Jews were required to report there after four o'clock in the afternoon. There were still signs of an old *mikvah* and other community institutions. However, since the local congregation sold the property to the Shell Oil Company, the area has been cleared and all that remains are fragments of the wall and pieces of the ferry boats Jews used in order to transport themselves to the center of the town.

The old cemetery was consecrated in 1659, and until 1680 it

was the only one used by the Jewish community in Curacao. Though another Jewish cemetery was consecrated, the old burial ground is still in use and, undoubtedly, is the oldest in the Western hemisphere. The cemetery covers an area of about three acres, and more than 2500 graves are still discernible. The oldest legible inscription is on the tombstone of Judith Nuñes da Fonseca, who died in January 1668.

One grave at the Curacao Cemetery which should be of more than just passing interest to American visitors, is that of Eliao Hiskiao Touro, who died 3 Ab 5434 (1674). He was the uncle of Ishac de Abraham Touro, whose family came to Newport, Rhode Island, and founded the Touro Synagogue there. This synagogue is the oldest still standing in the United States and has been designated as a national historic shrine.

The stone of Avigail Nunes Redondo, dated in 1747, shows her riding on a donkey surrounded by soldiers handing a gift to King David.

The tombstone of the *hazan* of the community, who died in 1791, bears an inscription which starts (with words cut in bold Hebrew type): "We shall sing to the Lord and make music to Him." Below, is a carving of a harp and another musical instrument. Further down in Hebrew is a list of the departed man's merits. On a second stone, whose date cannot be deciphered, appears a line: "And Moses ascended," followed by two hands with fingers forming the priestly benediction.

A tombstone from 1768 reads in Hebrew: "Beneath this stone lies the body of a truthful and Godfearing man, Joshua De Na-' har.' Above this inscription, larger letters read: "And God spoke to Joshua saying, Fear Not."

On the stone of a woman named Esther a passage from the Book of Esther is carved.

Among the most recent graves is a stone bearing no inscription other than the name, and date of passing: Anna Yakubovitch, August 11, 1945. It marks an episode in the great Jewish tragedy of our generation, when 85 Jewish refugees who escaped Nazi Germany, had traveled from port to port, each one barred to them. Liberal Queen Wilhelmina of the Netherlands granted them permission to land at Curacao. There, three of them died. Side by side, in the old Jewish cemetery in Curacao, the first victims of the Spanish Inquisition rest peacefully next to the latest victims of Nazism. Other victims of the Nazis who lie in the old cemetery are J. L. Maduro, who was killed in action while fighting with the Dutch army against the Nazis, and Mordechai Gandelman, who was granted a scholarship by the Jewish community in Curacao to study in a Yeshivah in Amsterdam, and was caught there by the Nazis.

The Curacao congregation, Mikve Israel, has a tradition of generously supporting the establishment and maintenance of Jewish communities and places of worship in other countries. In 1729 considerable financial assistance was given the oldest Jewish congregation in New York, Shearith Jacob, now known as Shearith Israel. This enabled the congregation to build its first synagogue on Mill Street, New York City. Repeated financial support was given for the building and maintenance of the Touro Sinagogue in Newport, Rhode Island.

The inside of the Mikve Israel synagogue is very impressive. Four massive 24-candle chandeliers are suspended from the ceiling. Made of solid brass, they are copies of similar ones that adorn the famous synagogue of the Portuguese Jewish congregation in Amsterdam. On the mahogany balustrade of the *Hechal* (Holy Ark) and *Teva* (reader's platform), stand eight huge brass candlesticks, also exact replicas of those in Amsterdam. The design of the candlesticks forms a complete Havdala set, consisting of a candle-holder, a winecup and a *besamim-box*.

The *hechal* (Holy Ark) with its eighteen *Sefarim* (Scrolls of the Law), is a masterpiece of richly carved mahogany, standing seventeen feet high and fifteen feet wide. At its top are the two mahogany tablets, bearing hammered, solid silver letters of the Ten Commandments in relief. Several of the *Sefarim* and the oldest of the Scroll covers served in former synagogues. The silver scroll ornaments likewise are actually older than the present building. All the wooden furniture of the building, the seats for the members, and the women's gallery are of heavy, dark mahogany. On the north side of the building, which is the left wall as

85

one faces the Ark, is an elegant baldaquin with five seats for the
Parnasim. Sand is strewn on the floor, the explanation given that
it serves as a reminder of the *Ohel Moed*, the Tabernacle built by
the Israelites when they were wandering through the desert, before they reached the Promised Land. I also saw strewn sand on
the floor at the Portuguese Etz-Hayim Synagogue in Amsterdam
where it was explained as a symbol of the destruction of the
Temple. The synagogue contains many remarkable sacred objects:
Torah scrolls, crowns, breast plates, artistically executed, and
handed down from one generation to the next.

Temple Emmanuel of Curacao is one of the finest structures
in town, located next to the government buildings on Queen
Wilhemina Street. From any point in the city the temple dome
is visible, its Star of David rising majestically over the charming,
Dutch-Style cottages. Services are recited mainly in Dutch, and
include some Hebrew songs, a prayer for the ruling Dutch Monarch, and a sermon by the rabbi. The entire service with its
formality, its accompanying organ and choir, and even the rabbi's
sermon, was reminiscent of an American Reform temple. Both
the rabbis of Curacao, incidentally, are paid by the Dutch government, as are all clergymen.

The two synagogues (now united) serve as a reminder of the
sharp conflict that raged in Curacao for two centuries, between
the "Cohanim" and the "Levites." It started when a group of
Jews in one part of the city—Otrabanda—formed their own synagogue, and the members of the original congregation were deeply
offended. Since the cemetery was located in the Otrabanda section,
the Jews of Funda, where the synagogue was located, were forced
to bury their dead in a special spot set aside for paupers. On the
Day of Atonement, in 1746, a fist fight took place among the Jews,
and the Governor, representing the Prince of Orange, had to use
his authority to settle the squabble. Traces of the debate are still
visible, though the "Cohanim" have not left a single priestly
officiant, nor the "Levites" any sacerdotal assistants. What remains are the two synagogues. In 1963, however, the Orthodox
Mikve Israel and the Liberal Temple Emanuel congregations
united. The congregation is now affiliated with both the World

Union for Progressive Judaism and the Federation of Reconstructionist Congregations. The official prayer book is Reconstructionist.

Curacao's Jews occupy a prominent place in the island's industry, finance and transport. Some years ago, when the well-known Maduro firm marked its centennial, the island's press featured a number of articles on the important contribution the Jews have made to Curacao. This firm was founded in 1837 by Rabbi Solomon Levy Maduro. Today it is Curacao's largest concern, controlling banking houses, shipping companies, transport firms, and import and export businesses. The Maduros can properly be called the Rothschilds of Curacao, and the celebration was observed as if it were a national holiday. The second bank of importance, that of Edwards, Henriquez & Co., is also Jewish. Other well-known Jewish firms are: De Sola, Castro, Henriquez, Penha, Delvalle, and others.

In 1927, Ashkenazi Jews from Eastern Europe came to Curacao and organized the Club Union. In 1959, Eastern European Jews organized Sha'arei Tzedek Synagogue. The Governor of the island, the Prime Minister, members of the Curacao Parliament, and representatives of all religious faiths and political and business organizations, took part in the dedication, and paid tribute to the contribution of these immigrants to the island. This congregation also has a Hebrew school.

Curacao's largest gold business is run by two Jewish immigrants from Austria, Spritzer and Fuhrman, who started a small business selling and repairing watches. Their names became synonymous with both fair dealing and successful business and, for their part in making the island known in the far corners of the world, the proprietors were decorated not long ago by the Queen of the Netherlands.

Other Jewish organizations in Curacao include the Jewish Relief Committee, the Curacao Ladies Benevolent Society, Alivio del Pobre (Help to the Poor), the Montefiore Fund, the Jewish Culture and Sporting Club, Maccabee, the Keren Kayemet Committee, the Ladies Committee of O.S.E., the Curacao branch of WIZO, and a number of others. Hias and the American Jewish

Joint Distribution Committee are represented by the Jewish Relief Committee of Curacao, and there is a representative committee of all congregations.

↗   ↗   ↗

Half an hour's flight from Curacao lies the serene and peaceful little island of Aruba, an area of 20 square miles with a population of 50,000. The island is the site of very large American-owned oil refineries, and the black gold flowing in from the pipelines of nearby Venezuela is processed here. Aruba makes an extraordinary impact on the traveller, with its pervasive atmosphere of repose and tranquility, a quality strengthened by the essential friendliness of the islanders. Its beauty is particularly impressive in the very early morning when, in the moments just preceding dawn, the tongues of fire, flashing from the refineries, light up the darkness all around.

In the 1930's, a group of Jewish wanderers, looking for a home, stumbled across this island, and were captivated by the idyllic environment and the hospitality of the islanders. They decided to remain and started to earn a livelihood by the classic Jewish method peddling with a pack and selling to the islanders on credit. Their trade prospered and they became small businessmen. In time, through relatives in the U. S., they made the necessary connections and became importers.

As soon as they felt secure in their new home, they rented a house to act as a center for worship and social assembly. In 1965 the small community of thirty families carried out a campaign to build a handsome synagogue. This was carried out in addition to the regular fund-raising drives they conduct for Jewish organizations abroad. They are now planning to bring over a Hebrew teacher to instruct their children.

CHAPTER VII.

The Abandoned Jews of Trinidad

The noisy carefree laughter, the slurred accent of speech, the brightly colored clothing and the slow movement of the inhabitants of Trinidad are all reminiscent of the Deep South of the United States. The population of half a million is a mixture of various races: 40% are East Indian; a large proportion are Chinese, Moslems, Javanese and Portuguese; and others are among the wide assortment of pigmentations and ethnic types.

On the baking pavements of the city a continuous din assails the ear. The hawkers do not let you rest. A bronze-faced peddler accosts you, his head wrapped in a turban-like bandanna. Grinning through pearly-white rows of teeth, he offers French perfumes and Panama hats. A Hindu with a French beret like a Parisian apache thrusts some English drapery material under your nose. Long rows of open shops display home-made jewelry in loud, discordant colors—all at astonishingly low prices.

At night, Chinese melodic patterns mixed with a Spanish tango float in through your window from nearby night clubs. A noisy American jazz band makes a deafening racket. The desperate shouting of some one being robbed is followed a little while later by police whistles. The daily newspapers are full of stories of robberies and murders.

The island is now undergoing a serious crisis. In World War II when thousands of American soldiers were stationed in Trinidad, the island received a steady stream of gold: the laborers were paid more, the middle class got used to a higher standard of living, all factories worked around the clock, and the goods in the stores were sold immediately. Now, with the Americans gone, it is not so easy to revert to a lower living standard. The officials complain that the Americans spoiled the Trinidad population.

Trinidad and its neighboring island Tobago were discovered in the year 1498, and for years were under Spanish occupation. For a long time England, the Netherlands and France fought for possession of the islands. In 1797, Trinidad was taken over by England; Tobago was next, in 1889.

Trinidad has a population of more than 100,000. A third of the population are descendants of immigrants from India. Between the years 1845-1871, 26,000 Hindus and 32,000 Moslems arrived. The island is rich in tropical fruits, sugar, cacao, coconuts and citrus fruits, and is of great importance to Britain, first because it is strategically located between the two American continents, and secondly because it is the greatest producer of gasoline in the British Commonwealth. It is also the main source of asphalt for Great Britain. It exports many other products.

The 30,000 inhabitants of Tobago are mainly occupied with farming. The island, 116 square miles in area, has a beautiful coastline, and is an ideal tourist spot.

When I first visited Trinidad it was still a British colony. The Governor at that time was the former secretary of the British Governor in Palestine during the Mandate. When the Irgun blew up the King David Hotel in Jerusalem, he had been saved from certain death, because those who set the bomb had sent out prior warning. Since then he has looked upon the Jews with friendship, and when the Queen and her consort visited the island, a Jewish deputation was invited to attend the royal ball.

However, among the British officials in Trinidad were others who had been hostile to the Jews at the time of the Palestine Mandate. On one occasion, when a suicide had occurred in the Jewish community, the police was asked by the community not to carry out a post mortem, as this is against Jewish religious law. The chief of police is said to have rejected the request with a sarcastic retort: "I was in Palestine for quite a while, and this won't be the first autopsy I've ordered for Jewish corpses!"

The early history of Trinidad's Jewish community is closely bound up with that of the nearby British West Indian islands of

Jamaica and Barbados, where Jews fled from the Inquisition after the Portuguese recaptured Brazil from the Dutch in 1654. One can still find traces of an old Jewish community which existed in Trinidad about 300 years ago. To this day, there is an old Jewish cemetery on the island, dating back to that period.

A small group of Sephardim settled in Trinidad in the 18th century, and on the shops the signs read: Mendes, Rafael, Gomez, Acosta, etc., names of aristocratic Sephardic families who long ago merged with the island's population. I was told of two interesting cases which led to the trail of the island's Jewish past by a local community leader and Zionist, Chaim Beer Auerboukh. One concerned a wealthy industrialist and millionaire, whose family had been living in Trinidad for generations. When his unmarried sister died, she left a will in which she asked to be buried in the Jewish cemetery. The little Jewish community filled her wish. When he himself took sick he asked that after his death his body be put in a boat, taken out to sea, and cast into the water.

The second case involved a man who had been a pious Catholic. Mr. Auerboukh, who had done business with him once happened to tell him about the tragedies that the Jewish immigrants had suffered before they finally reached the shores of Trinidad. The Catholic began to show interest in the fate of these refugees, and this interest grew to the extent that he opened up a special office to assist the newcomers. He began to neglect his business and devoted himself entirely to the noble work of helping refugees. He made no secret of the fact that he was of Jewish descent, and later he converted to Judaism, came to the synagogue, and became a pious Jew despite the strong protest of his family. When he was afflicted by leprosy, he was taken to a hospital where he still carried out his assistance to refugees. His disease grew progressively more malignant, he suffered great pain, and was distressed that his friends had abandoned him at this critical moment. His family could not forgive his having become a Jew, and the Jews no longer showed much interest in him. In a moment of despair, in the last moments of his life, he again reverted to Christianity and left a request in his will that he be buried in a Christian cemetery.

Today, the island's Jews consist of somewhat less than 150 souls, remnants of an unplanned, panic immigration during the years when the Nazis were overrunning the countries of Europe. Trinidad was then a free port, and offered a temporary refuge for the wanderers who hoped to move on to some other country. At one time, 2,000 Jewish refugees were living in Trinidad. Many found work in various American war projects; some moved on —to the United States, to Canada, and to various Latin American countries. A few hundred Jewish immigrants remained in Trinidad, to peddle and later to open up small businesses, restaurants and hotels. Gradually they organized a semblance of Jewish community life and institutions, including a free loan association.

As soon as the war was over and economic conditions deteriorated, Jews began to leave Trinidad. Of the more than 500, only about 100 remained, and they, too, are thinking of leaving. Their business is based predominantly on credit, and now it is difficult to collect old debts (and quite risky to grant credit for new ones).

As the Jewish community shrinks, its loneliness and isolation is felt more deeply. The sense of alienation is heightened as children grow up, and there is no one for them to marry. All the children of the Jewish families with whom I came in contact in Trinidad were studying either at American universities, in Europe, or in Israel. Parents work very hard in Trinidad to support their children who are studying at a higher institution of learning abroad, knowing that in the island there are no prospects for them. They hope that as soon as their children will meet with success abroad they will send for them. Others, whose children are still small, have an even more distressing problem. The children are growing up without any semblance of a Jewish education. For the most part these are East European Jews, each of whom had in his former home ties with Jewish life on some level.

One Friday evening I served as the tenth man in a *minyan*, and heard that the tiny synagogue which was rented from a native would have to be given up, and the Torah Scrolls moved into a private home where a *minyan* would meet each Sabbath. The pathetic, rented little synagogue typified the mood of the small group of isolated Jewish wanderers. On the wall was a large portrait of Dr. Herzl, in the familiar pose in which he is looking down from the bridge over the Rhine in Basle. In the stifling heat inside, a middle-aged Jew, wrapped in a yellowed Turkish *tallit* was standing in front of a wooden pulpit and singing the *Lecho Dodi* to an old hazzanic tune. Dog-eared, torn prayerbooks were lying about in disarray on the benches. The Holy Ark was hung with a white *parochet* embroidered with inscriptions in memory of departed persons.

A few days later I was a guest at a Jewish wedding. A Jewish Trinidadian from Bessarabia was solemnizing a double wedding: both his son and daughter were getting married. His daughter's groom was an American Jewish soldier from the nearby United States base. His son's bride was the daughter of a Jewish family from Belo Horizonte in Brazil. Every Jew in Trinidad, without exception, shared the joy of this occasion, as if it were their family. Two canopies were set up, in old East European style, under the open Trinidad sky. Since no rabbi or other religious functionary was available, the official Jewish community was represented by two laymen. One was the father of a local citizen, Dr. Ullrich Schechter, a man who had been saved from the death camps. (He had been brought to Trinidad by his son and who was planning to go from there to Israel.) The second man was H. Gendelman, an old local resident who was one of the first Bessarabian Jews to settle in Trinidad. A native Trinidad orchestra played wedding songs just like East European *klezmorim (shtetl* musicians). For some weeks Dr. Schechter had drilled them in Yiddish music, and they played the songs with zest, insinuating Jewish groans and sighs into the melodies of a *"Chosidl"* and a "Bessarabian *Volechel."* "What a treat," the Trinidad Jews told me, "having this kind of *simcha* in our town! Two Jewish weddings at once! It is rare that there is any Jewish wedding here at all! The daughters and sons generally go abroad to study, and to seek a mate. If they are successful, they send a wire home, and their parents generally go abroad to attend the wedding."

The bride's relatives danced the "Mitzvah Tenzl," the parents of the groom being somewhere in America. Again, a second time, the same *machutanim* did the Mitzvah Dance for the bride whose parents were living in Belo Horizonte in Brazil. The brown-skinned Trinidad musicians played a *Freilachs*, madly tapping their feet on the ground, tossing their musical instruments about, and generally increasing the hubbub.

Watching the scene, I became quite *unfreilach* at heart. Now that the sticky, humid heat had caked the face powder, wilted the stiff, starched collars, drenched and twisted their black formal suits and frilled dresses, the loneliness fairly shouted from their careworn faces. It seemed to me that in dancing, they were trying to forget for a brief moment their bleak prospects for the future, the years they had irretrievably lost, the horrible heat which had drained their marrow and life-blood, the many years of trudging on the baked pavements with a peddler's pack. And now, what was their future?

The brown-faced musicians grew more frenzied, and the sense of loneliness and misery became sharper. The weary Jews whirled around like marionettes in an automatic jig, and in the very midst of the deafening, braying music I seemed to hear the unanswerable query of these isolated Jews: "The little Jewishness we still possess will soon perish, and what are we to do with our children here?"

On my second visit to Trinidad, I was met at the ship by Mr. Auerboukh. He drove me to a newly developed district which only a short while before had been of swamp land, and pointed out streets named "Sinai," "Theodor Herzl," "Chaim Weizmann," "David Ben-Gurion," "Queen Elizabeth," "King George," and even one called "Chaim Beer Auerboukh Street." With pride he told me how he, the Jewish immigrant from Eastern Europe, had cleared the swamps and erected the modern up-to-date structures.

On my last trip to Trinidad, only a few years ago, the number of Jews had again diminished, but there is no doubt that a Jewish community will survive there. Many of those who were once willing to leave for anywhere at all, have now changed their minds. I recalled the words of the Jew who had said: "I'm tired and broken. I'm in my sixties. Where can I begin all over again?"

Chaim Beer Auerboukh, the community pioneer who devoted so much work and effort on behalf of the tiny community, was no longer alive when I was last there, but his widow had taken over his community duties and Zionist activities.

CHAPTER VIII.

Barbados: Remnants of an Ancient Jewish Community

An hour's flight from Port of Spain, Trinidad, brings the traveler to Barbados, one of the most beautiful and picturesque islands of the Caribbean. The airplane lands at Bridgetown, the capital city. The airport, encircled by palm trees, is an impressive sight, and, as you take your first walk on the island, you quickly learn why it is such a paradise for tourists.

One can live on very little on this island. A small sum pays for a comfortable room in a splendid hotel, with all necessities, and you have a view of the ocean, three meals and service included. Most of the hotels are constructed with all the rooms opening onto balconies overlooking the ocean, where mild breezes blow night and day. At night, one gets the feeling of sleeping on a ship far out at sea.

This remarkable island has been a British possession since its official discovery in 1627. There is some indication, however, of an earlier discovery. In 1536, when the Portuguese were seeking new territories, the navigator Pedro Campos landed in Barbados on his way to Brazil. The island is sometimes called "little England" or "the sanitorium of the West Indies," both for its mild, healthy climate and also for its pure water, a rarity in the isles of the Caribbean. Water may be drunk quite safely in undistilled form; it will be free of the various disease germs so prevalent in these areas. This, of course, accounts for the island's dense population which is 70% Negro, 7% white, the remainder of mixed race. More than 70% of its 166 square miles is cultivated and, of this, half is devoted to sugar. The sugar plantations have attracted wineries and rum distilleries.

On the main square, guides were soliciting customers, offering to take them to the most beautiful and most interesting sections of the city.

"Do you want to see the beach? It's called Bathsheba," I am assured by a Negro guide wearing a broad straw hat and white and black checked trousers. "Or would you prefer the cathedral —the oldest in all the Caribbean islands?"

He tried again, noting that I had not yet reacted, "The historical museum that all the tourists go to?"

"No," I reply, "none of these interest me as yet."

"What then does interest you?" he asks looking at me curiously.

"Do you know what Hebrews are? Jews?"

He thinks for a while and then grins again, showing me two rows of gleaming teeth. "Yes, sah, I know."

"Can you show me where one lives?"

"Come with me."

A few moments later we were standing in front of a neatly-built house surrounded by a garden. My guide pulled a bell and a woman appeared. The guide introduced me to her as a "landsman." She greeted me with a familiar "Gutn ovent" (good evening). "A good year," I replied in the traditional way.

Then came the inevitable question that arises when a Jew meets other Jews abroad; "Where are you from?"—followed by an invitation to come in. I paid the guide and noted how well he had guided me, bringing me to the very house that served as synagogue and meeting-place for the 35 Jewish families on the island. That evening I was the guest of these families who came together to hear some news of the Jewish world. They were all refugees from East European countries who managed to escape Hitler's Europe before the annihilation process started.

They had started out as pack-peddlers and, as they told me they would often find traces of a long forgotten Jewish past. In one place they would see an old Holy Ark, in another a large synagogue platform and pulpit, and sometimes, even sacred ob-

97

jects used in the Jewish ritual. On Rosh Hashanah when they first worshipped as a *minyan* and the islanders saw them wrapped in their prayer shawls, some came running in with shreds and tatters of old *taleithim* which had belonged to their grandfathers. One even boasted that he remembered his grandfather leading the worship. It is a peculiar coincidence that the businesses currently owned by Jews are all located on Swanstraat which once was the Joodenstraat, the "Jewish Street," site of the former synagogue and graveyard of the Jewish community of three centuries ago.

According to the Barbados historian, Shomburgh, Jews were in Barbados in 1628. *(The History of Barbados,* 1848). In 1655, Oliver Cromwell gave permission to two Jewish doctors to practice their profession in Barbados. The Brazilian historian, Dr. Arnold Wischnitzer, in his book *The Record of the Earliest Jewish Community in the New World,* writes that Abraham Mercado was one of the first pharmacists and doctors in the New World, and the organizer of the Tzur Israel congregation in Recife (Pernambuco), Brazil. According to his signature he was president of the congregation. In 1654, when the Portuguese recaptured Brazil, Mercado left for Amsterdam and from there to London, where he and his son, David Raphael de Mercado, received permission to settle and practice medicine in Barbados. The synagogue records reveal that the first tombstone, that of Aaron de Mercado, was erected in 1660.

In passing, it is interesting to note that medicine was a Jewish profession in 16th and 17th century Portugal. Even the physicians at the royal court were Marranos, who were hastily baptized. It was on their behalf that King Manuel passed an ordinance in 1497—at the beginning of the persecutions in that country—permitting those doctors not knowing Latin to make use of Hebrew medical books. In the New World, too, many of the Marranos were medical men and exerted a great influence on the medical history of Brazil.

A Jewish congregation, Tzemach David, was organized in Speightstown by Joseph Jeshurin Mendes, also known as Lewis Diaz. He had been a member of the Recife (Pernambuco) synagogue from 1649 to 1652. The historian I.S. Emmanuel indicates (American Jewish Archives in Cincinnati) that he and his father had joined a synagogue in Amsterdam in 1654.

After these early pioneers came other groups of Jews from Brazil who undertook the cultivation of sugar plantations—an industry which brought prosperity to the island. In 1657 emissaries of the island's Jews went to Amsterdam, to bring back Torah scrolls, an altar and various liturgical items. The Bridgetown congregation, Nidche Israel, was led by Abraham Gabay Isidoro, a native of Spain whose parents had fled to London, where he was circumcized. Later he studied in Amsterdam.

In 1833, after severe hurricane damage, the synagogue was rebuilt and was at the same time enlarged and improved. According to the records of that day the non-Jewish population participated in this effort, as the Jews were a signifficant element in the general community. The dedication ceremony was attended by all segments of the population, including high government officials and notables who participated in the event.

From this time on the Jewish community began to grow smaller, partly due to the hurricanes that damaged the coffee plantations and partly because of the emancipation of the slaves who worked on the Jewish-owned plantations. Many of the Jewish families left for England where they maintained business relations with Barbados; others left for the United States. In 1848 only 70 Jewish families remained in Barbados. Intermarriage and assimilation due to the distance from larger Jewish communities had also taken their toll. Of these 70 families, only 38 were enrolled in the community.

Anticipating the demise of the community by its constant diminution, and fearing the eventual loss of the synagogue, cemetery and other institutions, the community leadership took steps in 1869 to prevent this property from falling into the hands of strangers. They made legal arrangements to ensure that for the next hundred years—as long as there was even one Jew living in Barbados—that he would have a place to pray and a burial plot. Should no Jews remain any longer, the two institutions were to pass into the possession of the Bevis Marks Spanish and Portuguese Synagogue in London.

By 1905, the trustees who had signed the declaration were no longer among the living. Only two Jews remained on the island —the brothers Joshua and Edmund Baeza, both prominent merchants. Joshua died and Edmund Baeza remained as the island's sole surviving Jew. Realizing that the time had come to give thought to the communal institutions, he wrote to the Bevis Marks Synagogue, outlining the situation and asking for power to proceed, which he received. On March 27th, 1928, he sold the community possessions to Henry Graham Yearwood, a Bridgetown solicitor, for the price of $600.00. The contract stipulated that the burial ground should be maintained: its grounds, fence and gate be kept in good order, and that it not be used for any other purpose. The sellers kept the right to investigate whether these conditions were being met.

The purchaser let it be known that he wanted to contribute the synagogue to the government as a national museum. He proposed to the Bevis Marks Congregation that he would discard the broken tombstones and cut the others to a uniform size in order to restore some semblance of order to the burial grounds. The Bevis Marks Congregation rejected this proposal on the grounds of religious law, and Mr. Baeza was asked to seek another customer who would bind himself to their terms. Because of the strictures of the Londoners, Baeza sold only the synagogue, the former home of the rabbi, and the surrounding land for the same sum of $600.00. The cemetery, however, remained unsold, and in the possession of the Bevis Marks Synagogue of London. A sum of money was extended to Baeza to repair the cemetery. An inquiry from the London synagogue brought the answer that some tombstones had been cut down to size and that the grounds and graves were in desperate need of repair and maintenance.

In 1934, Barbados' last Jew died, closely followed by the solicitor who had purchased the properties. The synagogue and other possessions were taken over by a second purchaser, a Mr. S.C. Hutchinson, also a Bridgetown solicitor. A public auction was held of the furniture and sacred objects, and a large part of the heavy massive furniture found its way to antique dealers in the United States. Smaller items were purchased by the islanders. Mr. Hutchinson paid little heed to the clauses of the contract with the London Spanish and Portuguese Synagogue and cut a road through the cemetery, got rid of the old tombstones, and built a garage on the spot.

It was more than a coincidence that a newly arrived immigrant, Moishe Altman, whose body, I am told, now lies buried in the same cemetery, passed by this burial ground at the very time the new owner was shovelling aside the broken fragments of stone. Moishe Altman reprimanded the garage-builder and said: "You haven't God in your heart. You are desecrating the graves of the dead—and this is a great sin." A little while later, the story goes, Mr. Hutchinson fell sick and died. In his will he returned the cemetery to the Jews. His wife maintained that his death was due to his having desecrated the graveyard.

In the meantime negotiations were under way between the Spanish and Portuguese congregation in London, and the new Jewish community of Barbados, to whom, by contract, the cemetery had reverted. A sum of money was determined for repair and restoration; a committee was formed which included a representative of the Museum Historical Society and a statute was passed, at its initiative, giving the cemetery the status of an historical and religious site which must not be violated.

The London congregation wanted some assurance from the Jews living in Barbados that they would be there permanently. If they could guarantee this, the synagogue, too, would revert to them. However, since many of them only considered the island a place of transit, and they eventually planned to move to a larger community, this plan was not fulfilled. The synagogue is now the office of the Barbados Turf Club.

The history of the old Jewish cemetery on Barbados has been recorded by E.M. Shilstone, a Barbados barrister, in *Jewish Monumental Inscriptions*. As a little boy, he was frequently taken by the daughter of the synagogue's last Torah reader *(ba'al koreh)*, a man named Daniels, to walk in the cemetery and look at the curious writing on the stones.

After Mr. Shilstone had become a barrister, his office was, for many years, located opposite the entrance to the synagogue, and he would often watch the ceremonies the Jews observed there. More and more his interest was aroused by the strange inscriptions on the ancient tombstones, and he began to copy them down. He found the Portuguese, Spanish, and English words and phrases not difficult to transcribe or understand, and he began to publish these in a quarterly issued by the museum. With great effort he dusted off the old stones and started to copy the Hebrew inscriptions which were totally unreadable to him.

In 1938, he went to the United States and met Mr. Edward Coleman, librarian of the Jewish Historical Society, to whom he showed his copies of the Hebrew inscriptions. Both Mr. Coleman and Rabbi David de Sola Pool of the New York Spanish and Portuguese Synagogue encouraged him to proceed with the task. Mr. Shilstone made an attempt to acquire some knowledge of Hebrew and familiarize himself with the inscriptions. Mr. Coleman visited Barbados twice, and showed enthusiasm for his findings. Finally, Shilstone gathered and published almost 400 inscriptions taken from this burial ground, and his book is an excellent record of the Jewish past of this Caribbean island. Mr. Richard Barnett, Honorary Archivist of the Spanish-Portuguese Congregation in London, edited, indexed and prepared Mr. Shilstone's work for publication.

When I visited Barbados I went to see the Jewish graveyard. The inscription over the entrance has been repaired and is now legible:

Hayilodim l'maveth v'hamethim l'hahayot.
(The born are destined for death; the dead for resurrection.)

The partly destroyed stones are now repaired and have fairly legible epitaphs, inscriptions which reflect the character of the community of this island. Those no longer readable can be traced in E.M. Shilstone's book, in which all the data and wording has been carefully and patiently registered. Explanations of missing ornamental and decorative symbols are given, and the inscriptions include the supplementary letters, words and phrases which have been obliterated through time and erosion.

Since Joshua Baeza was buried on July 19, 1925, five new graves have been added to this historical cemetery, among them that of Moshe Altman, one of the founders of the new community.

The two most important monuments are those of the pioneers of the communities of Bridgetown and Speightstown. The stone of David Raphael de Mercado is dated 1685, and its text is in three languages—English, Spanish and Hebrew. The text reads as follows:

> Here lyeth ye body of
> David Raphael de Mercado
> Merchant who departed
> This world ye 14th of August 1685

The second monument is that of Joseph Jeshurin Mendes, also known as Luis Diaz, who died in 1690 at the age of 83. The inscription reads:

> Here is buried the Body
> of Mr. Lewis Diaz who was beloved
> and Respected by all men, in his time
> he died on the 27 of December 1690
> 83 years of age
> (Joseph Jeshurin Mendes-
> Lewis Diaz was his alias)

Another noted figure whose remains are interred in the Barbados Cemetery was Rabbi Raphael Haim Isaac Carigal, who once served as rabbi in Curacao, and later became rabbi of Kehilla Nidche Israel in Barbados. His epitaph reads:

> Here lyeth the remains of the
> Learned & Rev. Rabbi Raphael
> Haim Isaac Carigal
> Worthy Pastor of the Synagogue
> N.I. who departed this life on
> the 19 of May 1777 age 48 years

The thirty-five Jewish families of present-day Barbadoes are the successors of their forerunners of long ago, legal heirs to the communal property of a *kehilla* that existed in quiet isolation for centuries, and heirs also to the spirit and traditions of this *kehilla*. Those who established the original Barbados community escaped, against all odds, from ruthless persecution, and those who form the present-day community likewise escaped, providentially, from fiendish oppression. The rise of the first Jewish community on this distant island has in it an aspect of the miraculous, and so, too, does that of the later community. A community was born, it endured, then slowly disappeared, only to be reborn. Here, surely, lies profound meaning, an unmistakable message from a by-path in Jewish history.

CHAPTER IX.

The Jewish Community of Surinam

A brilliantly and throughly cleansed sunshine brightened the windows of the plane as it landed at the airport of Paramaribo, in the capital of Surinam, after an all-night flight through a tropical downpour. A large placard in the arrivals building welcomed the travelers in English, Dutch and several other languages, and announced that the population of Surinam was composed of many different religious groups: Moslems, Presbyterians, Lutherans, Hussites, Roman Catholics, Greek Orthodox, etc. Further down the list appeared the category, "Israelites," followed by the figure: 830.

Along the road from the airport to the city stretch broad open fields, dotted with houses surrounded by tropical foliage that serves to protect the inhabitants from the extreme heat. As the traveler reaches the center of the city, however, the tropical environment gives way to a European-Dutch motif. Finally, one arrives at the governor's palace, and other modern government buildings in the very heart of the city—a metropolitan area happily lacking the noise and confusion of most cities.

A special kind of calm prevails—a calm one is no longer accustomed to in the daily desperate chase of life. The calm seems to be emphasized in the statue of Queen Wilhelmina standing in the city's central square. The figure looks down over the square with a serene smile, the smile of a mother watching over her brood—quite a contrast to the monument of a general on horseback, gripping a weapon, which one sees in most South American capitals.

At 1:30 P.M. both the business streets and the waterfront

became quite silent and empty, as everything stops in Paramaribo because of the intense heat. Shops are locked, shutters are closed and the siesta lasts until four in the afternoon when the sun's burning rays are somewhat softened. Then the people of the city appear once more: Chinese, Javanese, Indians, Bush Negroes, Japanese, Indonesians, and from time to time, a white (well-tanned) European face. The babel of languages includes the official government language, Dutch; a pidgin-English called Papiamento (mixture of Spanish, Portuguese and English); a dialect of the natives called Toki-Toki; and then Chinese, Japanese and Javanese. The Bush Negroes have their own language, as well as a highly original type of clothing: trousers, which must be the fig-leaf breeches that Adam and Eve made for themselves in Eden. Japanese merchants walk about wearing respectable silk skull-caps and broad rimmed hats, while the Javanese wear a small narrow type of headgear. The Chinese wear odd looking caps and long pointed moustaches.

Surinam lies on the east coast of South America and has a population of about 250,000. In 1499 it was discovered by Alfonso Ajedo, a Spaniard, but the first to take an interest in it were the Dutch who, in 1613, organized a trading company on its shores, and the English who started tobacco plantations in 1630. Four years later, a group of Hollanders, under the leadership of David Pieters de Vries, settled in Surinam. It is probable that they were Marranos who had previously escaped to Holland. According to the documents noted by a local Jewish historian, Philip Samson, the name De Vries appears among the founders of Surinam's Jewish community.

In 1640, the French tried to settle Surinam, but failed in their attempt. A few years later, the English allied themselves with the Indians and established an English colony, but after five years war broke out between England and Holland, and the Dutch became masters of the whole territory. Clashes continued until a pact was finally signed whereby Holland agreed to cede New Amsterdam on the Hudson to the English in exchange for clear title to Surinam.

The Jewish community in Surinam has a remarkable history

going back over 300 years. In 1654, when the two Jewish communities of Brazil: Recife (Pernambuco) and Bahia, were retaken by the Portuguese, the Jews who had taken refuge there from the Inquisition were again forced to flee. Some fled to Cayenne, the nearest island. At that time, a large group of Marranos also chose to leave Leghorn (Italy) and settle in Cayenne, among them the poet Daniel Levi Barros. A year after their arrival the French took over the island, and promised the Jews religious freedom. When they did not keep their promise, the community broke up and many moved to Surinam, where some Jews had settled previously. They had received a permit to engage in agriculture in a certain area, and it was they who first established sugar plantations in Surinam.

The new wanderers also settled in this territory, which was pure jungle, and set about cultivating it. The territory became known as, Jooden-Savanna, the Jews' Savanna. They erected a synagogue and developed their own communal structure. The government gave them complete autonomy, and they even had their own militia to protect themselves from the Indians and the slaves who often threatened revolt. They maintained their own courts of justice whose jurisdiction was recognized by the authorities.

Documentation of this fascinating period is available, and is full of interesting tales about the Jooden Savanna. Among the members of that *kehilla* one finds the names of high ranking civilian and military officers. One of the records relates the case of a remarkable verdict handed down by the Jewish court, and tells how the defendant appealed to the government to annul its decree. A Jew was found guilty of shaving on one of the intermediate days of one of the festivals *(Chol HaMo'ed)* and was sentenced to banishment from the Jooden Savanna. His appeal to the government availed him nothing, for the government recognized the Jewish court's verdict as fully binding.

The Jews of Surinam have always been staunchly patriotic. As far back as 1689, when Surinam was attacked by the French, the Jews, led by Samuel Nassi, one of their elders, fought heroically alongside the Dutch. The Nassi family still exists in Suri-

107

nam; one of its members, a physician, has been studying leprosy with the aid of a grant from the Dutch government. In a later attack on Surinam, one of the chief defenders was Captain Isaac Pinto, a Jew.

An incident involving Jews once almost led to an international dispute between Great Britain and the Netherlands. At a time when all the other countries of Europe were expelling Jews, these two countries vied for them. When the English left Surinam they wanted to take the Jews with them to Jamaica, knowing that they would contribute to the island's development. The Dutch, of course, also appreciated this, and insisted on the Jews staying where they were! Something similar happened in our day when, during the First World War, Jewish diamond merchants fled Belgium for Holland and introduced the diamond trade there. Later, at the end of the war, both countries wanted these Jews: Belgium asked them to return, and Holland wanted them to remain.

Surinam has had two congregations: the Sephardic Tzedek Ve'Shalom and the Ashkenazic Neve Shalom. As usual, there was a long standing dispute between the two congregations, and they co-existed as two separate communities. In the course of years, the diminution in their numbers brought them together, and they finally made peace. In a mutually, agreeable compromise, they decided to use the Ashkenazic synagogue on Swanstraat, but for worship services to follow the Sephardic ritual.

From the outside, the building with its garden closely resembles the Portuguese Synagogue in Amsterdam, in the Meier Jonas Plain district. The interior has a beautifully decorated Holy Ark and the central platform *(Bimah)* is built of mahogany, and is encircled by ornaments and massive menorahs with bronze tablets. These bear the names of those who have made contributions to the synagogue, and also have inscribed on them historical data going back to the period of 1590-1730. The floor is strewn with sand, as is the custom in Amsterdam, in remembrance of the destruction of the Temple of Jerusalem.

One row of seats is marked off with a cord, and is reserved for guests. In the past they were used by the special envoys assigned to the Jews by the government. The Queen of the

Netherlands sat there on several of her visits, and listened to a *MiShe'berach* prayer made for her welfare. A bronze plaque commemorates the dates of her visits and of her gift of a medal to the *parnass* of the synagogue.

A few years ago the Dutch postal authorities of the colony issued a stamp depicting the Neve Shalom Synagogue of Paramaribo. The government announced a project of repairing and restoring the synagogue in the Jooden Savanna where the Jews once had an autonomous "state," for the purpose of turning it into a national museum. It is the oldest synagogue in the Western Hemisphere.

Jewish autonomy in Surinam lasted for 200 years, until 1825. By then, partly because of the frequent slave uprisings and partly because of the difficult climate, the Jews had begun to leave the Savanna. Some migrated to Curacao, some to Holland, and some to North America, until the ranks of the Jewish colony were decimated. Traces of this earlier community remain in a neglected graveyard with collapsed tombstones bearing inscriptions in Portuguese, Dutch, English, and Hebrew. On one stone, dated 1732, the dead man is described as a *shochet, mohel* and *sofer* (ritual slaughterer, circumcision surgeon, and Torah scribe). The Hebrew word *meshuba* is also added. This word, meaning "sworn," indicates that he also acted as a notary, a profession still highly regarded in the colony.

Paramaribo today abounds with traces of its rich Jewish past. There are streets bearing Jewish names such as the Joodenbree Straat (the same name is used for Amsterdam's Jewish quarter), Jessurin Straat, Da Costa Straat, and even Lovenstein Straat. (The latter is named after an orthodox rabbi born in Surinam. His son later served as rabbi in Denmark and Switzerland.) There are houses that still have *mezuzot* attached to their doorposts, though Jews have not lived there for years. The present dwellers have not taken them down out of a mixture of respect and superstition, looking upon them as a sort of good luck amulet. Names like Abiezer, Rafael, Aboab, Prado, Messias, da Costa—all distinguished names of Portuguese and Spanish Jewish families —appear on the shop windows. Their present bearers, however,

109

are not even aware of their Jewish ancestry. There are even Bush Negroes with Jewish names who use Hebrew words in their language—no doubt descendants of the slaves who worked on the Jewish-owned sugar plantations.

A story is told of those days of Negro slaves. Once a member of a community of runaway slaves living in the jungle kidnapped a servant in one of the Jewish homes and forced her to tell them when the best time would be to attack the Jewish community and rob their homes. She told them to wait until Yom Kippur night, when all the Jews would be at Kol Nidre services in the synagogue. After she had given them the information, they let her go, threatening to kill her if she revealed their plans to anyone.

For a while the servant kept silent, but her Jewish owners were so kind to her, and she liked them so much, that as Yom Kippur approached, the girl risked her life, and told the Jews what the runaway had in mind.

What were the Jews to do? At length a secret plan was decided upon. As Yom Kippur eve was about to begin, everyone went to the synagogue as usual. But each man carried a gun. All the guns were stacked at the back of the synagogue, and the *Kol Nidre* service began. Imagine the state of mind of those praying. Each man, standing in his white *kittel* (robe), asking God to forgive him his sins, expected that his life might end at any moment.

The evening wore on. Outside there were stirrings in the grass. Slowly the runaway approached and surrounded the synagogue. As they came closer they rose from their crouching positions and looked into the windows. A shock passed through the group. In Africa, from where these people had come, white is the sign of victory. And here were all the Jews dressed in white, as if they had already won, chanting loudly. After one horrified glance, the runaways took to their heels. They fled without ever having seen the guns. The Jews were able to go home that Yom Kippur night in peace, and never again did the runaways disturb the Jewish Savanna.

Surinam's Jews have tried to end their isolation and have sought contact with world Jewry. They have created a Central

Committee which coordinates the various local activities and is in touch with international Jewish bodies in the United States and Israel. Zionist activity is carried on, and a Wizo branch exists. The tiny Jewish community is actively concerned about its continuing existence. An examination of the community's register of weddings, births and deaths reveals that the ranks of the families of both communities—Ashkenazic and Sephardic —are perceptibly thinning. Seldom is a Jewish wedding celebrated in Surinam. Some young people migrate to North America or to Holland; and the number of mixed marriages is on the rise from year to year. The distress of the local community is openly manifest in their publication, *Teroenga* (Hebrew *Teruah:* trumpet blast), a symbol of their desperate appeal for help to the Jewry of the world.

During one visit in Paramaribo I was interviewed by the editors of the two newspapers in Surinam. Their first question was whether I was a delegate of the Freeland League which, for years, has been talking of Jewish colonization in Surinam. After I assured them that I was not, they both looked quite relieved. Then came the second question: As a Jewish journalist, what do I think of the Jewish colonization in Surinam? My reply was that Jews are ready to pioneer in a land of their own, and at the present time there is no need for Jews to turn to a country strange to them in language, culture and climate, when they have a land of their own. This pleased them even more.

"You must understand," said the elder of the two editors to me, "that we are sympathetic to the idea of Jewish colonization here in Surinam. It would bring in labor and, what is even more important, capital which we need so badly, but"—and here he paused, lest he hurt my feelings—"but Jews are not capable of farm work. What I mean," he hastened to add, "is that under the local circumstances they will tend to go into urban types of business and the professions."

"You needn't feel uneasy," I reassured him, "Jews will not come to Surinam, except for some who may have taken leave of their senses."

The next day my interview was on the front page of both

111

newspapers, under the heading, "Jewish Journalist from America Says Jews Will Not Come to Surinam." That night as I sat in the hotel dining room, I heard the government radio carrying the story on its newscast. The people in the dining room listened with interest, and I would even say I detected some satisfaction in their reaction.

I found out later that the majority of people in Paramaribo were opposed to the Jewish territorialist plan for Surinam. The project had been accepted by the Rikstag (Parliament) which had later revoked its assent because of the many protests it provoked. The few Europeans in Surinam feared possible competition from Jews, with the businessmen and professionals warning against a dangerous invasion of 30,000 Jews who would bring misfortune to the country. The time-honored anti-Semitic stereotypes were used, accusing Jews of being Communists, capitalists, profiteers, bloodsuckers, etc. I was told that even the creoles, the great-grandchildren of the slaves, now accuse the Jews of having enslaved and robbed their ancestors who were the true owners of the land.

The woman who managed the hotel in which I stayed, not knowing at first who I was, told me that everyone was afraid of an invasion of Jewish immigrants "something that would bring calamity to the country." When she later found out that I was a Jew she modified her claim, saying that she meant the Jews from Europe, not me, an American Jew, and certainly not the Jews of Surinam who are fine people and staunch patriots. (I later found out that she was employed by a Jew named Fernandez who owned the hotel.)

Who was pressing for the Jewish territorial colonization of Surinam? As far as I could tell, certain local interests were attracted by the sums of money they thought would be brought into the country, some part of which they hoped would find its way into their pockets. A mythical figure of several millions was bandied about which, it was said, certain American Jewish organizations were willing to invest.

I broached the subject to various Jews in Surinam and found that most of them were opposed to it. An exporter named L. Benjamin told me that as soon as the plan was proposed it had created anti-Jewish agitation, especially in the Nationalist Party, because of the fear of Jewish competition in trade. He himself dismissed the plan as "fantastic." The area in question, Saramacca, is a jungle area and has a climate worse than Paramaribo's. He reminded me that every year he who lives in Paramaribo takes a trip to New York for a change of climate!

A prominent Jewish communal leader who occupies an important government post told me that some Jews looked favorably upon the project as it would end their isolation. Jewish life would be revitalized and they would no longer feel cut off from the Jewish world. However, those who evaluated the situation quite soberly and clearly, and divorced themselves from sentimental overtones, were unequivocally opposed to Jewish immigration to that area. Neither climate nor living conditions were suitable, and any Jews who tried it would perish. "I was born in this country," he said, "but it would be impossible for me to settle in Saramacca. What, then, could be said about Jews who have never experienced the climate of the sub-tropics?"

I did, however, find one strong Jewish advocate of Jewish colonization in Surinam—a Viennese Jew who owned Surinam's only cafe. When I entered his establishment I received a rather rude reception. Perhaps, having recognized me as a foreigner from my clothing, and having heard the radio report of my views, he said to me immediately, *"Wider ein verdammter Jude da, welcher ist gegen immigration."* "What are you doing?" he complained, "carrying on atrocity propaganda?" He grew a little softer. "What would I have to lose if more Jews came to Surinam? Business would certainly improve." From him I learned that I was the fourth *verdammter Jude*, as he put it, to visit them who was against immigration. The others were the Israeli journalist Medzini, the American Zionist leader Mrs. Archibald Silverman, and Dr. Chaim Shoshkes. "Why," he wondered, "are the only ones who come here; those who oppose immigration?"

When I returned to New York and published my impressions of this fanciful immigration scheme in the *Jewish Daily Forward*, I was challenged to a "court of honor," by the late Dr. J.N. Steinberg, head of the "Freeland" movement. I accepted the challenge and was willing to submit to a panel designated by the I.L. Peretz Writers' Association. The Freeland League, however, designated its own people for such a panel, and I declined to come before a one-sided arbitration board. The Freeland movement then issued a statement that I refused their offer and their lawyer pressed me to a litigation before the courts.

Oifn Shvel, the Freeland organ, attacked me as a "Zionist crusader," and a propagandist who peddles atrocity stories. The story stated that the Israeli correspondent of *Haaretz*, Medzini, and the late American Zionist leader Mrs. Archibald Silverman, the late Dr. Chaim Shoshkes, and I were part of a sustained propaganda campaign seeking to spread lies and defamation in order to keep Surinam from becoming a competitor with Israel for Jewish immigration!

CHAPTER X

Jews in Ecuador: Land of a Thousand Hues and Colors

Some of the most breath-taking vistas in Latin America are to be found in Ecuador. The country has everlastingly snow-capped mountains which rise to a height of twenty thousand feet above sea level. There are active volcanoes that spit hot lava, luxuriant landscapes, rich varieties of flowers, and dark islands where it rains for months on end. Ecuador has sixteen such islands, including Galapagos, where Darwin spent five years. At every step your eye meets the most wonderful scenery painted by Nature.

Ecuador is a small country with an area of 171,500 square miles. The Ecuadorian will tell you his country is much larger, by at least another hundred thousand square miles, but this is denied by Ecuador's neighbors who have taken away whole stretches of territory that Ecuador refuses to renounce.

Ten percent of its population of three million are white, about 25% are *mestizos* (mixed-breeds), and the rest are Indians, living in the same primitive conditions as they did centuries back. They speak their own languages: Quichua and Aymara. The capital, Quito, with over two hundred thousand inhabitants—founded in 1534 by Diego de Almagro, one of Pizarro's lieutenants—is situated only fifteen miles south of the border of Colombia. It is bathed in an air of quiet and peace. The Ecuadorian is calm and restrained. He hates getting excited. He tries to keep his composure even when there is a revolution going on in the country —and revolutions occur quite frequently. More Presidents have been deposed in Ecuador than have retired after completing their term of office. The country has gone through thirteen new Constitutions and more than twenty Presidents in a very short period.

The Ecuadorian doesn't take revolutions as seriously as the people in the neighboring countries, where every revolution brings victims and bloodshed. A revolution—as the man in the street knows—is the concern of the army. Every fresh revolution in Ecuador begins the same way—with the tramp of army boots through the main streets, and windows being smashed in the Presidential Palace. Sometimes a shot or two is fired. Sometimes there is not even that.

The deposed President and his family slip away to Argentina, Chile or some other Latin American country. A new man takes his place as President. The following day the Press reports the accomplished Revolution. The Ecuadorian reads about it in his paper over his *cafesina* in the cafe, and doesn't even think it worth a *"Viva el Presidente."* It has nothing to do with him; he knows that the new revolution and the new President will do nothing for him.

The population of Ecuador is divided into two parts—Sierra and Porteño. The western and the eastern parts of the country are so different that they might as well be two different countries. The inhabitants of the Sierra live in the hills and jungles that cut deep into the Amazon basin. Though nature is very beautiful, the life of the people is hard. A native will tell you that this lovely scenery is only for the tourists. He himself goes to the town in search of a crust of bread to quiet his hunger. You will meet him on a cold night carrying a heavy load twice his size, made fast to his body with a leather strap.

Away from the big towns, barefoot Indians shuffle lazily through the streets in colorful dress wearing red, blue, purple or brown ponchos, and strange hats of various shapes, depending on the tribe to which they belong. The man walks first, and the woman follows submissively, trailing a string of a dozen or more children. On a market day, the whole family will drive a skinny cow or a pair of fowl to the market, miles away, to be sold. They may buy a little kerosene, a comb, a needle, perhaps a pair of scissors—quite a luxury. Then they go to church and offer their last bit of money there.

The Indians are devout Catholics, and there are many missions and priests in the area. I once saw a procession of hundreds of Indians taking gifts to the priests. In front went the band, playing on primitive instruments—barefoot Indians playing Indian tunes, nostalgic and sad. Behind came hundreds of Indians with their children, ragged and barefoot, carrying a huge wooden cross, hung all over with fowl, turkeys, ducks, rabbits and piglets. When they get to the church they hold a party. Such a fiesta sometimes lasts a whole week, with food and drink galore. The Indians drink *chicha*, a home-brewed liquor made from corn.

One of the Indians is chosen for the great honor of being host, and he pays for the fiesta, Rich or poor, he never refuses, even if he has to borrow and mortgage himself for years. After the fiesta, the participants lie around in a drunken stupor for days. Life passes between fiestas and siestas, without any time left to think about their poverty.

Ecuador was once called New Granada, and during the Spanish period had its own Inquisitorial Commissar. According to the Argentine Jewish historian Boleslao Lewin, in his *La Inquisicion En Hispano-America,* in 1770 a quarrel broke out in Cuenco between the Minister for the Indians and the Commissar of the Inquisition. The Minister for the Indians had under his jurisdiction all those suspected of not observing Catholicism. When he appealed to the Viceroy in Lima he was told that these matters (i.e. affecting Jews) did not fall under his competence and should be handed over to the Holy Tribunal of the Inquisition whose final verdict would be determined in secrecy. From this we can conclude that the Inquisition was supreme in Ecuador as elsewhere, that the *conversos,* as they were called, who fled to the most distant areas to be able to practice Judaism were still harried by the Inquisition.

Traces of that older Jewish past in Ecuador can be found in the names of well-known families. For instance, the man who founded the Opera House in Guayaquil was Isaac Aboab, which was the name of one of the first rabbis on the American continent: Isaac Aboab da Fonseca, a son of Marranos, who came to Brazil in the 16th century as rabbi in Pernambuco.

Until 1903, no non-Catholics, not even Protestants, were allowed to live in Ecuador. A year later, a small group of Sephardic Jews, originally from Arab countries, came to Ecuador as citizens of neighboring Latin American countries. But the official date for the beginning of modern Jewish immigration to Ecuador can be reckoned as 1910, when a Jewish engineer from Austria, named Robert Levi, settled in Guayaquil. He soon assimilated and took the Christian name Castillejo, but his son returned to Judaism and was for a time President of the Jewish Community in Guayaquil. Jewish immigrants from neighboring countries started coming to Ecuador in the early 1930's. But when the government prohibited peddling they lost their means of livelihood and returned to the nearby countries from which they had come.

Around 1936, when the Hitler regime was driving Jews in Germany to consider possible places of mass-immigration, Ecuador was one of the countries suggested. Samuel Zitlovsky, brother of Dr. Chaim Zitlovsky, was sent by a committee in New York and Paris to conclude an agreement with the Government of Ecuador for a large-scale Jewish colonization project covering an area of 500,000 hectares. Benjamin Mezibowski for many years an administrator of the Jewish Colonization Association (ICA) and an expert in colonization matters, reported on the plan in the "Shriften" of the Argentine *Yivo* (Yiddish Scientific Institute). He wrote: "I met Samuel Zitlovsky and Boni, who had already accepted the Government's proposal, and had even settled a few families there. I stayed in Ecuador about six weeks to make a thorough investigation of the plan. I found that these few families had not been settled on the land which had been offered. I was able to see only part of this offered land with my own eyes, for it was impossible to get to all of it. There were no roads, no communications and no means of transport. Some places could be reached only with mules."

He came to the conclusion in his report that colonization there would be dangerous even for people who had escaped from the

118

Nazi hell. They would soon succumb to disease, wild beasts and poisonous snakes. He recommended that the project be abandoned, as indeed it was.

Nonetheless, as Hitler strengthened his hold over Central and Eastern Europe, 5000 Jews from Germany and elsewhere sought refuge in Ecuador. They were mostly businessmen and professionals. The Joint Distribution Committee and the Hicem tried to settle them on the land, by starting poultry farms. Sixty such farms were established, but owing to climatic and other difficulties they were complete failures. Then the settlers opened small factories in the towns, but in a country like Ecuador, where less than ten per cent of the population of three million are consumers, it was difficult to make the factories pay for themselves. Nonetheless, Jewish initiative overcame the difficulties.

At first the small factories were only workshops in the homes of the manufacturers. They experimented and found that balsa wood makes wonderful furniture. Then they started producing iron and steel furniture, which was previously unknown in Ecuador. Next came factories for textiles, clothing, knitted goods, underwear and shoes. They even opened a *matzah* factory. Ecuadorians started eating *matzah!* Jewish women discovered that the belts the Indians weave can be used as a fabric for handbags, lamp-shades and women's hats. A shop was opened in Quito employing a dozen Ecuadorians. Soon, these articles were being copied all over Latin America.

Jewish refugees started laundries and dry-cleaning establishments. Next came shops selling ready-made clothing. Doctors secured posts in government hospitals. Women who knew languages got employment with firms engaged in foreign trade. Former hotel owners and managers took charge of the leading hotels. The Windsor, Ambassador and Savoy Hotels were transformed; today they are the equal of the best hotel in Europe, and are frequented by the best families. The Syrians and Cubans, who had run the hotel trade before, felt the pinch of competition, and started an anti-Jewish campaign. A shoe manufacturer told me he had applied for a permit to open his shoe factory, but the Minister of Economic Affairs had turned down the application.

119

He had managed to get an interview with the Minister, and suggested that in a country where eighty per cent of the population goes about barefoot it seemed unreasonable to refuse a permit for producing shoes. He got his permit.

But the anti-Jewish agitation succeeded, as it did in the other Latin American countries. Prompted by envy of the successful immigrants, and incited by the Germans who lived in Ecuador, a feeling grew that moved the Government in 1938 to order the expulsion of the small Jewish community in Ecuador. The order was withdrawn after intervention by the World Jewish Congress. The following year, the Chamber of Commerce launched a press campaign against the Jewish immigrants, charging that they were not working in agriculture, though they had been admitted on condition that they would. In March 1952, a government order was issued requiring all aliens to produce evidence that they are working in the occupation listed on their immigration papers. After intervention by the World Jewish Congress this order was also shelved.

Jewish life in Ecuador centers round the organized Jewish community, the Beneficencia Israelita, which embraces the entire Jewish population. German Jews are in the majority; next in number are the East European Jews, and then the Sephardim. The community building is in the center of Quito. Inside it gives the impression of a Viennese or Berlin cafe: tables with clean white cloths, newspapers on holders on the walls—among them the New York *Aufbau* and the community's own paper,which bears the names *Beneficencia*—and reports on local Jewish life: a theatre group performance, a Chanukah Ball, engagements, dinner parties, births, business opportunities, etc.

The Beneficencia is a well-organized body which includes various agencies—the Zionist Federation, WIZO, B'nai B'rith, the Jewish Loans and Savings Bank, and a women's organization, "Chesed We'Emes." The synagogue and the *mikvah* are in the building, and there is a hall for concerts and plays. The classrooms of the Jewish school are there, and until recently children were flown in to Quito from Guayaquil by plane. But now Guayaquil has its own Jewish school, with a teacher from Israel. Guayaquil also has its own community house, a synagogue and a Jewish club. There are several Jewish families in each of the more remote small towns like Bambo, Cuenco and Baños.

The Jewish immigrants brought much experience from Europe in the area of social and intellectual activity, and this has won them the respect of their intellectual neighbors, which counteracted, to some extent, the anti-Semitic propaganda of the Germans in the country.

One of the things the Jews did was to organize Bible exhibitions in Quito and Guayaquil. The idea was put forward by Dr. Karger, who had been a member of the Executive of the Jewish Community of Berlin. He submitted his plan to the Archbishop, and got the Church's approval. The exhibits were arranged to trace the evolution of the Bible from the earliest periods to the days of the later Prophets, and also included many ritual objects. More than 30,000 visitors came to the exhibition in Quito. In Guayaquil the Bible exhibition was held in the Cathedral, by permission of the Archbishop.

But the Jewish population of Ecuador is diminishing in numbers, both in Quito and in Guayaquil. Jews are leaving for Israel, the United States, or other Latin American countries where there is a larger Jewish community and a more active Jewish life.

There is no question in Ecuador of assimilation, in the sense of merging and being lost in the general population, as happened centuries ago with the first Jewish immigrants, the Marranos, and with the second wave of Jewish immigration in the 19th century which was composed mainly of German Jews, who had been assimilationists even in Germany.

However, too many things have happened since then. Hitler did not spare the assimilated Jews, not those who were baptised —not even their children and granchildren who were born Christians. The creation of the State of Israel also played its part in changing the attitude of the Jews. Moreover, the exclusiveness of the upper strata of society in these strictly Catholic countries, bars Jews from their ranks unless they undergo public conversion, which few Jews care to do. And the lower classes are terribly poor, illiterate, backward, and offer no inducement for assimilation. This leaves two alternatives: to organize a Jewish cultural life on the spot, or to emigrate.

✓   ✓   ✓

In the center of the capital, Quito, stands the Palacio Nacional, where the President of the Republic receives his visitors. The building, a mixture of old colonial and modern architecture, stands out among the other buildings, which are all built low because of the frequent earthquakes. A bronze plaque on the front of the Palace, records that Simon Bolivar came to this place for the first time on June 16, 1822. The list of names on the plaque of those who gave their lives for the liberation of the country includes several names that sound Jewish.

I had occasion to appear at the Palacio Nacional for an appointment with the President, Velasco Ibarra. I had asked him to receive me as a representative of the Jewish press. And the letter from the President's secretary fixing the appointment said specifically that the interview was with the Jewish press.

A young adjutant calls my name and I find myself in the President's study. The President receives me with a friendly smile and a warm handshake, and waves me to a seat. He stands.

"Mr. President," I say, "you are, I think, aware that I am the correspondent of a Yiddish paper."

"Yes, I know," he answers with a smile. "You may tell the Jews and the whole world through your paper that I am a sincere friend of the Jews, *buen amigo del pueblo Israel*. My teacher in France, where I studied law, was that great Frenchman and noble Jew, Victor Basch. I know the Jewish people not only from the Bible. In my book on the rights of nations I gave a lot of space to the Jewish question, and condemned Britain for not carrying out the Mandate to establish a Jewish National Home in Palestine. I am a friend of all who are oppressed—and who today is more oppressed than the Jews?"

I wrote this down in my notebook. The President stood silently, watching me write.

"You are writing Hebrew?" he asked me.

122

"No, Yiddish."

"Isn't it the same?"

So I had to explain briefly to the President of Ecuador, who listened attentively, the difference between Hebrew and Yiddish. Then I asked the President what he thought of the debates about the Middle East.

"Palestine was proclaimed the Jewish National Home," the President answered, "and Jews had every right to go to live there. That is why I instructed my representative at the San Francisco Conference to vote for Palestine as a Jewish State. I believe the whole democratic world owes a debt to the Jews. Ecuador is doing her bit by admitting Jewish immigrants."

"Does this mean," I asked, "that your country is open for Jewish immigration?"

"Yes," he said. "Ecuador has no restrictions against Jewish immigration. Our Consulates everywhere have instructions to issue visas to Jewish immigrants who wish to settle in Ecuador. It is, of course, important that Jewish immigrants to Ecuador should bring some money with them, not to become a burden on our State in the early days. It is also desirable that the immigrants who come here should be able to adapt themselves to agriculture."

"This means," I suggested, "that you want an immigration of specially selected people, who are fitted for agriculture."

"Ecuador," he took me up immediately, "also has good opportunities for people who can develop new industries here. I know of the contribution which Jewish immigrants have made in recent years to the light industry of our country, and I value their services."

Then the President spoke of the great contributions of the Jews to world civilization, culture and progress. He spoke particularly of the achievements of German Jews in science, art, literature, industry, and commerce. The Jews gave so much to Germany, he said, and Germany treated them abominably.

Ecuador has always been a good friend of Israel. In 1946 its representative, Antonio Quedo, proposed that the Jewish Agency should be recognized as a Jewish government in exile.

✦   ✦   ✦

"Jews! Rabbi Nahum Gitlin is speaking to you. It is time you abandoned your sinful ways and adopt the way of truth, the holy light of Christianity!" I heard these words on the radio in my hotel room in the beautiful town of Baños, nine hours distant from Quito. Herr Wolff, a German Jewish refugee from Breslau, who owned the tourist hotel, told me this was the "religious hour" which once a week was "devoted" to the Jews. Herr Wolf lit the third Chanukah candle that evening and in his German-accented Hebrew intoned *Ma'oz Tzur*. How strange and yet familiar to see the Chanukah candles glowing on a warm Ecuadorian night in a community of Indian tribes with broad *sombreros* and colored *ponchos*. The little flames were enchanting in the soft warm night. "*Sie verstehen,*" Herr Wolff argued, "*dieser verdammter mission-arischer 'Rabbiner' hat mich veranlasst zünden diese Chanukah Lichte. Ich bin doch ein Jude,*" (You see, this confounded missionary "rabbi" is the one responsible for my lighting the Chanukah candles. After all, I *am* a Jew).

Baños, a mineral spring resort, has three other hotels, each owned by German Jews, all constructed on the model of Swiss chalets in the Lucerne area. The President of the republic and his cabinet are regular clients here. Other guests are Jews from Quito and Guayaquil who come to take the baths and to enjoy a change of air. Many of these are former habitues of the European spas of Carlsbad and Marienbad. In the season one sees vivid contrasts: severely pressed trousers, a neatly tied cravat, and a tattered poncho; a woman elegantly attired in the newest style, and a ragged shawl wrapped about half a dozen children. Here "*wird Deutsch gesprochen,*" and even Galician Jews aspire to High German. The Catholic Church apparently feels it can do some fishing for souls here, and for this reason it has the "rabbi" on its radio hour every Sunday.

✦   ✦   ✦

Jews in Ecuador: Land of a Thousand Hues and Colors

The hundred Jews who live in Guayaquil have quickly acclimatized and acquired the ways of the land. Their homes have become fortresses, barred and bolted against prying eyes. The general social center is the Cafe Calmonia where anyone meets over a coffee. During the day it is hard to work because of the fiery tropical sun, so many Jewish men meet in the cafe to talk. Then, when the sun is less fierce, they go back to work. Late in the evening they go back to the cafe for some relief from the blistering heat, and then home again—all but two bachelors who stay on in their loneliness. I met two such bachelors: one a Bessarabian and the other a Galician.

The Bessarabian has been so buffeted by life that he has become an embittered misanthrope who speaks only in curses and anger, and is shunned by people hoping to avoid clashing with him. The troubles and loneliness of the Galician have led him to adopt the pose of a patient saint who willingly bears his burden of sorrows as a good, pious Jew should, and who seeks applause for his fortitude. Both types are equally burdensome—one with his anti-social bitterness and the other with his overdose of virtue —and very few townspeople will have anything to do with either.

And so it was that both seized on me—a stranger who was willing to listen to their stories. The Bessarabian complains, "I haven't been inside a home here in twenty years! As a peddler I broke a leg and lay in my room like a dog, perishing in loneliness. It's unheard of for Jews to be so mean!"

The other interrupts: "What do you want from these poor Jews? They work hard and long to support their families"— and here his own complaints start. "I injured my shoulder from carrying my peddler's pack on my back in the hot sun. The doctor says it will be permanent; one shoulder will be lower than the other. Well, let's hope that that's my worst *tsorre*. There were Jews who suffered far more in the concentration camps. True, it's not good to remain alone as one gets older but what do the Jews of Guayaquil owe me? If one could move to a larger community where there are more Jews it might be different. Believe me . . . ," and here he blushes like a girl, "I could make a woman very happy. I have a few thousand dollars in the bank, but . . . ," and suddenly he turns sad—"what can you do when the tropics have crept into your very bones? I no longer have the energy to tear myself out of here. If only I could find a relative of some kind, an heir ... " He looks at me sadly. "Someone with pull assures me he can get me a visa to Chile. There are lots of Jews there— different Jews. I'm told, in fact, that it's possible to get through the border to Peru. What do you think?" He is silent for a while and then answers his own questions. "I've stolen through enough frontiers in my time, I've starved and served in prison for it ... how much can a man bear?"

I met a Jewish leather merchant when my *baat* of bamboo stopped at a primitive and forlorn port half a day's journey from Guayaquil. Indian huts of lime that looked like cages, palm leaves and bamboo strewn everywhere. Soon the senses are dazzled by the shining brown backs and gleaming white teeth of the natives and their carefree, loud chatter. After a long walk one reaches a row of bazaars offering the traveller cushions, Panama hats, and articles made out of animal skins. I entered one of these bazaars which had a placard, "English spoken." After hearing the proprietor's first few words of "English," I tendered him a *"Sholom Aleichem, Reb Yid,"* and his reply was, *"Fun vanent kumt a Yid?"* We had no time to talk, for soon the little shop was filled with tourists buying Indian leathercraft work.

That evening the merchant came to visit me with his wife, and took me to his home. Here I heard the lament so familiar to me in these remote corners: "Business is good, but what good is it? One is cut off from other Jews and alone; I want to live with other Jews. Is $50,000 enough to settle in Israel with?" I assured the childless couple that with this sum—in fact with less—they could live quite well in Israel. "I'm sure I'll leave here eventually," he went on. "Of course we will," added his wife. "What is the alternative—to finish our days here among the Indians? We must get away from this wilderness."

It was decided on the spot that the next day he would go to Guayaquil with me to get his travel documents. "For years," says his wife, a warm, friendly person, "we've been thinking of getting away."

126

In the morning when I went to his shop the man hardly noticed me, he was so engrossed in selling his articles to American tourists to whom he spoke in his English. That night the same story was repeated: they begged and entreated me to stay for another day, they received me warmly and repeated the same arguments: "How can we waste our lives in this wilderness? The loneliness is killing us. Tomorrow I'm definitely going to Guayaquil. I know someone there who for a few dollars can fix me up a passport. Please stay for another day."

When I returned to Guayaquil I received letters from him, he was coming the next day, in two days. Before I left Guayaquil I wrote him I was leaving and he came to see me off. When the boat pushed off he shouted he would escape immediately, and was getting his passport the next day.

Now, in the cool of the late evening, as my boat is churning its way out of the harbor of Guayaquil, heading for Peru, I see his wife's gentle, weary face, and I hear her saying: "Are we to end our days here among the Indians?" I see the distorted desperate faces of the two lonely old bachelors, and the nervous face of my friend saying: "Tomorrow I go to get a passport."

The tropics and loneliness have totally consumed the entire spirit of these people. The Jew in the Indian pueblo, earning his dollars from his tourist customers, and from the Indians from whom he buys his stock—will live out his days there as a disjointed, displaced soul.

CHAPTER XI.

Peru: Jewish Life in the Land of the Incas

I entered Peru at Tumbes, on the Ecuador border. It is an old-fashioned town with sturdily built houses and a plaza of sand and stone. It once belonged to Ecuador, and for this reason the police are extremely watchful at the border. There is a great deal of illicit trade, but the police are more interested in your passport than in your baggage. If you are an Ecuadorian your stay in Tumbes is limited, you must report to the police, and you may not proceed to another part of Peru.

From Tumbes to Lima is a journey of several days along the Pan-American Highway. The road cuts through dry, sandy wastes devoid of human habitation. When you reach a town you must stop overnight and take a different bus in the morning. For a thousand miles you see nothing but empty, rocky stretches, parched and faint under the burning sun, longing for a little water. Then, as the bus approaches a settlement, rich green fields appear, like a magic garden in the Arabian Nights. Immediately after leaving the town, you are back in the desert, with the sun blazing down like a furnace.

When the bus reaches a town it stops, and the passengers get out to wash the dust and grime out of their face and hair, and have something to eat. But there is nothing but *chicha* and hard *galletas* (biscuits).

The town generally consists of a few small streets, a police station, and a tavern which always rocks with the carefree song of a few drinkers who have had a drop too much. The people who live in these towns have permanently red eyes as a result of the irritating and pervasive dust.

The bus stopped at a small town named Talara. Suddenly, I caught sight of a sign on a storefront: Moses Furmann. I stepped in and was greeted with a warm *"Sholom Aleichem"* by a Jew who hailed from Bessarabia. There were four Jewish families in the town during the war, he told me. Business wasn't bad then. They are now gone, and he is the only Jew left.

At Puira I found ten Jewish families. The delegate of the Keren Hayesod had just preceded me. All had contributed beyond their means. In Chiclayo, I was told, there was a somewhat larger community—about twelve Jewish families. The bus stopped for half an hour, and I had time only to take a look at the shops on the main street, note a few Jewish names on the placards, and pick up a copy of one of the New York Yiddish dailies!

Trujillo is one of Peru's most beautiful cities, famous for its university. Known also as a center for Peru's finest aristocracy, it is crowded with historic monuments. I was to remain only overnight in Trujillo, but the city's Jews learned I was there and would not let me proceed. They insisted that I stay to tell them what was happening in the Jewish world—a world from which they were isolated and remote.

Sabbath eve I was the guest of the fourteen Jewish families of Trujillo. After the Sabbath worship which, in my honor, the prayer leader converted or confused into a High Holy Day chant, I conveyed greetings and a report of Jewish life in other lands. They were intensely interested in what I had to say. "Do you see my daughter?" said one of them, indicating a charming, olive-skinned brunette. "I tell her about the *Judios*. But there are no other young Jews! And do you think it's any better in Lima? The young men there want a dowry. There's no decent living to be made here as a salaried man or a worker, so a young man has to turn to trade, and for this of course he needs capital, so one can't blame the young men I suppose. . . . Do you have some advice perhaps? Should I send my daughter to Israel? I'm sure the *chalutzim* don't ask for a dowry. And once she is over there, the rest of the family will be sure to follow."

129

When I took my seat in the bus the following morning, I found myself sitting between two passengers who were speaking German with a thick Berlin accent. When I entered and sat down, they looked at each other as much as to say, "Who is this stranger?" At first they spoke softly, but seeing that I paid them no heed, they grew bolder, and began speculating on the nationality of the new passenger:

"Is he an American?" "No," said the other, "more likely French. Can't you see he's dark?"

"Then why is he wearing an American hat? Perhaps he's English. And what in the world is he doing here? Could he be a secret agent of the American security police?"

"What ideas you get, Fritz!" interrupted the other. "What of it? The Peruvian Government has admitted us legally since we have Peruvian wives. Americans can't do anything about it."

"Anton," warned the other, "you've no idea what kind of devils these Americans are. Have you forgotten Marseilles? We already had visas for Peru then, and how close we were to being arrested!"

My face was burning; I could no longer conceal my feelings. I wanted to avenge myself on these two Nazis who probably had more than one Jewish victim on their conscience. The question was how to do it? Suddenly it occurred to me. I remembered the Yiddish newspaper given to me by the Jew in Chiclayo. I quickly took it out of my pocket, unfolded it, and spread it out before me with the bold Hebraic script staring the two Nazis in the face. Their faces flushed and then one of them suddenly turned pale. They looked from me to the newspaper and back, and began to blink nervously. The one sitting to my right hissed under his breath, *"Donnerwetter, ein Jude!"*

"Dammit!" I shouted in my best American profanity. The other Nazi looked at me, about to say something, but at the look of undisguised contempt on my face, he looked away. He began to mumble something unintelligible.

"You swine!" I shouted again with all my might. Both began to look around for some way to hide their faces. At this point the bus stopped. The driver called out that there was a thirty-minute recess for lunch.

When the passengers boarded the vehicle again the seats near me were empty—both my neighbors had vanished.

As you near Lima the carpet of green grows broader and brighter. And when the bus enters the first streets of Lima you forget that you have just been travelling through a barren expanse of sandy waste-land. There are broad avenues with fine tall buildings, beautiful parks, masses of flowers, statues, crowds of people, heavy traffic. You go to your hotel, wash and brush the dust from your clothes, and mingle in the streets with the crowds. The people are strange mixtures of old traditional and modern types. Certain parts of Lima look like the Brazilian capital Rio de Janeiro and its movement is like that of a big bustling North American city. But the architecture is more Spanish than in any other Latin American town, and when you walk along the plaza and see the scores of cathedrals with their spires rising to the skies you think you are in Madrid or Barcelona. Then, when you turn into the business section, you are back on Fifth Avenue in New York, the sidewalks densely thronged; the fine shops crammed with customers choosing from the latest fashions and furnishings.

Peru, with more than eight million inhabitants, can be divided into three distinct parts, each different from the others in appearance, character and way of life. The first is the sandy desert and the plains along the coast. The second is the Andes, where the villages are situated high up on the lofty mountains. And the third is called the Montaña, a completely undeveloped area, where the people still live in primitive conditions.

Three towns in Peru express the three characters of the country—Lima, the capital, proud of its status as the old Viceragal residence, favored as such above all the other Latin American capitals during the Spanish rule; Cuzco, with its ancient Inca past; and Inquitos, the Amazon border town, rich in rubber plantations, sugar and minerals.

Arequipa, the second city of Peru, boasts of its liberal spirit.

All the revolutions against the various governmental regimes started in Arequipa. In Peru it is known as Ciudad Blanca, the White City. The streets and houses, built of white marble, are a mixture of three civilizations: some are Spanish-Colonial, some Indian in style, and others modern. There are structures erected by the best Spanish architects of the Colonial period with stones taken from ancient Inca buildings, and there are modern skyscrapers put up by leading American architects. The different styles of architecture make this "White" extraordinarily picturesque.

Arequipa has ten Jewish families with their own little synagogue. In the very center of the town is a doorway bearing the name Leon Feldman, and you feel sure you have located a Jew. But Leon Feldman is more; he is a poet who writes in Yiddish and Spanish. Arequipa is a university town and Feldman is a close friend of many of the professors who have crowned him as Peru's national poet. Feldman has also written a Yiddish volume of nostalgic poems, stories and experiences. It is difficult for the outside Jewish world to imagine that at the edge of the giant Cordilleras lives a Jewish poet who both sings of the beauties of the Peruvian landscape and bitterly bemoans the ruin of his Bessarabian birthplace.

Half the large Indian population of Peru knows no Spanish. They speak the two Indian languages, Quichua or Aymara. They are illiterate, dreadfully poor, and ignorant even of what is going on in their own capital, Lima. The barren soil of the snow-covered mountains among which they live yields little sustenance, so the Indian is drawn to the big town to satisfy his hunger.

✦   ✦   ✦

Next to Brazil, Peru has the richest Jewish past in South America. Of this faraway epoch there remain today not only historic vestiges, but even living descendants. Though these persons are no longer part of the Jewish people, they often seek the occasion to meet Jews and talk of their common origin, sometimes with longing and regret.

Peru: Jewish Life in the Land of the Incas

The earliest chapter of Peru's Jewish history is one written in blood. Soon after Francisco Pizarro conquered the country, Jews started to arrive in Peru. One theory claims that there were Marranos among the members of his expedition.

In 1564 the mercury and silver mines of Peru were discovered by the "Portuguese" (Marrano) family of the Salcedos, who contributed in no small measure to Peru's economy. A great-grandson of this family, Augusto Legua Salcedo, was President of Peru from 1919 to 1930.

By 1583 a large number of these "Portuguese" had secretly established a well-organized Jewish life, maintained own doctors, teachers, and other functionaries. The building that they used as a community center still stands in Lima today, very close, as it happens, to the old Inquisition offices, and directly facing the Franciscan Church. The location was undoubtedly chosen to avoid suspicion. It was constructed in such a way that those inside could look out on all four sides. In order to ward off suspicion the building included a public inn for wayfarers. The Inquisitorial officers would not be suspicious of people walking in and out of such a public place, I was told.

One day, on Yom Kippur, a drunken sailor who lost his way in the inn reached the secret place where a group of Marranos with their leader, Manuel Perez, wrapped in *taleisim*, were praying *Kol Nidre*. Manuel Perez, who was known as *El Gran Capitan*, was a man close to the Viceroy. The sailor immediately brought his tale to the Inquisition and all of the men were immediately slapped into the Inquisition's dungeons. In addition to the offense of practising Jewish rites in secret, Perez and his men were charged with conspiracy against the State and of plotting with the Dutch who at that time had their ships on the Pacific coast ready to invade Peru. As proof, it was pointed out that only a few weeks before, Manuel Perez had volunteered to assume command of the arsenal, and to repair the artillery at his own expense.

The men were held in the Inquisition cells for three years. On January 23, 1639, Perez was taken, with twelve other leaders of the secret *kehilla,* and burned by the Inquisition in the public square of Lima. They were led through the streets of Lima mounted on donkeys, and were reviled and spat on by the mob, on the way to the *auto da fe*. Perez' two brothers-in-law were burned with him. One of them had recanted. The other, Sebastian Duarte, was allowed to approach Manuel Perez before the fire was lit, and embrace him with an *"osculus pacis"*—a kiss of peace. Also among those who were burned, was the Chilean Marrano, Dr. Francisco Maldonado da Silva, who had been tortured by the Inquisition for 14 years. The other 88 arrested men were sent to Spain to serve on the galley ships.

In the records of the Inquisition one still can see the inscription which was placed on the clandestine synagogue:

> *Que en lo que digo no miento, pongo por testigo a Dios; esta casa es la de los Judios del prendimiento.*
> (That I am telling the truth, God bears witness; this is the house of the Jews [taken] in the great seizure.)

In Peru the Inquisition was abolished on Septempter 23, 1813. Two years later, when King Ferdinand assumed the throne, it was restored, but it was finally abolished by the South American liberator, San Martin, on February 8, 1822.

The second period of Jewish life in Peru (after the Inquisition had wiped out the Marranos) began after the unrest in Germany and Austria, which followed the revolution of 1848 when Jews from the Posen district started coming to Peru. They found that the surviving descendants of the Marranos had been absorbed into the indigenous population. The German immigrants established a rudimentary form of community structure—a free loan fund (*gemilat chasadim*), and provision for the sick (*bikur cholim*)—and on Rosh Hashana and Yom Kippur they prayed in the Masonic Temple. It was only in 1870, when an English-Jewish engineer who built the railway across the Andes contributed land for a cemetery, that the community was officially registered.

A Zionist community worker resident in Peru, Moshe Nimand, collected the accumulated records of the community and gave them to Ben-Zvi, the late president of Israel, to deposit in his museum. Some of the German-Jewish surnames, dating back to this period, appear on the business establishments in the fashionable parts of Lima, and these families, now Christian, are part of Peru's aristocracy. From time to time, when they come to pay their respects to the memory of their grandparents and great-grandparents, they can be seen at the Jewish cemetery standing before the tombstones, their heads bare, making the sign of the cross. In January 1958, an aged Jewish woman was buried in the Jewish cemetery. Her children and grandchildren sang Christian hymns at her grave.

The sons and daughters of this immigration intermarried and left the Jewish faith. Senorita Gladys Zender, a former "Miss Universe," the daughter of a Christian mother and a Jewish father, belongs to this element. Ambassador Berkmeyer, Peru's envoy to Washington, and his brother who is an important political personality in the country, are descendants of these Jews. Their grandfather, an immigrant from Posen, was named Berko Meyer.

The Peruvian diplomat, Arias Schreiber, who served as Ambassador to a number of states including the Vatican, is a descendant of these German Jews. For a while, prior to the Second World War, he was Peru's Ambassador to Japan. Ten months before the attack on Pearl Harbor, in 1941, he obtained information, from a Japanese woman employed in his Embassy, about the feverish preparations of the Japanese Army and Navy for attack upon an undisclosed base. The Ambassador's calculation pointed to Pearl Harbor. Later, in a private conversation with a Japanese university professor who spoke too freely after a few glasses, he obtained confirmation that Japan planned to attack the United States. He immediately informed the American Ambassador in Tokyo of his suspicions, but the latter did not take it seriously. The Ambassador informed his government of the possibility of an attack, but did not convey it with any sense of urgency. Cordell Hull confirms this in his memoirs.

In 1952 Schreiber was Peru's Foreign Minister. On his mother's side he is a great-great-grandson of the famous Rabbi of Pressburg, the Chatam Sofer. His mother lit candles every Friday, fasted each Yom Kippur, and bade her Christian son to be proud of his Jewish origin, but the Peruvian diplomat Arias Schreiber has little to do with Jews.

Many other stories can be told about the disintegration of the German-Jewish community in Peru. A former mayor of Lima was buried in the Jewish cemetery in accordance with a promise made to his mother who had threatened suicide if this were not done. The files of the *Beneficiencia* contain a record of a dispute that arose about a Jew named Fratzell, whose grandchildren are today fullfleged anti-Semites. Moshe Nimand, the Zionist leader in Lima, told me that in a far-off corner of the country there is a family grave surrounded by a heavy iron wall. This is the grave of the last Jewish family in that area who, according to their wills, were brought to Jewish burial by Gentile friends (who later walled up their family grave). I saw a similar family grave in Belem, Brazil.

There are 5,000 Jews in Peru today, most of whom live in the capital, Lima. A small number live in remote areas among primitive natives, and tiny Jewish communities may be found all through the interior, from the border of Ecuador on one side, to the border of Chile on the other. Most of the Jews who settled in Peru came there directly from East European countries. It was mainly Bessarabian Jews, from the hamlets of Novi-Selitz, Sikureni and Yedinitsi, who discovered that the land of the Incas could be a source of livelihood for them. These Jews will tell you that the "United States of Novi-Selitz," starts at Peru and extends up through to the north, as far as Nicaragua. Costa Rica, the next state, is the "territory" of Polish Jews from Ostrowce and Zelichow.

For many years Peru was a sort of America for Bessarabian Jews, who came there to make a few dollars peddling, and then return home to their shtetl. After World War I, however, it became increasingly difficult to live in the stifling anti-Semitic atmosphere of the East European countries, nor was there much impulse to return to these lands which were in the throes of an economic depression. It was time to think of establishing Jewish community life in Peru.

A few Jews live in the *pueblos* which are scattered along the Pan-American Highway winding its serpentine way over the most primitive areas of Ecuador, Peru and Chile. A cluster of small houses set in the midst of a patch of fertile fields breaks the arid, barren landscape from time to time. Often, the only commercial establishment in a town is the general store *(almacen)*, frequently run by a Jew. These stores, generally, have a permanent sign hanging outside, which reads *Remate* (Sale) !

So it went, all along the Pan American Way. Whenever the bus would stop for a few minutes in the center of a *pueblo*, I would see stores, some small, some large, bearing familiar Jewish names. Jewish eyes looked out at me, identifying me without much trouble among the *criollos,* though I was covered with dust from head to foot. As the bus drove past one of these *pueblos*, which consisted only of a town hall, an *almacen,* and a crude tavern with a squeaking gramophone, I could read on the store front, "Casa Bessarabia."

The Jews in Lima have chosen as their meeting place two of the city's finest cafes. During the week, the cafe serves as a locale for business transactions and friendly chatter. Peruvians look upon the cafe as a home away from home, and the Jews have adopted this Peruvian attitude. On Sunday, a different cafe serves as a center, and there the week's news is told, re-told and digested. Stories of the quarrel with or about the rabbi or the new Hebrew teacher, gossip and banter told not with malice, but merely to pass the time. If a guest comes he is brought to the cafe and served endless cups of coffee.

The Jews have also established social clubs, with upholstered leather easy chairs, and porters dressed in gold-braid uniforms who open the heavy ornamental doors. There are two such clubs: Tendler Club, named after the President, and the Club Sharon, also called the "Lord's Club" in friendly fashion.

Lima has three Jewish communities: Sephardic, German, and East European. These are all united through a Central Committee, and the Presidency is regularly alternated among the three *kehillot.* There are two rabbis, one a Sephardi and the other East European. The fact that many of these Jews maintain regular business contacts with the United States has put them in touch with Jewish communal affairs in that country which has widened and enriched their horizons.

The impressive Hebraica community-center, the cultural and sports center for youth has every modern appurtenance including, of course, a swimming pool, gymnasium, lounges, and rooms for many different activities. It is built on the model of the Hebraica of Buenos Aires, an indication that the Jews of these communities have acknowledged the need to approach the youth in its spirit, to accept the *Nusach America* or, as it is called in Latin America, the New York or American experiment.

Proof of the yearning for a modern type of Jewishness was given in a chat I had with the young director of the Hebraica Institute. As he escorted me about the building he said, "We need a young, modern, American rabbi who can understand our mentality and relate to our youth." Recently, a young American rabbi from the Lakewood Yeshiva was engaged as a rabbi. He organized the first Junior Congregation in Peru.

The sons and daughters of the immigrant-peddlers have absorbed Peruvian culture, studied in the local universities, and now occupy a place of respect in the country's political, economic and cultural life. One is professor of agricultural science at the university, and often represents Peru at international conferences. Alexander Grobman-Twersky, a descendant of the well-known rabbinical dynasty, is one of the most important heart specialists in the country. Engineer Rosenzweig is the leading expert of the petroleum industry, and president of the Jewish school. The younger generation of Jews also play vital roles in the country's literature, poetry and plastic arts, and are identified with Jewish organizations.

Eighty percent of the community's children get a Jewish education. Mixed marriages are less frequent in Peru than in other Latin American countries.

The small Jewish community of Peru is the best example of the transition and change now taking place in the Latin American Jewish centers where the younger generation is now beginning to take over the community reins. The former community head in Lima, Michael Rodzinsky, an immigrant from the Polish town of Siemiatych near Bialystok, and now one of the country's foremost textile manufacturers, handed the presidency over to Azi Wolfenson-Ulanowsky, dean of the Engineering School, and one of the country's outstanding professional men.

In doing so Rodzinsky stated:

"We came to this country alone, destitute, and without the language on our lips. We worked hard and built up our institutions; we felt that if we did not, the same would happen to us as did to the earlier generation of Jewish settlers a century ago. All that has survived of those Jews of 1870 are their tombstones.

"We are handing the community leadership over to you. Though you do not speak Yiddish and are not fully conversant with our culture and traditions, you possess good Jewish hearts and feelings as children of Jewish immigrants from Poland and Bessarabia, proud, of our historic past and of the New Israel which has brought you closer to your people."

The new communal president responded:

"I know that I am assuming the leadership of a 400-years-old community. I know where the Inquisition tribunal stood, where our forefathers were burnt at the stake. To this day there are streets named *Matar Judios* (Slaughter the Jews) or *Quemados* (the Burnings). I can show you Pilatus House—as the Peruvians call it—in the cellar of which the Jews recited their hidden prayers, declaiming the *Kol Nidre,* and where they were taken by surprise along with their spiritual leader Bautista Perez. They were all burnt alive.

"I, Azi Wolfenson-Ulanowsky, who can barely decipher the words in the Hebrew prayer-book, am now called upon to be the spiritual heir of these martyrs. I hope that the God who

139

gave strength and sustenance to all our generations to resist and not yield, will also show me the way of leadership and responsibility in our sacred task."

The two Vice Presidents of the community are Isaac Sternthal who is an outstanding engineer, and Jose (Pepi) Ludmir, the most prominent radio and television commentator in Peru. They represent that country at each Oscar Award ceremony in Hollywood. This new administration has been responsible for having the pupils at the Jewish school recite the daily prayers and put on *tefillin* each morning before classes.

The Jewish school is named after the Marrano, Leon de Pinelo, who bore his mother's name. His brother, Diego Lopez de Lisboa y Leon, bore his father's name. Both were central figures in Spanish colonial culture. Leon Pinelo, was a poet, theologian and student of colonial culture, as well as historian. He wrote the history of the Indians. Diego Lopez de Lisboa y Leon was Rector of San Marcos University, the first university in America. The Inquisition discovered that in Portugal his family was accused of practising Judaism and one of his uncles had been burned at an auto-da-fe. Thanks to the protection of the Archbishop of Lima, however, he himself succeeded in escaping the Inquisition. He was the author of *El Paraiso es el Nuevo Mundo* and *Las Leyes de los Indios*, a book of the laws of the Indians.

The Leon Pinelo school is a structure comparable to any in New York. Its enrollment includes a number of non-Jewish children who are taught the Hebrew part of the curriculum along with the others.

Together with the Pinelo brothers, another pioneer in Latin America's science and culture was a Marrano, Pedro Peralta Barnuevo Rochay Benavides (i.e. Ben-Avidoth), mathematician, astronomer, chemist, and one of Latin America's most famous poets who served four times as Rector of San Marcos. When Peralta was an old man, sick and broken, the Inquisition recalled his Jewish origin and began to pursue him. He withdrew to a tiny cell in

San Marcelo Street, far from the town center, and ailing and alone he breathed his last there.

In November 1964, three hundred years after his death, scholars came from all over the world to take part in celebrating his anniversary. The only missing guests at this celebration were the Jews, to whom the martyrdom of this great scholar is generally unknown.

A modern day visitor to Lima can walk around the Franciscan monastery on a bright, sunny morning and note how the sunbeams are incapable of lighting up the dark, grim crucifixes on the walls. He can walk on the massive flagstones leading to the steps of the monastery in the Plaza de la Inquisicion, which have been soaked with the blood of martyrs. In the middle of the square is a small space marked off with heavy chains; here the fire was lit. Through the massive gates, now crumbling with age, the victims were led in chains, to confess their sins in the church. Inside the cloister there is an odor of incense and candle wax; women are kneeling, their heads covered with black shawls. Approaching the main altar, beneath one's feet one feels an iron trap-door which leads to the dungeons below. Though the trap door is closed with heavy locks, the staircase down is visible. Those stairs lead to the torture chambers of the Inquisition. The walls are covered with inscriptions now difficult to decipher. So you go from place to place. Each corner has its silent, eloquent testimony of torture and death. You can hear the last death-cry "Hear O Israel!" hanging in the air.

Nearby, on Ancash Street, there is today a center for leather merchants (including, of course, some Jewish dealers). I chatted with some of the Jewish leather merchants, immigrants from Eastern Europe whose shops stand on the site of the old Spanish Inquisition. "You see," I said, "the fires of the Inquisition were unable to extinguish the faith of our people. These Jewish shops, a few doors away from the site of the terror are symbolic."

Not long ago, Golda Meir, Israel's former Foreign Minister, stood at this very site, watching a military parade in her honor, and she was decorated with Peru's highest order. When she was given the key to the city, Peru's Foreign Minister greeted her with these words:

> The first victim here of the Inquisition, hundreds of years ago, was the Jewish woman, Manzia de Luna. In 1736, the Jewess Maria de Castro was the last victim of the Inquisition to die here. Both died as martyrs. And the first woman to receive these honors from Peru is, likewise, a Jewess.

At the time of the creation of the State of Israel a number of aristocratic families in Peru stated that they were descendants of Jews. It is preferable to be of Jewish descent than of Indian origin, or to stem from the Spanish *conquistadores*, who to this day are hated because of their greed!

Many Christian writers have done research about the earliest Jews in Peru, and some articles have been reprinted in the Spanish-language, Jewish periodical, *Nosotros* ("We"), which has appeared in Lima since 1931. One writer, Onofrey de Taran, claims that ancient Hebrews and Phoenicians sailed to the River Amazon, which they called the River of Solomon. Pinelo, too, thought that Peru was the land of Ophir, whence Hiram, King of Tyre brought gold to Solomon, and that the Hebrew for gold, *zahav*, got its name from Peru.

Dr. Moshe Cohn, the Brazilian Jewish historian, refers to this theory in his book on the Jews of Brazil, and has published reproductions of stones found in the interior that bear, what appears to be, Hebrew inscriptions. He also maintains that the Indians there use in their speech, what may be corrupt Hebrew words.

Moshe Nimand relates that he is often visited, in his bookstore, by prominent citizens who seek books of Jewish content. One of Peru's leading attorneys came to buy a *mezuza*, and asked that its contents be read to him. The following day he came with his wife to ask for a picture of Moses, saying that he regarded him as the greatest man in history. The attorney's name is Prato. He explained that he is a descendant of Marranos and has, since his childhood, been attracted to Judaism.

Another noted jurist, Dr. Elias Alvarez Calderon, came to ask for a picture of the prophet Elijah. He explained that it is a family tradition always to have one member named Elijah, so that when the forerunner of the Messiah comes he will find someone of that name.

Peru provides the best example of the changes taking place among Jews in Latin America as a result of Israel's existence. The first time I was there anti-Semitism could be felt quite tangibly, but it has since changed for the better. President Fernando Belaunde was a sincere liberal, and the country enjoyed genuine democracy. He successfully carried out a number of reforms for the peasants and workers. He improved diplomatic relations with Israel, and sent delegations there to study its methods of co-operative farming. Even Peru's Vice-President has visited Israel.

At the time when all the Israeli ambassadors to the Latin American states met in Lima they were invited to a banquet in the presidential palace. Care was taken not to include pork on the menu. By "coincidence," the representatives of the United Arab Republic scheduled a press conference in Lima for the same day, and heaped abuse upon Israel. However, the U.A.R. delegates left in disappointment, having failed to make an impression on the public. In contrast, the local newspapers responded warmly to the Israeli ambassadors. One of the columnists said that from Egypt they could import only the third plague of Pharaoh, but from Israel there was much to learn. On the recommendation of a military delegation which had been on a study mission in Israel, the Peruvian Government is carrying out an experiment in frontier army colonization. And Israel irrigation experts have come to Peru to undertake experimental work in its desert area.

CHAPTER XII.

Jewish Life in Chile: Past and Present

The Pan-American Clipper cleaves through the air and speeds on like an eagle thousands of miles above the Cordilleras, the mountain range that divides Argentine and Chile. Every now and again the plane rises higher and higher above the clouds, and you would expect that it would soon pierce the skies. Then suddenly it dips. Seasoned travellers by air are used to this sort of thing, but when you make your first flight it is alarming. Only the sight of your fellow passengers taking it calmly reassures you. Next, the plane turns and shoots straight ahead, as if nothing had happened. Now we are in the midst of a long chain of mountains, one higher than the other, covered with snow that sparkles in the light of the sun—real snow in these hot, tropical Latin American countries. The white snow dazzles your eyes. The plane passes between two snow-capped peaks, so near that you feel you can reach through the window and scrape together a handful of snow and fling it down on the world.

The American pilot informs us that we are flying at an altitude of more than 35,000 feet. Nothing but snow is around us. Looking down we see a red mass—dead lava from volcanos that suddenly erupt, and then become dormant. No human foot has ever trod there. Its immense mineral wealth lies unexplored.

Heavy black clouds gather in the skies. Our plane rises higher and higher, but we have not escaped the storm that is now beating like mad around us. The battle between nature and the machine is on. The plane is buffeted about. One blow after the other. It reels, and then rights itself. The machine has won the battle. It rises high above the clouds. The sun shines once more. We hear

144

the steady throb of the engines. Then we see scattered dots below. They grow larger and come nearer. The plane descends and we land in Santiago. Immediately, one feels lighthearted. There is friendliness in the air, something like the French *insouciance*. The sun is shining brightly in a clear sky. Now you know why the Chilean is such a friendly, cheerful soul. Santiago is like a young bride still wearing her wedding finery and refusing to take it off though the wedding is long over. Nature is extraordinarily beautiful here. There are cool refreshing breezes in the evenings. From the open windows come the strains of serenades and tangos.

As soon as one has passed through the main streets, the picture changes. Leaving the modern skyscraper buildings and luxury shops behind, you enter an area steeped in poverty and want —children pale with hunger, holding out their hands for alms. People live crowded together, three and more families in a wretched hovel. But the Chilean takes his poverty cheerfully. He takes no thought for the morrow; when he has some money, he spends it all.

The Chilean is friendly and easy-going, unless you offend his *dignidad*, his dignity. Then he loses all control. He doesn't attempt to make the most of his time; he wants plenty of leisure. His siesta is sacred. In summer the "official" hours of rest are from noon till four. And then there are the "unofficial" rest hours, in addition.

The Chileans, fond of poking fun at themselves, tell this story: There was a revolution in Chile. The two sides fought bitterly till noon. They then both laid aside their arms, sat down, and took their midday meal, followed by the *siesta*. After that they resumed their fighting. As it happens the Chileans are good fighters. In both its wars, against Peru and against Bolivia, the Chileans won.

Chile has an area of 286,320 square miles, with a population of 5,860,000. Over thirty percent are whites, sixty percent are *mestizos* (half-breeds), and a small number are Indians (about 50,000). Spaniards hold first place among the white communities. Next come the Germans and the British-English, Scots and Irish-

145

Slavs, and about 40,000 Jews. Each of these groups has contributed in its way to the growth and development of the country.

The name "Chile" derives from the Indian words, *Chi-Le,* which mean "end of the world." In this "end of the world" there are traces of two Jewish communities which preceded the modern one. First came the tragic epoch of the Marranos who practised their faith in the New World, though hounded by the Inquisition. Because of its distance from the Tribunals, crypto-Jews found Chile a convenient place to hide from the Inquisition; also served as a transit area to Argentina, Paraguay and Uruguay.

The initial period of the Jews in Chile goes back to 1562 when the Chilean city councillors complained to the Spanish King, Philip II, that people whom the Holy Inquisition had forbidden to enter had come with false documents—among them Jews and Moors—and asked to expel them.

Gunther Behm's book, *Jews in Chile in the Colonial Period,* published by the Chilean Academy, and printed at the University of Santiago, lists a hundred and fifty names of Marrano origin, now borne by families of the Chilean aristocracy. The names are taken from the Spanish genealogies and peerage records of the sixteenth century. Luis Ajedo, Chilean historian, lists four hundred Chilean names that indicate a Jewish origin. Carlos Lorrain de Castro, a member of the Chilean Academy of History, writes of pioneers of Chile who were Marranos, among them, Rodrigo de Arganos, lieutenant of Diego de Almagro, who carried on a campaign against the Araucanian tribe of Indians whose ranks had been joined by many fugitive Marranos. It is noteworthy that both in Brazil and Chile Marranos fought against Marranos during the Colonial wars. Among other descendants of Jews Lorrain de Castro also listed: the Viceroy of Chile, Francisco de Villagra; the Provisional Governor, Diego Garcia de Caseres; the national Chilean poet, Alonso de Ersille; the author of the well-known poem *La Araucania,* Pedro de Salcedo, who fought together with Pedro de Valdivia at the siege of Araucania; and other Chilean pioneers.

There was one Marrano in Chile who worked and fought for his faith until his last breath at the stake, and whose martyrdom will long be remembered. A native of Tucuman in Argentina, Francisco Maldonado da Silva (known as *Eli Nazareño,* Elijah the Nazarite) practiced medicine in the Chilean city, Concepcion, and was arrested by the Inquisition. Many historians have told his tragic story, though the details differ with each writer. This account of unbelievable sacrifice and suffering for his faith has been a favorite topic of chroniclers, beginning with Dr. Isaac Cardozo, who, in *Las Excelencias de los Hebreos* which appeared in Amsterdam in 1679, pays tribute to da Silva as a great figure of Jewish martyrdom. Because of the greater accessibility of certain documents in Lima, the locale of the execution, more information has recently been obtained about him.

Francisco Maldonado da Silva came from a Portuguese Marrano family. His father, who was also a physician, had been arrested by the Inquisition for observing Judaism. He confessed, and was given an opportunity to be "reconciled" to Catholicism. Da Silva had two sisters who were pious Catholics, one of them a nun. It was they who betrayed him to the Inquisition, saying that he had not been to confession for a long time and was observing the Jewish Sabbath.

Da Silva was shipped to the Inquisition headquarters in Lima. At the first examination he declined to take the oath in the Catholic manner. "If I must swear," he said, "I will swear in the name of the living God who created heaven and earth, and who is the God of Israel." Though the officials of the Inquisition were reluctant to do so, they permitted this, as they hoped it would enable them to get a valid confession.

At the hearing, Maldonado da Silva openly stated he was a Jew, just as his father and grandfather were before him. His father had confided in him that all his own kin and forbears had been Jews and had died faithful to their beliefs, but that on his mother's side he was descended from Christians. Until the age of eighteen, he told them, he considered himself a Christian. Then he read the book of the apostate, Shlomo Halevi, who, upon baptism, had taken the name Pablo de Santa Maria, and became the Bishop of Burgos. This book, *Scrutinium Scripturarum,* though written as a Christian tract, had the opposite effect on him and

147

led him to a study of the Scriptures and eventually to Judaism.

At the next examination, Maldonado da Silva stated that he had observed the Sabbath according to the law of Moses as a commandment incumbent upon all Jews; that he had circumcised himself with a scissors and razor; and that he had attempted to convert his sister to Judaism.

The Inquisition was most anxious that da Silva, more than any of the other prisoners, be reconciled to the Church. Attempts were made, by torture and by persuasion, to win him over. None of this, however, caused him to recant, and he was bold enough to declare the basic belief of Christianity to be false. A keenly-argued disputation arose, which consisted of fifteen sections, but he stubbornly held to his position.

The disputation of March 4, 1634 found him on the verge of death. It was the result of a long sickness brought on by an 18 day fast, and the torture-machines. After a period of unconsciousness he came to, and immediately asked those debating with him to repeat to him the chapters in the Bible on which he had challenged their interpretation. This time the Inquisitors were certain that he would abjure his heresies, but after a three-hour discussion they were exactly where they had started.

Maldonado da Silva had collected a great many leaves from corn stalks, which he had asked for in place of bread. With these he had made himself a rope, and with this rope he let himself down through his prison window and reached the other prisoners. He urged them, on their release, to go to the synagogue in Rome where they would be welcomed. The Inquisition found out about this and when he was questioned, he admitted it freely.

In his last disputation with the Inquisitors, Maldonado da Silva produced from his pocket two handwritten quarto-size books made up of scraps of paper "so neat, that they seemed to have come out of a stationer's shop." He had made his own ink from charcoal. One book consisted of a hundred and three pages and the other of a hundred. This fifteenth, and last, disputation left the Inquisitors in great fury, as their prisoner stated that all the arguments for the messianic nature of Jesus were invalid.

For twelve years Francisco Maldonada da Silva lay in the underground dungeons of the Inquisition under acute physical pain, but nothing could break his rocklike adherence to Judaism. On January 23, 1639 an *auto da fe* was staged in the public square, the Church encouraging public attendance and granting pardon for their sins to loyal Catholics witnessing the fearful spectacle. This was the day da Silva was led to the stake, bearded, grey, and skeleton-like. He bore around his neck the two books he had written; this the Church had required, in order to have the flames consume his heresies as well as his emaciated body. An eye-witness has left this record:

> After the act of condemnation was read, a wind blew up such as has not been seen by the oldest residents of Lima. The wind blew off the curtain over the stand where *Eli Nazareño* was confined. He shouted aloud that this had been done by God, so he could look upon him face to face. And so, Francisco Da Silva, Elijah the Nazarite, was swallowed up with his books by the fires of the Inquisition.

The news of his martyrdom reached Europe and aroused great mourning, especially in the communities of the former Marranos. A Jewish poet in Amsterdam, Miguel Barrios, himself originally a Marrano, wrote a poem mourning da Silva's death, which concludes:

> *He faces the fire unflinching,*
> *To which Isaac brings the wood*
> *Following his father's order.*
> *Like Elijah, he is borne to heaven*
> *On a chariot,*
> *And leaves only his dust on the ground.*

In 1885, needing the assistance of technicians to develop its copper, nitrates and other minerals, Chile permitted the immigration of non-Catholics. Among the technicians who came from Germany at that time were a number of Jews. For the same reasons that applied in Peru—the paucity in numbers, the isolation from other Jewries and isolation from each other— assimilation

149

took a heavy (almost complete) toll among this group. Only a few descendants of this group still know of their origin and speak of it on occasion.

In 1941, a meeting in memory of Theodor Herzl, the founder of political Zionism, was held in Santiago. Among those attending was a woman of a leading Chilean family and her Chilean husband. It turned out that she was of partly Jewish parentage, and a relative of Dr. Herzl. Her husband was the Chilean Minister in France. Their son was in France when Hitler invaded that contry, and he helped rescue Jews from the Nazi claws, providing them with Chilean visas.

Another characteristic case is that of the family of Eliyahu Braun, a Polish Jew who came with the German Jews in that period and settled in southern Chile. His eldest daughter married a wealthy Chilean. Her brothers were taken into the brother-in-law's business, and the family soon merged with non-Jews. The synagogue of the *Circulo Israelita* possesses a copy of *Bereshith* in Hebrew, printed in Vilna in 1863, which belonged to Eliyahu Braun. On the fly leaf, the birthdates of the children, Sarah-Itta, Moritz, Oscar, Anita, Fanny, Mayer and Juan, are listed. The former Sarah-Itta Braun, later Señora Valenzuela, noted in Chile for her welfare work and philanthropy, identified herself as a Jewess when she visited the United States.

In the Protestant cemetery there is a mausoleum belonging to a Jewish family which is decorated with various Jewish symbols. The souls lying there are in limbo, between Jew and Christian, neither entirely one, nor the other. It was about such as these that Heine wrote before his death, when he remorsefully felt his own tragedy:

> *Keinen Kaddish wird man sagen....*
> *Keine Messe wird man singen*
> No one will say Kaddish for me,
> They will sing no Mass for me.

When the Balfour Declaration was issued, a reporter asked the Chilean Archbishop, the late Msgr. Crescente Errazuriz, for his reaction to the event. The Archbishop replied that this was a means of righting an old wrong done to the Jewish people, and he added that perhaps it is no secret that the head of the Church in Chile himself is a descendant of these secret Jews of old.

A high-ranking official of the Chilean Ministry of External Affairs insisted on embracing the liaison officer of Israel when announcing that Chile had recognized the State.

In a debate in the Chilean Parliament, the writer Ricardo Lachos listed a long series of distinguished Chilean families who come of Jewish ancestry. Among the descendants of the Marranos was Agustin Edward McClure, the owner of Santiago's most important newspaper, *El Mercuro,* who never denied his origin. For many years he was Ambassador to Great Britain.

✼   ✼   ✼

The present Jewish community of Chile recently celebrated its first half century. Unlike Jewish migration to other parts of Latin America, the movement to Chile was not a direct influx of families or *landsleit.* Jews who had not found success in Argentina, and who had enough wanderlust or imagination, would look beyond the towering mountain ranges of the Cordilleras to seek their fortune. The first Jewish adventurers who were enterprising enough to cross the Cordilleras were sons of the Moiseville colonists from the so-called Jerusalem of Argentina. On an earlier trip to Santiago I was able to talk to one of these pioneers, the late Nechemia Trumper, who was the first President of the Jewish Center and of the Zionist Organization. He was virtually the founder of the community, a typical son of the Argentine farm colonies. His was a simple, cordial temperament, and his attitude to all that were Jewish was warm and serious.

The original means of earning a livelihood among the Jews in Chile, as throughout Latin America, was pack- peddling. There it was called by the Spanish-Yiddish word, *semanalchik,* from the Spanish word for "weekly payments." They were also known as *klappers* (knockers), as they would knock on doors offering everything under the sun on weekly installments. Gradually, the isolated peddlers, scattered in remote parts of the country, began to look each other up and to settle in the larger towns in order to form some kind of group life. In 1906 the first *minyan* was held in Santiago. In 1909 the first Jewish association was formed. Among its statutes is a clause stating that in order to be eligible for membership persons must have a decent occupation. This was an attempt to protect themselves from those who may have brought with them the shame of Buenos Aires—the white slave traffic.

From that point the Jewish community of Chile made rapid social and economic progress contributing significantly to the country's development and occupying a meaningful place on the world-map of Jewish communities. There is not one area of Chile's economy where Jews are not to be found. In many ways they were the creators of its industry. According to government statistics, there are four hundred Jewish-owned industries employing 20,000 workers—an imposing contribution in a country of this size.

The Jewish community has grown both communally and culturally. Many important community and welfare institutions have been created. Chilean Jews are concerned about their children, and all means are being utilized to retain the loyalty of the second and third generation. Santiago has a magnificent school building which houses a Jewish day school. Its budget is over $100,000 a year. Israeli teachers sent by the Jewish Agency give Hebrew instruction although, as in other Jewish day schools in Latin America, the curriculum concentrates on general education.

The fact that Jewish immigration to Chile was not of uniform composition has handicapped the development of a cohesive Jewish life. Alienation of the youth from traditional Jewish life, so prevalent in Latin America, has been particularly marked in Chile. Nevertheless, there is no need to be utterly pessimistic about this community. In conversation with the leaders of various community organizations—many of them second-generation Chileans—one gets the impression that their approach to Jewish life is changing.

There is unmistakable evidence of a trend among the second-generation to return to Jewish life—largely because of external pressure. The Chilean-born Jew does not suffer the inferiority complex of his immigrant parents. The immigrants will never admit to you that anti-Semitism exists in Chile, and they seek consolation in the news that in New York, too, there were synagogues daubed, with swastikas.

The second generation Jew, however, will tell you that a ghetto exists without walls, and that he is proud of being a Jew. He will tell you that the doors to non-Jewish society—especially upper-class society—are barred and bolted. A middle class, as such, does not exist in Chile. The masses are on a cultural and social level that is so low that the Jew can create no contact with them. He, therefore, has no alternative but to create his own social and cultural environment. Envy of the foreigner—especially of the Jew—because of his rapid economic success is much stronger than in the United States. The same envy is directed toward the Jewish student and professional for their academic and professional success.

The present period in Jewish life in Chile might be described as the birth pangs of a new era—a transition period leading to a new *nusach*, a Latin American Jewish way of life. Proof of this might be in the success of the B'nai Israel congregation, the country's newest community, formed by German Jewish refugees in 1939.

Since its formation, B'nai Israel has been an important religious, cultural and communal institution, the center of a wide periphery of activities, modeled on the American synagogue, which does not restrict itself to a purely religious program. B'nai Israel has a sisterhood, a junior congregation, youth clubs, a school and library, a cultural circle, a broadly-based welfare organization, and even a kosher restaurant—the only one in Santiago. Two rabbis, Dr. Manfred Lubliner and Dr. Egon Lovenstein, helped to create this imposing apparatus, which takes in all elements of Santiago's German Jewish population.

With the assistance of the American Jewish Committee, B'nai Israel conducted a study of Jewish University students in Santiago, disclosing important data on attitudes toward the country, Judaism, local institutions and Israel. It also helped to create a Seminary for Jewish Leadership in Santiago (along the lines of the School for Community Leadership in Buenos Aires).

153

As in other Latin American countries, anti-Semitism is an imported product in Chile. The native Chilean is not anti-Semitic. Chile has a large German population, concentrated in centers such as Valdivia, where even the second generation speaks German, and are strong German nationalists and anti-Semitic. When, in 1932, a Chilean Nazi party was organized with the name Popular Socialist Vanguard, or as they are called in Chile "Nazistas," many Germans joined this movement. The Arab League has also started anti-Israel and anti-Jewish propaganda as in all the Latin American countries. Until then there was harmony and friendly relations between Jews and Arabs, and for many years they had business connections with each other. The present democratic government under the leadership of liberal minded Eduardo Frei Montalva is anti-Nazi.

On the advice of, and with the cooperation of the American Jewish Committee, the Comite Representativo— the central body of Jewish organizations in Chile—made contact with the Catholic Church, Cardinal Raul Silva Henriquez, the highest ranking dignitary of the Church accepted an invitation of the B'nai Israel congregation, and gave a lecture in the synagogue on the topic "Human Rights and the Old Testament," which was published in *Comentario* in Buenos Aires, and then in a special edition of *Cuadernos*.

The Chilean Jewish community, like those of neighboring countries, is comprised of various divergent elements: The Eastern Europeans, Hungarians, Germans and Sephardim. All these are linked by means of the central body—a committee on the model of the Argentine Daia—in which each bloc is represented.

Chilean Jewry has taken a long step forward, in terms of organization, since the day the first East-European Jewish immigrants founded the "Filharmonico Ruso," and the Sephardim, who had been there earlier, founded their "Centro Macedonia." Today all second-generation Chilean Jews are "Israelitas."

Outside of the capital there are Jewish communities in Valparaiso, Temuco, Valdivia, Concepcion, La Serena, and in other towns throughout the length of the country.

✓   ✓   ✓

When I first visited Chile, I passed through the town of Arica and met the solitary Jew who lived there. I settled down in a hotel cafe to relax after an exhausting journey along the Pan-American Highway. I sat listening to a group of musicians strumming a sort of Chilean tango on guitars, when my eyes caught those of a Chilean wearing a broad straw hat, his face bronzed like the others, but with a somewhat different look about him. Our eyes met a few times, and I could have sworn they were Jewish eyes. I thought: I must be in error—many Latin Americans look like Jews. But he kept looking at me curiously. I went up to the table where he sat nursing a glass of beer. He began talking first.

"An American?" he asked in English. He looked a little closer and added softly, "And perhaps a Jew?" "Of course," I replied. He responded with a joyous, *"Sholom Aleichem!"*

"Well, well—a Jew! Where are you from and where are you heading? Jews are so rare hereabouts!" he kept repeating in great excitement. "A Jew!"

Soon he took me up to the second floor to meet his family, who were equally delighted to meet a Jew in this most unlikely place. He told me his name: Samuel Kreikerman.

I asked, "What are you doing in this remote corner?"

He told me that he had moved to Santiago several times to be near a large Jewish community, and to be with Jews, but something drew him back to Arica each time.

"What is it?" I asked.

"You see," he replied, "I often come across Jews here who have been wandering about the world—some with a purpose and some without. Sometimes there's a favor to do for them—an immigrant might need some kind of legal access to the three countries that are close by—Peru, Argentina and Bolivia. I'm the one who can do that favor. I have enough contacts here for it. What would the Jewish wanderers who stumble across this place do if I weren't here?"

In the center of the city this man had a business. He was known to all as a *Judio*. His business was a sort of advice-agency and traveller's aid office for Jewish emigrants who wander over the face of the globe.

On a recent trip I visited Arica again, and I found no less than 200 Jewish families settled there. On 21 de Mayo Street in the center of town I counted at least twenty Jewish business establishments. On the 18 de Septiembre Street where other Jewish shops are located stands a white-washed building with a well-tended garden attached, called the "Centro Dr. Theodor Herzl." This is the social club, school and synagogue of this small, remote Jewish community.

How did Jews come here and establish this community in the space of very few years? First, one must know something about the history of these *casas* (stores), all of which started out in the same way. In the early years it was the custom for three, four or five young immigrants to live together in one room, sleeping in portable cots known as *catras*. Each had his own package of merchandise lying next to his cot. When dawn broke each would get up, put his load on his shoulders, and start knocking on doors to sell his wares to the natives, to be paid for in weekly or monthly installments. Each carried a set of business cards and contract forms printed with names like Casa Jaime, Casa Samuel, Casa Miguel (for Mendel), etc. From time to time the purchaser might want to exchange an item he bought from Casa Jaime, and would come on a Sunday, to the address shown on the card, asking for Casa Jaime. The other *"casas"* would direct him, saying, "The cot on the right of the sink—that's Casa Jaime."

Today, those make-believe *casas* of Jaime and Mendel are real *casas* with as many as a dozen employees—elegant shops provided with the best of imported goods, all in the height of fashion. They are either importers or manufacturers, employing some hundreds of people, in direct touch by wire with the largest factories in the United States, Italy and England. The well stocked shelves of these shops display a wealth of handicrafts and goods from North America, Asia and Europe.

Señor Mendel, of Casa Miguel, who is both a manufacturer and an importer, took time off to tell me how the Jews got to know about Arica and why they chose to settle here. Arica has almost no rain all year long, and very little grows there. The sky is the color of copper, and it is an odd experience to find that your hotel room windows are on the ceiling. Since it does not rain at all, is the explanation, why spoil the wall? Should you happen to awaken in the middle of the night you have the feeling of sleeping in the open air.

The population in this arid unproductive area is quite poor. The territory is surrounded by lofty mountain peaks so barren they suggest the unformed void of Genesis. On the slopes of these crags are small huts inhabited by the local natives called Rotos. For years, these people lived their primitive life totally isolated from the rest of the world. Suddenly, they became aware of a world of railway trains, automobiles and fine clothing. All this, the native will tell you, was due to the airplane. Once the airplane penetrated the mountain fastnesses, it brought with it all the curses of civilization. 'It is destroying our youth," he will complain. "All they want to do is dress up in fine clothes and leave home."

In order to assist this province, the government created a free port in Arica, and soon it was invaded by merchants from the two neighboring countries: Bolivia and Peru. From Chile itself, thousands moved in to take advantage of the cheap prices or to seek employment. As a result, Arica soon became a busy, bustling city and lost its primeval calm. The shops are packed with customers who come from the bordering countries, and with Chileans who come to get bargains, paying much less than in their own towns. How do they get the goods out of the free zone?—They have ways and means of managing this.

The Jews of nearby Bolivia, as well as the Jews of Santiago, were quick to scent the possibilities for commerce in Arica. Moreover, political and economic conditions had not been too stable in Bolivia. Jews began to leave for Arica and, before long, a new Jewish community developed.

✓   ✓   ✓

While Santiago was still blanketed in darkness, our motor car slid out on the road to Mendoza. When dawn began to break and rays of light pierced their way through the morning blue of the sky, we found ourselves in the midst of the gigantic Cordillera Range, which blocked out the rising sun. At this moment, between night and day, the giant peaks are of an undetermined color and look like sleeping silhouettes wrapped in eternal slumber.

Our automobile cut its way through a narrow pass chopped out of the giant mountain chain. We ascend the range, going higher. The greatest peak of all, Aconcague, standing in stately dignity, is over 23,000 feet high, and is the second highest in the world, and the highest in America. Thousands of feet down from its peak, it is still covered with snow.

At the foot of the mountain is Punta del Inca, a natural bridge formed of various minerals into a natural overpass. Nearby is a fenced off space. This is the grave of the "Unknown Warrior," who fell off the cliff with his horse. Here lie also the remains of people, and the carcasses of cattle, who fell victim to the dangerous road. Soon we come across cataracts and waterfalls reflecting the thousand colors of the rainbow.

We arrive at a small Chilean town lying at the edge of these huge mountains, and there we stop to rest and eat. The inhabitants, people with fresh faces, smile at us pleasantly. The warmly dressed women and children wear hobnailed shoes that enable them to climb the mountain trails more easily. You can feel the mountain air filling your lungs, just like good wine, and you know why the people are so good-natured and friendly. Finally, we arrive at the tunnel which connects Chile and Argentina. It was impossible to cut a pass through the high peaks here, and a tunnel had to be dug through their interior instead.

Mendoza was the first Argentine city I had seen after an absence of 25 years, and I arrived in the very midst of the carnival. The city was decked out and festive. Young and old were dressed in holiday clothes; all sorts of fanciful, bizarre costumes and masks were seen. Everyone was out on the streets in a happy, carefree mood.

I felt as though I were an uninvited guest at a wedding—a guest who aimlessly wanders about, a stranger to all. How I longed to see a brother Jew! But how was I going to find a Jew in the midst of the Mendoza carnival, when all the shops were shut tight? Then, on a corner of Avenida San Martin, in the midst of all the hubbub and noise of the carnival, I caught sight of one face from among the thousands of carefree holidayers. I saw a person, tired, weary, hung about with belts, chains and purses. I looked at him closely and said, "A Jew?"

"Yes," he replied, somewhat surprised. "My name is Yampolski. And you?" A smile appeared on his weary face. "Where are you from?"

"From New York," I quickly replied.

"From New York," he repeated a few times. "What are American Jews there doing for Israel?" he asked. "They do have some power to do something, don't they?"

Then I was swept away by the stream of merry-makers, and I lost this fellow-Jew hung all over with little belts, chains and pocket-books. People are celebrating their carnival, I thought, and we Jews sell little trinkets, and carry about Israel. . . .

The International Express traveled with great speed on the way to Retiro. Towns and villages flashed by the coach as the train passed. I stood near the window feeling quite uneasy and restless, and as scenes and pictures of twenty-five years earlier flashed through my mind, I felt that a demand was being made upon me to give an accounting of all that intervening time.

The flames of thousands of little lights from the homes of Buenos Aires dotted the window of the coach. This is just how the port looked that night twenty five years ago when our boat slid into the port. Memories rushed back into my mind. My heart was full. "Retiro," announced the conductor casually.

It is a sticky, hot night; I can't sleep at all. I am weary from the long trip, but I go down into the street. I seek memories of Buenos Aires of twenty five years ago. Here is the old street, dear old Corrientes, and here is the Rio Bamba, the *Hachnosses Orchim* (the refuge for travellers). In the old days we used to gather there and spin our fantasies. Here I am again on Lavalle and Junin Streets. Again I am troubled. There, in that very house, for 50 centavos a night, I slept on a cot when I first came as a

159

young man to Argentina. There, in that house, I had my first dream in this sunny land. I remember the girl with the black braids and the fiery eyes, the landlord's daughter. She had blushed seeing me, and I was embarrassed.

The house has become larger . . . the other houses also have increased in size. Just as they did, twenty five years ago, people sit outside, unable to sleep because of the stifling heat. I look at the people-strange, cold faces. Where is the girl with the fiery eyes and the black braids? A middle-aged, Jewish housewife looks at me with some suspicion. "What does the *Señor* want?" I look at her in the darkness and I think I detect traces of the girl with the black braids. It seems to me her eyes might be somewhat similar. "What do you want?" she inquires with some irritation.

"What do I want?" I feel as though I could fairly shout it, but I am silent. I am looking for twenty-five years of my life which have vanished like the clouds!

CHAPTER XIII.

Argentina: The Melting Pot of South America

One can best appreciate the changes which have taken place in a country when one returns to it after an absence of years. Walter Rathenau, the German-Jewish statesman, once said, "If you want to know your own country, you must first see the world." Since I first landed in Argentina as a young immigrant in 1922, I revisited the country six times. Each time I entered by a different route, using planes and ships, and even an automobile, through the Cordilleras of Chile. Each time, marked changes were clearly visible.

On my first return, Peronism was in its honeymoon period. Juan Domingo Peron was seated firmly in the saddle, the land was swimming in an artificially inflated prosperity. Everywhere one could hear the deafening shouts: *Viva Peron! Viva Evita! Viva Peron!*—like a magic incantation designed to shut off any embarrassing inquiry into the questionable or the dubious. For instance, at the Customs, half your baggage might suddenly vanish from under the hands of the inspector, and you could not redeem the rest of your belongings without giving *mordida* (i.e. the "bite") to the official who openly demanded it. No sooner had you dealt with one, when a second official appeared with a similar demand. And then, at the government depot, the locks of your baggage might be broken open, and the officials would make off with your property. Your complaint before the higher official is met with a *"Viva Peron!"* implicitly suggesting it is best to keep quiet and write off your losses; it is healthier to make fewer complaints.

161

Peronism was on the decline when I visited Argentina for the fourth time. The dictator's bust was no longer seen everywhere. Peronism was rapidly coasting downhill. The workers, whom Peron had accustomed to an easy life, were in a state of utter demoralization. The *campesinos* whom he brought from the outlying areas of the pampas and settled in city hotels to solidify his support, had to be evicted from the hotels with water-hoses. The country was suffering from a food shortage—a country which so long had been the supply center of meat, and the wheat granary for so many lands. Agriculture was in ruins and industry in collapse. Many industrialists had simply handed over the keys of their factories to the government, unable to maintain the constant increase in wages in the face of diminishing production.

When I visited Argentina the fifth time, Juan Domingo Peron was in exile. By now the deep wounds caused by his regime were apparent: unlit, broken streets; faded, unpainted buildings; boarded up shop-windows. Buenos Aires, known as the Paris of Latin America, had lost all its charm. Florida, its famous boulevard, looked as if it had been hit by earthquake or bombardment. The American financier John Nureen of Chicago estimated that the various Latin American dictators such as, Peron of Argentina, Rojas Pinilla of Colombia, Perez Jimenez of Venezuela, Batista of Cuba, and the lesser dictators of the smaller countries, had in the course of twenty-five years robbed their countries and their peoples of one billion, three hundred and seventy-six million dollars. The Argentine dictator well belonged at the head of this list.

Argentina's half million Jews is the world's third largest Jewish community. Officially, this community came into being in 1860 when, on November 11th of that year, the first Jewish wedding was solemnized in Argentina. In 1862 the first Jewish congregation, the Libertad Synagogue, was established. Its founders were mainly West European Jews from Alsace-Lorraine.

Unofficially, however, there are historical traces of the Marranos who fled from the Portuguese Inquisition. Buenos Aires was a free port and the Marranos sought refuge there, especially after

Portugal reconquered Brazil where the refugees had built up prosperous communities in Pernambuco, Bahia, and other centers. In 1654, the same year in which the first group of Jews came to New Amsterdam, eight ships with "Portuguese" passengers sailed into Buenos Aires, and despite official refusal to admit them, the travelers found ways and means of entering the country.

In his book *Historia de Buenos Aires,* the historian Romulo Zabalo writes that as early as 1601 the influx of "Portuguese" into Argentina was so great that it was proposed to set up an Inquisition Tribunal in Buenos Aires, to include the neighboring areas of Chile and Paraguay. Another Argentine chronicler, Ruiz Guinazu, writes in his book, *Inquisition in America,* that in 1636 the immigration of *"Judios"* (he calls them directly by their name—Jews) to the shores of the La Plata was so great that the city fathers of Buenos Aires became alarmed. They applied to the Viceroy at Lima asking that a tribunal of the Inquisition be established in Argentina. The Argentine Jewish historian Boleslao Lewin and the Chilean historian Jose Toribio Medina have shown through documents, proclamations and records that in the seventeenth century an Inquisition Commission existed in Argentina and the surrounding provinces. Persons suspected of secretly adhering to Judaism were arrested and transferred to the Inquisitional Court in Lima.

The noted historian, Don Lucas Ayagarry, referred to several eminent Israelites of Spanish origin who played a role in Argentina's early history and held various political posts during that agitated period.

A second Argentinian historian, J.M. Ramos Mejilla, credits the crypto-Jews (Marranos) with being pioneers of the Argentine Revolution.

What the beginnings of Jewish life in Argentina looked like is described by Mordecai Alperson, the veteran of that country's Jewish colonization, in his book, *Thirty Years of Jewish Colonization in Argentina:*

On a muddy street in a narrow, dark little room stood a Holy Ark *(Aron Kodesh)* with a little pulpit and four benches on

163

which there lay a dozen prayerbooks. The rabbi was Henry Joseph, the congregation's first spiritual leader, who himself took a Protestant woman as his wife in a church, and who, in turn, married his daughters off to Christian bridegrooms also, of course, in a church.

In 1893, this rabbi, along with another intermarried German Jew, organized a *Gesellschaft für Beerdigung* (burial society). The ceremony of its founding took place on the premises of an organization called *Poalei Tzedek,* indicating that an organized Jewish workmen's group was already in existence. The burial society, originally was nothing more that its name indicated: an arrangement to ensure its members a passport to the next world. However, it did not remain this forever. It later became known as the *Chevra Kadisha,* and under the influence of the East European Jews who were by then the majority, it became the *Chevra Kadisha Ashkenazi,* from which developed the present central *Kehilla* or community organization.

The urban dwellers at that time consisted of two elements: the "defiled," as they were referred to (i.e. the white-slave element), who called themselves *Judios* (Jews), and the other Jews who distinguished themselves from this group by describing themselves by their countries of origin, as *Rusos, Polacos,* and *Alemanes* (Germans). These struggled against the former group until they succeeded in driving them out of Argentine Jewish life.

In 1910, five years after the abortive Russian Revolution, Argentina received an influx of revolutionary-minded immigrants to whom religion had no meaning, and who fought Jewish religion as the contemporary radicals did in New York, with Yom Kippur balls and anti-religious demonstrations. On the other hand, the colonist element on the farms had brought traditional Judaism with them from their small towns in East Europe. Many of the farm colonies had synagogues and even some religious functionaries. The ICA schools had a curriculum of teaching the traditional practices and ceremonies called *cursos religiosos.* Looking to the future they saw that in a Roman Catholic country a mere language devoid of Jewish content would be insufficient to maintain Jewish continuity. But the colonies had no influence on the metropolis. On the contrary, the metropolis overcame the colonies and fought the "Jews in the top hats" who were accused of planning to raise a generation of fanatics. The teachers were influenced to avoid religious subjects whenever possible.

When I returned to Argentina after an absence of many years, I found the face of Argentine Jewry quite changed. The former peddlers now owned factories, and were integrated into the Argentine economy. Thanks to their vitality, energy and connections abroad, they had built up important industries—especially during the two war periods when Argentina was neutral. Jews developed the furniture and leather industries, and weavers from Lodz and Bialystock built factories and developed a great textile industry. Near Buenos Aires there is an entire town of factories of former Bialystock weavers, named Villa Lynch.

What used to be small and primitive *Gemilat Chasadim* (free loan) offices— consisting of a desk and a few worn benches where the immigrant peddlers could get a loan of a few *pesos* to buy their stock of merchandise—had grown into large Jewish banks carrying on transactions in millions of *pesos*. The old *Chevra Kadisha*, whose sole function was to bury the dead, had become a centralized *kehilla* with facilities and personnel embracing all aspects of Jewish life, education, culture and philanthropy. Its budget ran into millions of *pesos*. Its building housed many insitutions including the DAIA, the Bureau of Education *(Va'ad Hachinuch)*, YIVO, a library, a museum, and a religious department.

The economic rise of the Argentine Jewish community made it possible to establish and endow cultural institutions on a fairly lavish level, and many fine modern structures were erected. The visitor is impressed at first glance, but when he examines things a little more closely he sees that the growth lies only in the height of the building. There has been a visible decline in Jewish education. The second and third generations, with very little exception, no longer speak Yiddish. The Bureau of Jewish education noted that the number of children receiving a Jewish education is between twenty and twenty-five percent of the total, and the situation is deteriorating from year to year.

The late A.L. Schussheim, a Jewish journalist writing in the *Yiddishe Zeitung* of July 4, 1954, gave an account of the children who were then receiving a Jewish education in Buenos Aires: The number attending first grade was 2,078, and in the second grade it was down to 1,512. More than half the children who enroll in a Jewish school, he wrote, leave in the second grade. In the fourth grades of the Jewish schools of Buenos Aires and vicinity there were then 661 pupils, in the fifth no more than 159, and in the sixth only 39.

After researching the field of Jewish education in Argentina, Dr. Chaim Armion, from the Israeli Education Ministry, came to the conclusion that in recent years only 15% of the Jewish children receive a Jewish education; the other 85% do not. The average Jewish child who went to an afternoon school received an hour per day of Jewish studies—with a four month vacation. There has been mechanical concentration on the Yiddish language—a language quite unfamiliar to the child, and totally alien to his environment, which is devoid of any kind of traditional Jewishness. And when one realizes that 85% of all Jewish children in Argentina have been getting no Jewish schooling at all, one cannot help but ask: In a country so overwhelmingly Roman Catholic, is a program consisting of mechanical Yiddish instruction sufficient to keep this community safe from complete assimilation?

The way back to Jewish tradition, which has been useful in North American Jewish life, and which establishes contact with the younger generation in its own language, simply did not exist in Argentina until recently. There was no Jewish literature in the Spanish language. A movement in this direction began only a few years after the establishment of the State of Israel. Jewish writers of the second Argentine generation began to write in Spanish on Jewish themes, but they have been opposed by the secularists whose chief obsession is with Yiddish. During one of my visits there, when a theatrical group performed a play in Spanish on a Jewish theme, it was totally ignored by the Yiddish press of Buenos Aires.

The Bureau of Jewish Education sent around a questionnaire

among the pupils in the schools which gives a clear idea of the position of Yiddish in Argentina. To the question, "What language is used at home?" 90% replied, "Spanish." To the question "Do you receive a Yiddish newspaper at home?" the answers were negative. The same applied to Yiddish books. This, however, does not mitigate against regular and frequent public proclamation that Argentina is the stronghold of Yiddish; Yiddishists from all corners of our little Yiddish world sing hallelujah panegyrics to the Argentine community.

The concentration on language at the expense of Jewishness in the program of the Jewish secular schools has served to bring Argentine Jewry face to face with a serious problem. The estrangement of its youth from Jewish life and Jewish interests does not forebode well for the Jewish future. The fact is that immigration ceased some years ago, and there are no new reserves of Yiddish-speaking immigrants arriving in the country. Yiddish has struck no deep roots and has had no influence on the generation born in Argentina. Over a fifty year period it has failed to inculcate any love or reverence for Jewish values. These schools have even failed to transmit the Yiddish language to the younger generation. Even the insignificant number who do speak Yiddish, do so in a mechanical manner, as if they were rehearsed by a stage director.

During my visit to Argentina in 1952, the *Yiddishe Zeitung* carried a symposium on the state of Judaism. It was reported that family purity, circumcision, *kashrut* and Sabbath observance were disappearing from the scene; *trefa* foods were served in synagogues on festive occasions. As far back as 1929, when Rabbi Solomon Goldman of Chicago visited Buenos Aires, he protested being given ham sandwiches at a public Jewish dinner. The same happened in my presence at a luncheon tendered in the Hebraica (a Youth Organization), for the well known American-Yiddish poet, J. J. Schwartz, who complained of being served ham sandwitches after reciting his Yiddish verses. In the jubilee issue of the Argentine *Yiddishe Zeitung*, M. Okrutny an Argentine writer wrote an article entitled, "Burnt Out Soil," stating that what our enemies did not succeed in destroying over so long a period, we are. The number of mixed marriages is rising. "We often pinch our cheeks to bring color to them," he writes. "In the hope that others will believe that all is well, we are committing an even graver sin by deceiving ourselves into believing that all is well."

Buenos Aires, a city of a quarter million Jews, has no more than seven or eight rabbis, and these are all imported from abroad. The second and third-sized Jewish communities of Rosario and Cordoba have no rabbi at all. In the provinces, the situation is virtually disastrous.

A scholarly conference took place in Buenos Aires in which the participants were Dr. Moshe Davis, Dr. Saul Asch of Israel, and Bezalel Sherman, the American Jewish sociologist. Its purpose was to inquire into the state of Jewish life, and to establish contact with the Spanish-speaking Jewish intellectuals. But the Yiddishists ignored this event since, of course, Yiddish was not spoken, and certain unpleasant truths were mentioned— truths which do not justify the claims of the success of Yiddish.

Visiting Yiddishists in Argentina find their lectures attended by an "inside" group of 500 listeners—though there are virtually none but gray heads among these. They do not see, or do not wish to see, the other side of the coin. They return to North America, and broadcast the message that Argentina is the most Yiddishized community in the world!

And when Argentine Yiddish writers visit North America, they do the contrary. In spite of the pitiful results achieved in their own country, they picture the United States as a barren wasteland. A director of an Argentine Yiddish school (who, incidentally, did not have his son circumcised) forecast, on his return from New York, an early demise for the North American Jewish community. "The Jewish schools," he said, "are located in old neglected and shabby buildings, sometimes in basements, in contrast to our splendid modern structures." By "Jewish schools," he meant the Yiddish-secular schools. Yeshiva University, the Chicago Theological College, the Hebrew Union College in Cincinnati, the Jewish Theological Seminary, the Lubavitcher *yeshivot*, and the whole network of *yeshivot* and day schools throughout the country—these, to him, are apparently not "Jewish schools."

168

Yet another group of champions of Yiddish are the Bundists. The Bund played an important role in Jewish life in pre-war Poland, but in America its communal role is a very minor one, so the battle for Yiddish is the last card it can play. It also gives the Bundists an opportunity to hit back at the Zionists who have undertaken to "destroy Yiddish." The Bundists set up a hue-and-cry that the emissaries from Israel, the *sh'lichim,* are driving Yiddish out of the Jewish schools of the Latin American countries. The alarm was taken up in Yiddishist circles and exploited in a most melodramatic fashion. The Zionists, it was alleged, have undertaken to destroy the tongue spoken by the six million martyrs. If things are not as well as they should be in the Argentine "stronghold," the propaganda machine stated, it is the fault of the Zionists.

What is the truth? Did the Israeli representatives drive Yiddish out of the Jewish schools of Latin America? Even forty years ago, when I was a teacher in the Jewish schools of Argentina and Brazil my pupils, except those born in the farm colonies, spoke Yiddish only with difficulty. When I returned four decades later, my former pupils were already fathers and, in some cases, grandfahers. Their children and grandchildren certainly were not speaking Yiddish. When Israel learned of the deplorable state of Jewish education in the Latin American countries, and the danger of assimilation confronting these communities, an attempt was made to encourage education in Hebrew. Whether the Israeli teachers and *sh'lichim* will succeed in bringing Hebrew and Jewish content into the schools is a question still unanswered. It is quite likely that they will at least be able to salvage a certain percentage from total assimilation.

Di Presse, in an editorial, drew a distinction between the attitude toward Yiddish in Argentina and North America: "Whereas in North America, even those not familiar with Yiddish have a respect for the language, and many English translations from Yiddish writers have been published, in Argentina this is not so. There, the ignorance of Yiddish on the part of the youth is accompanied by a snobbish and cynical attitude towards it." Because the Jewish cultural treasures of the past have not been trans-

169

mitted to them in their own day to day language, they have become alienated from the spiritual message Judaism has to offer.

Not long ago the DAIA carried out a survey in Buenos Aires which indicated that Jewish youth were estranged from Jewish life. Of 90,000 Jewish young people, 34,000 were enrolled in Jewish youth groups and, of these, only 8,000 were active in Jewish life. This means that more than 90% were not interested in Jewish life, and more than 62% were destined for assimilation. Among university students the situation is much worse. It is estimated that there are 70,000 Jewish students at the universities, and of these only eight percent are connected with Jewish organizations. A large number are associated with Castroite groups.

The official Jewish community of Buenos Aires (the *kehilla*) has in recent years expended millions of *pesos* on Jewish education, totalling more than one-third of its budget. Despite these costly efforts, the results shown are quite sad. At a dialogue conducted by the DAIA with Jewish students who are actively involved in Jewish life, one young man condemned those Jews who fled the Castro regime for their hostility to the new social order. A second denounced Israel because of its association with "reactionary foreign powers." A third demanded the acceptance of mixed marriages.

At a press conference in New York, the Vice-President of the DAIA, Dr. Gregorio Faigon, attempted to explain the presence of Jewish students in the leftist Castroite organizations by saying that at the Argentine universities the undergraduates are organized in the two extremes of right and left. Since the Jewish students cannot, and will not, go along with the rightist reactionaries, they had no choice but to join the leftist groupings.

The problem of Argentina's Jewish youth has been well studied by A. Guverstein, himself a young Argentine Jew. Writing in the youth journal *Yugnt-Ruf* (No. 6, 1966), he divides the younger generation into three groups. The first category is quite apathetic not only to the Yiddish language but to anything related to Judaism. Many of these have been drawn into leftist ranks, and nothing Jewish is of any concern to them. The second category does have some notion of Jewishness, but has little interest in the Yiddish language or culture. The third category, which is pitifully small, is nationally conscious.

THE PERILS OF ASSIMILATION

The serious peril to the young, Jewish generation was made quite clear at a symposium conducted by the American Jewish Committee on the theme of Jewish identity, which was attended by thirty Jewish intellectuals, among them sociologists, university professors and psychologists from Argentina, Uruguay and Chile. Señorita Sara Strasberg, a sociologist, stated that the lack of positive Jewish identification was a result of the type of Jewish education given in these countries. The condition of Jewish education in Argentina was described in general terms by Professor Olga Winters, as follows: 15% of its Jewish children attend Jewish schools; of these only 3% reach the secondary level. Sociologist Eduardo Rogowski stressed that the community was in a state of self-delusion when it constantly praises its insitutions as being the best organized in the world for they are completely devoid of content. The younger generation has failed to acquire proper substance, although it is seeking a new form of Jewish identity from which it can draw pride and satisfaction.

Several years ago, an anti-Semitic Deputy in the Argentine Congress attacked another Deputy, named Saporznik, as a Jew. Saporznik's "courageous" reply was that he had nothing to do with Jews. It was only through this incident that the fact that there were five Jewish Deputies in the Congress came to light.

Di Presse, a local Jewish daily, published an editorial pointing out that in the U.S. Congress there are 12 Jewish Congressmen, and that there are even Jewish Senators who vigilantly defended Jewish interests and the good name and honor of Jewry, and who were proud of their Jewish identity. Saporznik happened to be a Russian-Jewish name quite familiar to me from my early days in Argentina. This man's father or grandfather had stood at the helm of Jewish life in Buenos Aires, but as a result of the community's neglect of Jewish tradition and content, the young generation had grown up a stranger to its own people and history.

This serious problem was raised at a session of the Council of Communities, held in Resistencia. Dr. Gregorio Makowski in a basic analysis made of Jewish life in Argentina, stressed that the whole method of community work must be altered to fit the pattern of the new generation. He pointed out that the majority of the younger people have acquired a higher education. Many are professionals and academicians. They cannot be won over by the same approaches and techniques used, as were used in the preceding generation.

"The Jewish schools," he stressed, "are of vital significance for our approach. I am not an opponent of Yiddish. I know the language and I am a regular reader of the Yiddish press. Nevertheless, I believe that teaching Yiddish in the schools is nothing more than a waste of time. We teach the children history, literature and other such subjects via Yiddish or Hebrew and most lessons are lost, for the pupils do not follow what is being said. Wouldn't it be wiser to teach all the subjects in Spanish?"

I made a point of visiting the town of Resistencia to get a picture of Jewish life in the Argentine provinces. Resistencia was noted throughout Argentina for its Yiddish school which has existed for many years.

The town of Resistencia, in the remote Chaco region near the Paraguayan border, has a look of Texas about it: well paved streets still smelling of sand; modern parks; shop windows stocked with merchandise; up-to-date houses standing next to primitive hovels. The people in the streets were a mixture of all shades, some dressed in city clothing, others wrapped in *ponchos* of various colors.

The town is easily identifiable as a new center. It was built by immigrants from various lands who flooded into the Chaco in search of gold, just like in the California "gold rush." The area was invaded by Poles, Ukranians, Germans, Italians, Spaniards and others who had not found their fortune in Buenos Aires, and who were fed up slaving in the burning heat in the *tallers* (workshops) of the city. By contrast, the old American sweatshops were palaces. In the wilderness of the Chaco they cast off the troubles of the city, and lived close to nature, buying animal skins from the half-civilized *criollos* and selling them brass clocks, trousers, ties and shirts. Others tilled the free soil that the government granted them, and large farms and *ranchos* spread throughout the barren untilled stretches.

Among those who came here and accepted the Argentine Government's bid to help open up the Chaco, were Jewish colonists who had left the ICA farms, because of dissatisfaction with their bureaucratic management. Here I met a former neighbor of mine, Yudel Mariash, who was from the Narcisse Lewin Colony where I had been a teacher. Yudel was no longer a farmer, other families of that group are now wealthy estate owners, and hire men to work their lands. Many Jews who had not "made it" in the capital also came to the Chaco and opened small shops and trading posts in the most isolated spots among semi-savages. Maintenance and overhead were negligible, and the profits were high.

All had one goal in mind—to make a *tuler* in the shortest possible time (the Argentine Jew uses the term *tuler* for the *peso*; it is Yiddish, from *thaler*), and to return to Buenos Aires to live among Jews. But only a few have managed this. The others, while constantly planning the return trip, have gradually adjusted to the environment, to the peculiar climate, and even to the plague of mosquitoes. They struck roots and started to establish a Jewish life of sorts in this remote spot. They built a *Salon* (the name for a Jewish center), a Talmud Torah, brought in a teacher from the capital, and formed the rudiments of a Jewish communal society. There are today about 340 Jewish families in Resistencia. In contrast to other Jewish communities made up of people from the same East European area, Resistencia is a composite of Jews from every quarter: Litvaks, Poles, Galicians, Bessarabians, even Austrians (i.e. Jews from Austria proper). This was no influx of *landsleit* or family groups. No one brought over anyone else. It was a movement of individuals who came to seek their own fortune in the "wild west." If some of them brought in a friend or relative, it was from within Argentina, not from the "old country."

And as is usual when Jews come together under one roof, particularly when they are from different lands with different customs, they dispute, they quarrel, they make up . . . and then quarrel again.

The *kehilla* leaders sought to prove to me that they followed Jewish tradition, and boasted that they maintained a *shochet* (ritual slaughterer). No one, however, would tell me where he lived. It took a long time before I managed to locate him (he has since left) in an unfurnished dilapidated house. I found him, his wife and children in a distressing state. The children were shoeless and in tatters. The scene was in stark contrast to the well-fed community leaders who sat in armchairs and deplored the unlettered state of the younger generation. The *shochet* was a grandson of the first Moisesville Rabbi, Aaron Goldman. He invited me into the synagogue, which was quite disorderly and neglected, with prayerbooks lying on the seats and floor. Apparently it was in use only on the High Holidays.

The state of Jewishness in Resistencia was lamentable. Of 340 Jewish families, there were 100 mixed marriages, and the children of these unions are increasing in number. Even children with two Jewish parents know little of Judaism aside from a few broken Yiddish phrases or Hebrew words which they have learned and repeat by rote.

This situation, it must be said, holds true throughout all the provincial areas of Argentina. There are cities with as many as four or five hundred Jewish families which possess no religious functionary of any kind. In the whole province of Entre Rios, where the bulk of the Jewish colonies were located, there is not a single *mohel* or *shochet*. In the few cases where a *mohel* is desired, the parents send to Buenos Aires for one.

At a conference of communal representatives in Buenos Aires the delegates from the isolated provincial centers pictured their sad state, pointing to the rising tide of mixed marriages and the threat of total disintegration confronting them. One delegate told of a Jew who had walked into the office of a Yiddish newspaper with tears in his eyes, to tell about his grandchild who had called him a "Christ-killer."

At the request of community leaders in Argentina, the American Jewish Committee launched a broad program in 1948, to help prevent total assimilation in Argentina, and to bring Jewish youth closer to Jewish tradition and cultural values. The AJC's Foreign Affair's Department has been conducting its program in close partnership with the Instituto Judio Argentino de Cultura e Informacion, established in 1948. A Spanish language magazine, *Comentario*, was founded and edited by Maximo Yagupsky. It is read by intellectuals, educators and political leaders in nineteen Spanish speaking countries.

The AJC enlisted the service of a corps of Jewish scholars and community workers to produce materials specifically tailored to the local needs. Books and brochures on contemporary Jewish subjects—historical, religious and cultural—have been issued. Their subject matter is broadly inclusive. How to celebrate Jewish holidays; How to arrange a Bar Mitzvah ceremony; How to organize a seminar on Jewish history; How to prepare a *Shabbat* dinner: What is the Talmud?; An analysis of the philosophies of Orthodoxy, Reform, Conservatism and Reconstructionism; Edmond Fleg's *History of Jewish Literature;* A historical demographic and sociological report on the ten largest Jewish communities in the world; A selection of essays and articles on Jewish identity; Reprints from *Comentario,* and other publications; A sociological study of the Argentine Jewish community; Articles by non-Jewish authors about Argentine society; Problems of integration of immigrants, including Jews; Essays on Jews in American society; Dr. John Slawson's book on Jewish identity. A center for audio-visual materials has been set up, and an exhibit of synagogue architecture in Europe has been arranged. A Latin American Jewish Yearbook is produced, and a department for statistics about Argentine Jewry was created. A study of the Sephardic Jewish Community in Argentina was made for the first time.

During Book Month, arranged by the *kehilla,* books are sold at special, reduced prices. At the last Book Month the number of Yiddish books sold came to 2,879 (and slightly more of Hebrew books), whereas, the number of Spanish books of Jewish content sold amounted to more than 14,000. At an earlier Book Month event, when the figure of Spanish books exceeded 17,000, sober Jewish leadership clearly saw the situation and realized they had to face the fact of a changing community, and that they have to produce books of Jewish content in Spanish for the Jewish youth. To this end, the *kehilla* organized a special department, "The New Generation."

Recently, this department published an anthology (the third of "Today's Jewry" series), which includes essays and studies about Jewish problems, written by writers of stature, including, Albert Memmi, Joseph Kastein, Chaim Greenberg, B. Borochov, Dr. Nachman Sirkin and others. This decision created a stir among the defenders of Yiddish. Soon the usual hue-and-cry went up, that Jewish life is not possible without the Yiddish language. The *kehilla* replied: "If we intend to reach our youth with Jewish content, Jewish life, and Jewish national and religious values, we must do it in the language they speak. We have no right to scuttle our ship and abandon it to the sea of assimilation."

Dr. Leon Dujowne, an eminent scholar and writer, former editor of *Mundo Israelita,* and a leading figure in Argentine Jewry's cultural life who himself cherishes Yiddish, gave the champions of Yiddish a clear and unequivocal response: "No one is attempting to deny the great and historical importance of Yiddish down through the centuries. But it is a fact that the Jewish people existed and flourished for generations, and created great and significant works long before there was a Yiddish language."

Dr. Dujowne pointed to the rise of Jewish culture in our own day in languages other than Yiddish: the Hebrew renaissance in Israel, Jewish writings in French and in English. He cited from an article by Jules Brunschwig, in the organ of the Alliance Israelite Universelle, that there is no publishing firm in France which is not interested in publishing books of Jewish interest. The same certainly applies in North America. He pointed out that the American Jewish Committee did not stop being Jewish after giving up its Yiddish Department, when it became clear that maintaining such a department could not be justified.

The Latin American Bureau of the World Jewish Congress in Argentina, which also maintains branch offices in Uruguay and

Brazil, recently issued a series of translations from Yiddish and Hebrew called, *Biblioteca Popular Judia,* for the purpose of familiarizing Jewish youth with the rich Jewish historic and cultural heritage. This series includes biographies of a number of Jewish personalities, historians, scholars and writers who are recognized in world literature, starting with Maimonides and Rabbi Akiba to Walter Rathenau and Stefan Zweig, from Yehuda Halevi and the Baal Shem Tov to Heinrich Graetz and Simon Dubnow.

The series also contains translations of local Yiddish writers among them rabid Yiddishists, and other authors on the legacy of the Yiddish classics. Recently, this Bureau issued a series of publications about the uprising in the Warsaw Ghetto and its fighter-heroes.

Even Mapai, whom no one will suspect of betraying Yiddish, has realized the necessity of publishing, in its *Kium* publishing center, a series of translations into Spanish, among which are such basic works as Moses Hess' *Rome and Jerusalem,* and *Morning Star,* by Zalman Shazar, the President of Israel.

Years ago, some Jewish leaders in Argentina, looking to the future, felt the urgent necessity of creating Spanish language books of Jewish content. The pioneers in this effort were the brothers Mierlman, who founded the publishing firm Editorial Israel, and which has this far published more than sixty volumes of Jewish content works in Spanish.

The late Dr. Abraham Mibashan, Zionist leader and representative of the Jewish Agency in Argentina, established a second publishing center called Candelabro (i.e. Menorah) which published a number of translations in Spanish from Hebrew and Yiddish and also issued a periodical named *Eretz Israel.* At the time this whole project was regarded by the Yiddishist circles in Argentina with disdain, as a betrayal of Yiddish.

When the late S. Resnick edited a Spanish language periodical called, *Judaica,* he had to struggle constantly for its existence, and it finally failed. Today, aside from *Comentario,* there appears in Buenos Aires other periodicals, among them one called *La Luz* (Light), under the editorship of N. Elnecave. The various Jewish movements also produce their own Spanish-language organs.

Uruguay, Brazil and Chile which border Argentina each have now Jewish periodicals in the language of the country. Even much smaller countries in Latin America, such as Colombia, Venezuela, Peru and even Costa Rica have Jewish publications in Spanish.

The interest in Spanish books of Jewish content influenced the publisher, Paidos, to produce a library of historical and religious material. Among the titles issued by them are, Baeck's *The Essence of Judaism*, Heschel's *The Sabbath*, Adler's *The World of the Talmud*, Parkes' *Antisemitism*, and the first translation of the Babylonian Talmud in Spanish, of which the sixth volume, *Seder Zeraim*, has appeared. The World Council of Synagogues published a complete translation of the *Siddur* (Sabbath and festival prayerbook) in Spanish. A *Machzor* (High Holy Day Prayerbook) was translated into Spanish by Rabbi Marcos Erdey, a former resident of Morocco.

A number of Orthodox Jewish immigrants have arrived in Argentina during the last few years. The Mizrachi and the Agudath Israel have begun to function. Such religious educational institutions as Rabbi Kook Yeshivah, Beth Jacob School for Girls, Hechal Hatorah, Yavne, and Machon L'limudei Hayahaduth have been established. Upon the initiative of the former Chief Rabbi Yaakov Fink, now in Israel, a *yeshivah* was established for the purpose of training religious leaders. Four young boys, born in Argentina have already graduated from that *yeshivah*, went to Israel to complete their studies, and were ordained as rabbis. Now they serve as spiritual leaders in Argentine Jewish communities.

The Jewish Theological Seminary of New York recently sent six rabbis to Latin America to serve in Argentina and in various other communities.

The Torah Department of the Jewish Agency gives the youth of Argentina the opportunity to go to Israel to complete their education at the Machon Gold.

Another effort which has enjoyed great success and has had repercussions in nearby Latin American countries is the "New York experiment," as it is called in Argentina. Several years ago, some far-seeing community leaders of the Libertad Congregation invited an energetic young American rabbi, Marshall T. Meyer, a graduate of the Jewish Theological Seminary, to start a junior congregation on the American style. I was present at one of its Friday evening services, where hundreds of young people sang the Sabbath prayers, made *kiddush* and listened to the rabbi's Spanish sermon. The experiment has achieved popularity, for the Jewish youth living in a Catholic environment yearn for religious content, and the movement is growing.

Rabbi Meyer now serves a Conservative congregation named Beth El, which has a membership of more than 1,500, and a varied program of youth activities. He heads a Rama Camp which has now completed its seventh season, and where young people from Uruguay, Brazil, Chile and Peru come to spend their summer vacation with Argentine youth. The World Council of Synagogues has established a rabbinical seminary under the leadership of Rabbi Meyer, and guest professors from the Jewish Theological Seminary in New York are helping in the task of training future spiritual leaders of the Latin American Jewish communities. Graduates of the Seminario Rabinico Latinoamericano will continue their studies at the Jewish Theological Seminary in New York, and receive ordination there.

The Reform movement has established a Temple under the leadership of Rabbi Chaim Asa. A former leader of the *Hebraica,* Argentine-born, Leon Klinicky, graduated from Hebrew Union College in Cincinnati.

At the 1968 convention of the Rabbinical Assembly it was decided to send thirty rabbis to take positions as spiritual leaders in Latin American communities. Perhaps, Argentine Jewry has not yet missed the bus.

ANTI-SEMITISM IN ARGENTINA

While the Eichmann trial was taking place in Israel, I happened to be traveling on an Argentine ship on route from New York to Argentina, the land of which I was a citizen. It was my sixth trip after an absence of several years. As soon as I had settled in my cabin and handed my documents showing my occupation and religion over to the *comisario* (purser), I became aware of hostile glances directed at me.

My fellow-passengers, the ship's surgeon and the officers, kept dropping German words and phrases into their conversations. The situation grew more strained every day. In the evening when I sat on the deck chair I would hear phrases: "Heil Hitler! Heil Eichmann," to which I would respond loudly with, "Heil Einstein!" The couple in the next cabin kept up a constant refrain of German songs, to which my wife and I would chorus *Hatikvah*. Two other Jewish passengers who were aboard hid in their cabins, keeping totally out of sight. I complained to the purser and threatened that as a correspondent of one of Canada's most influential newspapers, the *Globe and Mail* of Toronto, I would report all this. The tension eased a bit; the purser was afraid that bad publicity might hurt the line's business.

My first impression on re-entering Argentina was that the country was undergoing a severe crisis. I could read it in the faces of the people, in their clothing, and in the general air of tension and depression. I grew even more disturbed when I saw the anti-Jewish slogans defacing the walls along almost all the streets. More than anywhere else, I saw these slogans on the street called, Estado de Israel, named for the Jewish state by the Buenos Aires City Council. A sensation was created when the Argentine philosopher Lanza del Vasta, a disciple of Gandhi, went along the streets from house to house armed with a ladder and brush, erasing the Jew-baiting slogans.

I read in the newspapers that when Bernardo Trilling, a young Jewish boy, was seriously wounded by the Tacuara, an anti-Semitic organization, a passing automobile refused to bring him to the hospital. I read that in Cordoba students daubed the walls with a threat to kill a Jewish professor named Hellman. At Plaza Once, in the heart of Buenos Aires' Jewish district, public meetings were held that were reminiscent of anti-Semitic demonstrations in Poland of the 1930's. One speaker hysterically shouted, "Jews to Palestine!" Another threatened bloodshed. Bombs exploded in Jewish institutions daily.

At this point I went to the Daia and had a talk with its president, at that time Marcos Diner. "I assure you," Dr. Diner stated, "we are not panicked. The quite substantial liberal and democratic forces in this country are with us. Anti-Semitism is foreign to Argentina. This lingering infection has been smuggled in by foreign elements." When I suggested that the Eichmann trial was the cause of this epidemic and that it might have been better had the Israeli commandos dispatched him on the spot (as some Argentine Jews think), he replied that most Argentine Jews are convinced that bringing Eichmann to trial in Israel was quite proper and justified, for the world had to be shown the full enormities of his crimes.

Every day the press carried front-page stories about Eichmann's capture and trial. When the pictures of Eichmann and the other Nazi criminals, Martin Bormann and Dr. Joseph Mengele, were published, *La Razon,* the newspaper which first broke the story about Eichmann's capture by the Israeli commandos reported that an Italian waiter in a fashionable restaurant in Buenos Aires recognized them and stated that they used to gather there and hold meetings.

Eichmann's wife, Vera, and family had disappeared from Buenos Aires for fear that the Jewish commandos would murder them. The reporters of the local newspapers began to search for them, but had no luck. Then, my telephone rang one day and a Spanish colleague notified me that Madam Vera Eichmann had been located. That evening some colleagues were to hold an interview with her, and knowing how deeply interested I was they were willing to take me along—only on condition that I must not ask any questions. I could only stand by as a silent witness, in order not to betray my Jewishness.

The same evening our automobile stopped in San Fernando, a suburb of Buenos Aires, on a quiet street, in front of a white plastered home.

Madam Vera Eichmann, a thick-set woman, held her youngest child in her arms and fondled him so as to awaken pity and sympathy. Eichmann's younger son was the spokesman. He stood at the end of the table holding a revolver in his hands which he waved before the questions of my colleagues began. "The govern-

ment permitted me to keep this weapon so as to defend myself
against the Jewish criminals who want to assassinate us," was
his first comment.

"Could you tell us how your father was caught?"

"It is not true," he began to bellow like an ox. "It is not true
what the newspapers wrote that the Jewish criminals caught him
at six o'clock when he came from work. It was eight o'clock, he
had already come from work and was going to a meeting..."

"What kind of a meeting?" a second colleague asked.

He became somewhat confused, looked at the questioner with
cold, steely eyes. "A...a... meeting of the syndicate (union) to
which he belonged..."

"Did you have a suspicion that they were searching for your
father?"

"Yes," came his swift answer. "We knew it full well and,
therefore, because of this, we never let him go out alone.... Suspicious persons loitered in our section, and the neighbors were
also..." He did not complete his sentence. Then he said: "This
time we had no time to escort him."

Madam Vera Eichmann interrupted the conversation in a
plaintive voice. In a broken Spanish with a German accent she
said, "He is innocent, my..." and embracing the child with a
German expression, *"Armes Kind"* (poor child) ...

I suddenly felt that my blood rushed to my face. I had all I
could do to control myself from shouting out: "And the thousands
of Jewish children that were burned through your husband, the
mass murderer—was there no pity for them?"

"Do you have a suspicion about anybody who was connected
with the capture of your father?"

"Yes," he answered, "Jewish criminals from Buenos Aires
helped the Israeli criminals." He named two Argentinian Jewish
young men whom he suspected.

"What do you believe will be the verdict of the court in Jerusalem?"

Young Eichmann jumped up. "Blood will flow in the streets
here in Buenos Aires and in all the countries where Jews live, if
they will dare touch a hair on my father's head. We," he bellowed

182

like an ox, "are not alone. Our people are found everywhere. They will take revenge. . . ."

❧   ❧   ❧

The Jews in Argentina have fought discrimination since the earliest years of their settlement. When in 1881, President Julio Rocco issued orders to Argentine Consulates abroad to issue visas to Jews, a French-language publication in Buenos Aires attacked the order, denouncing Jews as parasites and as a non-constructive element, and predicting that they would foment unrest. The president of the small Jewish community, thereupon, challenged the editor to a duel—and the latter withdrew his remarks and apologized.

The influx of immigrants from Czarist Russia brought with it some revolutionary elements, including adherents of anarchism. In 1909, when there was a workers' demonstration in Buenos Aires on May Day, the chief of police ordered his men to shoot at the demonstrators. A number of victims fell, and a Jewish anarchist named Simon Radowicki avenged himself on the police chief by throwing a bomb which blew him to bits. This provoked a stern reaction against the *Rusos,* and the Biblioteca Ruso, as the Jewish library was called, was stormed and its books burned. Reactionary rioters played havoc, attacking Jewish pedestrians on the street and breaking Jewish shop-windows.

In 1919, after the Bolshevik Revolution, reactionary elements again stirred up hatred against the *Rusos.* They were charged with wanting to set up a Communist regime in Argentina, with the Jewish author Pedro Wald as President. However, the government was immune to the influence of the chauvinists and protected the *Rusos.* When the Jews organized street collections for the victims of the European war many Argentines participated. President Hipolite Irigoyen permitted the entry of 100 Jewish orphans from the Ukraine, despite the restriction limiting urban immigrants which, it was believed, the country did not need.

Anti-Semitic incidents occurred in 1929 when the revolutionary government of General Uriburu was dominated by an inflated and chauvinistic nationalism. A few years later, Jewish schools of leftist tinge were padlocked. Yiddish newspapers were about to be suppressed and were only saved by the intervention of President Franklin D. Roosevelt who was apprised of it by the World Jewish Congress.

With the rise of Hitlerism, anti-Semitism began to take root in Argentina and other Latin American countries. Hitler was interested in disrupting Latin American trade with the USA and spent millions on propaganda, disseminating his racial theories.

Hugo Wast, (the pseudonym of Martinez Suveria who was then Minister of Education), wrote two anti-Semitic books, *Kahal* and *Oro* (Gold) which describe Jews in the same vein as Julius Streicher's *Stuermer*. When Jews held a meeting to protest Hitler's persecution, some hoodlums placed a bomb in a synagogue and attacked Jewish passers-by. When a Jewish delegation complained of this to the Minister of the Interior, he responded that according to the Argentine Constitution everyone had the right to express his opinions. "In that case," replied the Jews, "so do we! We, too are Argentine citizens!" Whereupon Maccabee youths attacked the hoodlums.

Nonetheless, the Argentine people as a whole did not follow the Nazi line. When the Jews of Buenos Aires carried out a demonstration against the brutalities of Hitler and closed their shops, dozens of Argentinians made common cause and closed their businesses, putting up placards which read, "We are not Jews, but we want to express our solidarity with our Jewish brethren in their hour of sorrow."

The man who raised anti-Semitism to a new height in Argentina was the dictator, Juan Domingo Peron. He had served as military attache in Germany and in Italy, and had absorbed the philosophies of Nazism and Fascism. After Hitler's defeat he arranged to bring 60,000 Nazis into Argentina with false documents. He entrusted fascists and quislings from various countries with important posts, and even chose his private bodyguard from among them. The former advisor of the Gestapo, Dr. Hissheim, became consultant to the Argentine police. Notorious Nazis who had fled Germany received jobs in various government departments and in the army. Among them were, Hans Ulrich Rudel, former Commandant of the German Air Fleet; S.S. Marshall Adolf Galland; Engineer Willi Tank; Von Leers, who was later to become Nasser's advisor; and Otto Skorzeny. Dr. Klagenfuss, one of Peron's advisors, arranged the necessary documents. Eva Peron's private secretary was a fugitive Nazi. Señora Peron donated a villa in the finest district of Buenos Aires to Ante Pavelic, the Croatian mass-murderer. When the West German government demanded the extradition of the noted executioner, Dr. Josef Mengele, who was practicing medicine in a fashionable neighborhood of Buenos Aires, the police replied that the request must be made in Spanish. The ensuing delay enabled the mass-murderer to effect his escape.

As an offshoot and by-product of Peronism, the notorious "Alianza Nacionalista" began to propagate anti-Semitism publicly. Juan Domingo Peron's demagogic role was played so well that he even went to the trouble of seeking out Jews and surrounding himself with a coterie of *Hofjuden* (court-Jews), among them the community rabbi on whose title the Jews playfully punned, calling him not, *Rav Ha-koillel* (chief rabbi), but *Rav-Hakoiler* (the slaughtering rabbi). He even permitted a group of Yiddish authors to settle in the country to conceal his anti-Semitism.

Later, when he was a political refugee in Spain, Peron showed his true colors. A Peronist deputy in parliament wrote a venomously anti-Semitic book about the "Zionist conspiracy" in Argentina, accusing the Jews of undermining Argentina's spiritual values and charging that a Zionist guerrilla commando unit was involved in the kidnapping of Eichmann. Peron praised the book in a letter stating that it reveals the goals of a people which now seek to dominate the world, and which should arouse the resistance of all those who do not wish their people to be enslaved.

In 1947, when Argentina voted in the U.N. against the Palestine partition plan, Peron received from Egypt the highest decoration ever given to a non-Arab statesman. Three years later, a street in Damascus was named "Argentina," and Peron was thanked at Arab meetings in Buenos Aires for his stand on the

Suez Canal. The slogans read: "Long live Nasser! Long live Hitler! Make soap of the Jews!"

The heir of Peron's "Alianza Nacionalista is Tacuara, formerly a branch of the Peronist youth movement, which went underground in 1955 and now numbers about 1,000 hot-heads. Since 1960 it has been vigorously led by two students, Alberto Excurra Uriburu and Jose Baxter. Their political platform is avowedly Falangist, with a strong emphasis on corporate fascism as the best form of government for Argentina. Tacuara distinguishes itself from Peronism by a strong pro-Church attitude. Its extreme chauvinist-reactionary position is not aimed exclusively at the Jews, but also challenges Argentina's democratic basis.

More recently much anti-Jewish propaganda has reached Argentina from the Arab countries. Egypt has sent 35 teachers (read: propagandists) to combat Zionist propaganda in Argentina and arranged a student exchange. Similar activities are being carried out in Brazil and Mexico. The example of Castro-ism, which shows that it is possible to expropriate and strip people of their possessions and still remain an "idealist" has also intensified anti-Jewish agitation in Argentina, and in certain other Latin American lands envious looks are being cast at the hard-earned possessions of the Jews. However, the Argentine people and the present government of Argentina are not anti-Semitic. Argentina's representative at the United Nations openly repudiated the compliments which Arab delegates paid the Tacuara for their anti-Jewish actions, praised the achievements of the Jews in his country, and associated himself with the condemnation of anti-Semitism.

The chaotic economic state in which Peron left Argentina lends itself to anti-Jewish feeling. The thousands of *"descamisados"* (shirtless ones) whom the dictator had brought from the fields to the city to solidify his power, cannot forget their seven fat years, and it does not concern them that this was at the expense of the Argentine economy. Their slogan now is: *Ladron si no ladron, queremos Peron* (Thief or no thief, we want Peron!). The discontent is exploited by sinister elements who instigate the grumbling masses against the Jews. Similarly, when

186

political parties are competing for power, they do not hesitate to use anti-Semitism as a propaganda tool. The established authority may be accused of having sold out to international capital (i.e., the Jews), or, conversely, of being influenced by "Jewish Communism."

Nonetheless, when the Eichmann trial was exploited by Nazi sympathizers to incite the Argentine people against the Jews, members of the government, leaders of political parties, intellectuals, and especially the press—all denounced the anti-Semitic attacks in the sharpest language. Dr. Alfredo R. Vito, former Minister of the Interior, said, "The outbreaks against the Jews do not express the sentiment of the Argentine people. The government will undertake all necessary means to put an end to the anti-Jewish acts which violate our democratic traditions. Our long history has been distinguished for tolerance—no distinction has ever been made of race or religion."

Members of the Chamber of Deputies introduced resolutions demanding that the government take immediate measures against anti-Semitic propaganda which was a foreign product imported from abroad, and must cease for the protection of Argentina's good name and tradition. The Jewish deputy, Zenon Goldstraj, said then in an address in Parliament, "I have not come to defend the Jewish people whose tragic history is free of crime and violence against others. I have come to defend Argentinian democracy which is in danger because of the anti-Jewish outbreaks."

From the leading newspapers, *La Nacion* and *La Prensa,* to the provincial press, a similar reaction was apparent: the Argentine way. We want no racist fanaticism! Anti-Semitism is barbarous and has no place here."

In one protest, the Union of Argentine Writers condemned the acts of Jew-baiting. "No normal person possessing any basic Christian feeling could possibly identify himself with any attack on a people who have suffered so much."

Presidents Arturo Frondizi, Arturo Illia, and General Juan Carlos Ongania (the present head of the government) have spoken out against anti-Semitism.

Although at least one Catholic spokesman, Father Julio Meinville, has made rabid attacks upon Jews and, in articles, has deplored that the Jews were released from the ghettos of the Middle Ages, this is not the view of the Catholic Church in Argentina. In a prominent Catholic journal, *Criterio*, Monsignor Gustavo Franceshi, a distinguished leader of the Church, wrote glowingly of his travels in Israel.

In a personal interview with me, Monsignor Franceshi said, "You certainly know my attitude toward Jews. As a believing Catholic . . . I deem anti-Semitism to be a phenomenon of sickness. After all, we have something to be grateful for to a Jew named Jesus."

"I should like to know," I asked "what impression the state of Israel made on you. But I am especially interested in your views about the Catholic holy places located on the soil of the Jewish state and its capital Jerusalem!"

"I can assure you," he replied, "that the declaration of the Israel government on the autonomy and protection of the Christian holy places will be completely fulfilled and will be observed with the greatest care. Catholics enjoy the fullest religious freedom there. The Israel government, at its own expense, has published a periodical for Catholics. I must tell you that travelling in towns and colonies in my priestly garb I was surprised at the tolerance, respect and friendship shown to me both by officials and by the man on the street."

The only complaint Father Franceshi had against Israel was that it lacked piety. "True, the Sabbath is an official day of rest, but the Jews are not strict in the observance. My feeling is that if the Jews regain their land, they should return to the law of Moses."

Monsignor Franceshi reminded me that Argentina bears traces of a rich and historic Jewish past. "If you really want to know the remarkable history of the Jews in Latin America," he said, "I advise you to read the history of the Inquisition in the La Plata River (*La Inquisicion en el Rio de la Plata*) by Jose Toribio Medina."

According to the latest report of the American Jewish Committee there are some 80 extremist organizations in Argentina, the most important of which are the Tacuara and the Guardia Restauradora Nacionalista. Although they have been declared illegal, these groups continue to exist, generally attracting dissident youth, many of whom stem from the upper social classes. Father Julio Meinville has been the spiritual mentor of the Tacuara group, and has stimulated its leaders to undertake numerous acts of violence, vandalism and provocation. A small number of other priests and bishops also supply encouragment. Periodicals published in Spain and distributed by the anti-Semitic Huemul publishing house in Buenos Aires, spread anti-Semitic propaganda, especially in religious, military and political circles.

The government of President Juan Carlos Ongania, has maintained that it does not approve of anti-Semitism and will not permit anti-Semitic groups to operate, and the number of public anti-Semitic incidents has decreased. When such incidents do occur, however, police action is minimal or non-existent. It must be pointed out, too, that under the conservative and strongly Catholic Ongania government, Jews play no role in public affairs, in contrast to former regimes where Jews participated freely in public life.

The Daia—the Central body of Jewish Organizations in Argentina, although it is affiliated with the World Jewish Congress, acts independently. It decides alone what requires to be done to combat anti-Semitism in Argentina, also what action is to be taken to encourage the Argentine Jewish youth to acquaint them with the Jewish heritage and values to safeguard them from total assimilation.

CHAPTER XIV.

Seventy-five Years of Jewish Farm Colonization

The story of Jewish agricultural colonization in Argentina is a unique chapter in Jewish history, and was a by-product of Jewish love and yearning for the land of Israel. It is a fact that in July, 1889, before Baron de Hirsch began his plan for mass colonization in Argentina, an attempt had been made by a group of Jews who left the city, Kamenetz-Podolsk, to make their way to the land of Israel to become farm workers there. The 130 families comprising this group were marooned in Germany, *en route*, without financial means and without any way of making their way further. The Alliance Israelite Universelle took an interest in them, but instead of sending them on to Palestine, diverted them to Argentina, where arrangements had been made for an Argentine estate owner to sell them certain stretches of land.

Upon their arrival in Argentina, however, they found themselves bitterly disappointed. They found the fields barren and they suffered from starvation. More than sixty children died of exposure and hunger during that first season.

In the ensuing months, the Jewish world rose up in alarm over this tragedy. Rabbi Zadoc Cohen, Chief Rabbi of the Jewish community of Paris, appealed to his community and interested Baron de Hirsch in the plight of these Jews. Baron de Hirsch had been considering the possibility of large-scale Jewish colonization, and he immediately convened a special meeting of colonization experts. This marked the organization of ICA, the Jewish Colonization Association, in 1896, which undertook to assist Jews to emigrate from Russia into countries where they could develop freely and become productive persons, earning their livelihood through labor on the land.

A special delegation left for Argentina, and there the first ICA-sponsored colony was organized. It was named Mauricio Hirsch, in honor of the Baron. The earlier pioneers had by this time, and in the face of all adversity, already founded a colony of their own which they called Moiseville, after the biblical Moses. To this day Moiseville is referred to as the "Jerusalem of Argentina."

These earlier colonists met with the delegation in the home of their first rabbi, Aaron Goldman, (grandfather of the leader of the World Jewish Congress in Argentina, Dr. Moshe Goldman), and the representatives of the ICA proposed that they transfer themselves to the new colony, Mauricio Hirsch. However, the pioneers did not want to leave the cemetery and the graves of those who had perished of hunger, frost and destitution. Baron de Hirsch then arranged to purchase the lands around the Moiseville section.

This marked the upward climb of Jewish agricultural colonization in Argentina. The Jewish Colonization Association purchased large stretches of land in the Argentine provinces and established a whole network of Jewish colonies. One was called Clara in honor of the Baron's wife; others were named Rosh Pinah, Rachel, Avigdor, Narcisse Lewin, and Lucienville, (named after the Baron's son who died very young). After the tragic death of his only son, the Baron said, "My only heir was taken from me—mankind is now my heir." It was not an easy process for the untrained pioneers from the *shtetl* environment to become agrarian workers. They faced the challenges of a capricious, unpredictable climate, barren and lonely wastes, and the depredations of the half-savage *gauchos*, the native Argentine vagabonds used to a lawless life on the steppes who stole the colonists' cattle, horses and even their last morsels of food. The robberies soon extended to murders. The police were altogether unable to prevent mass attacks on the colonists. Sometimes, the police themselves were partners and accomplices in the raids, and looked the other way. Sometimes, when the culprits were caught they were let off with light sentences, even in cases of murder.

The situation reached a head on March 26, 1898, when a cold-blooded murder took place, sending a shudder through the entire district of the Clara colony. After a struggle, outlaws had stabbed a colonist and his two children, aged 14 and 12.

The news reached the Argentine capital, and *La Nacion* sent a special correspondent to Clara, to get the details of the murder. Because of this tragic event the country at large finally became aware of the accomplishments of the Jewish colonists, who in the short span of five years, under the most difficult of conditions, had changed the barren Argentine steppes into fertile fields.

In his reports, Venesia Gallan, the correspondent of *La Nacion,* gave the details of the *gaucho's* brutalities, crimes and murders, and demanded that the government give more protection to the colonists. He had strong praise for the achievements of the Rusos. "In the district," he wrote, "there are more than 5,000 Rusos (on another occasion he refers to them as a "Judaic section of the Russians") and their cultural level is extremely high; in the Clara colony there are eleven schools where classes are given in Spanish and Russian (what he meant was Yiddish) under experienced pedagogues."

Gallan pointed out that the schools all displayed portraits of the Argentine national heroes along with pictures of Baron de Hirsch, and that every colony had a doctor who treated all who came to him without discrimination, whether they were Jews or *criollos.* This, however, did not prevent murder attempts being made upon the doctor. Gallan also mentioned that the colony had a school for learning trades such as tailoring, conducted by a skilled woman from Paris, and its own steam mill. The colonists, Gallan reported, had their own cultural association and had established a library. He was present at a play in which the younger colonists portrayed peasant life in Russia and also Moliere's comedy, *La Malade Imaginaire,* which the young farmers themselves had translated from the French. Revenue from the performance was to go towards the purchase of a battleship for the Argentine Navy, for which the entire colony was raising funds.

He pointed out that the sponsors of the colony were Frenchmen, Englishmen, and Americans who sought to help their people escape the despotism of the Russian Czar, who had persecuted them for their religion and race, and come to freedom-loving Argentina, where, as industrious settlers, they had found a haven and home.

From this report the Argentine people learned of the contributions the Jews had made to their country, the sacrifices they had made in order to wrest a livelihood from the swamps. After this, the Jewish colonists and their contributions were frequently mentioned with praise and respect.

Years ago, I was a teacher in an ICA school in one of the Jewish colonies on the pampas, and I well remember that when the then-President of Argentina, Señor Alevar, passed through that area the colonists turned out *en masse* to greet their honored visitor, the Jewish children parading with Argentine and Jewish flags and singing the Argentine national anthem with genuine enthusiasm. Señor Alevar in turn paid warm tribute to Argentina's Jewish farmers.

AT HOME ON THE PAMPAS

What were the colonies like in those days? Here I must glance backward forty years, to a time when a piece of the East European Jewish way of life was transplanted, bodily, to the pampas of Argentina.

Harvest time in an Argentinian Jewish colony of that era was one of the most beautiful and inspiring scenes one could wish to see. From the long row of neat little houses, still lit by kerosene lamps, emerged the figures of Jewish peasants, to harness horses to their wagons, look after the well with its high tower, where the cattle were to drink, set out on tractors or harvesting machines. When the sun shone full over the fields, one could see the athletic, broad-shouldered sun-bronzed sons of the colonists working feverishly. In the evening when cool winds blew from the pampas, one could hear the sound of Yiddish folk songs mingling with the creaking of large carts filled with grain. And when night fell, young girls, like their ancestors in biblical times, stood at the wells waiting for their sweethearts, while the eyes of vigilant mothers watched from nearby windows. The heavy gallop of the horse came nearer and nearer and the young hearts beat stronger:

"Buenas noches, Rosita!" (Good evening Rosa!)

"Como le va Jose?" (How are you Joseph?)

Then, soft voices were heard among the trees. ". . . Father, you must talk."

"What?" came the young man's angry voice. "He does not approve of me as a son-in-law? Is it a city *compadre* (sport) he prefers?

"My mother is more sensible. She wants you to come and bake bread at our house tomorrow. . . ."

Far away from the whitewashed houses grouped in clumps of three or four over a long distance, was the school house where the children were taught Spanish and Yiddish. Twice a day little dots appeared on the horizon: children wrapped in white *guardapolvos* (dust mantles) riding on horseback, two or three together, coming to school across the flat fields. There was a large garden at the school where the horses awaited their little riders until school was over. The Jewish children in the Argentine *pampas* rode horses from the age of four.

As a teacher in a Jewish school in the colony Narcisse Lewin, I was at the same time the pupil of my pupils in the art of riding a horse. The brown, speckled horse, a present from one of the colonists, which I used to ride, was nicknamed Methuselah by the children, after the famous story by Sholom Aleichem. One day, as I rode with several pupils over the fields, we suddenly noticed black spots on the sun, and children began to shout *"Pampero! Pampero!"* They jumped off the horses and placed them in a semi-circle, putting the smaller children down inside it. In a moment it became pitch dark and a lashing rain began pouring down. The wind raged and howled louder and louder, and broken pieces of wooden posts, or wheels and other articles carried by the wind flew over our heads.

The finest and merriest season of the year in the Jewish colony followed the harvest. If the harvest had not been spoiled by drought or locusts, the colony was decked out in festive array. The small towns in the vicinity did a thriving business. The storekeepers collected old debts. Agents came from Buenos Aires to sell subscriptions to Yiddish newspapers. Representatives of organizations came to raise funds, and musicians came to play at weddings. The girls, grown like mushrooms after a rain, were sunburned and hardened by work. The boys, young men, garbed in new red silk shirts, with the ends hanging down like *gauchos*, exchanged their old saddles for new ones.

Each young man made for a house where a thick wooden post stood at the door, apparently meant for horses, but in reality signifying that a girl in that house was ready to be spoken for. The young man remained standing in the door, and clapped his hands a few times to signify that a stranger was asking permission to come in. The host came forward and greeted the guest, who removed his knife and revolver, handing them to the hostess to keep during his visit. Father and mother withdrew to the kitchen while the girl remained with the young man, to treat him with *"mate"* (the national Argentine beverage, made from herbs) and pastry of her own baking.

When a marriage was negotiated, the girl received only a few oxen or a patch of field as her dowry or, if her father was poor, not even that. The parents, as a rule, preferred that their daughters marry a young man from the city. But the young people preferred otherwise.

Two Jewish authors who wrote in Spanish, Alberto Gerchunow and Jose Liberman, both sons of colonists, have described the tribulations and achievements of the Jewish colonists. Liberman wrote *Tierra Soñada (Blessed Earth)*. Gerchunow whose father was murdered by a *gaucho* in the colony of Rachel, wrote *Los Gauchos Judios (The Jewish Gauchos)*, which has been published in an English translation. Gerchunow became famous in Argentina as a columnist for the well-esteemed Argentine liberal newspaper *La Nacion*. The country named a railway station after him in the province of Entre Rios where a great many Jewish colonies are located.

195

IDEOLOGICAL AND RELIGIOUS ATTITUDES

At the edge of every Jewish colony there was a strip of land which even the non-Jews of the area identified as "Palestine." It was the custom for every colonist to contribute a strip of his own land for the Jewish National Fund. The harvesting of this "Palestine strip" was carried on with great zeal and ceremony. All the colonists, young and old, would gather together, dressed in their holiday clothing. Indelibly impressed in my memory is the picture of the colonists' faces, toughened and bronzed by the sun and wind, their sturdy bodies dressed in coarse peasant clothing, clearing the black earth with their primitive ploughs. The ploughs were decorated with blue-and-white fiags, and the children accompanied their parents in singing the *Hatikvah*. A sharp *pampa* wind would blow sand in everyone's eyes as it carried out over the fields the words, *"Od lo ovda tikvatenu."*

In the initial years of settlement, the religious life of the colonists reflected the spirit of the *shtetl* of Russia and Bessarabia. Each colony, upon its establishment, would build a synagogue, and services would be held each *Sabbath* and holiday, with most of the colonists attending as a matter of course. In some of the settlements weekday services were also customary, except during harvest time. *Kashruth* was observed, and the general pattern of life had a traditionally religious coloring. In each colony, the schools established by the Jewish Colonization Association included traditional religious instruction in the curriculum.

I will always remember praying on Yom Kippur, some forty years ago, in a primitive little synagogue in the far wilderness of the *pampas*. It was built by the colonists themselves, from wood and clay, in the style of a *"rancho."* The *cantor* was an aged colonist, enrobed in a shabby yellowish *talith*. His *Kol Nidre* melody stirred me more and penetrated deeper into my soul than any of the noted cantors or choirs whom I have had the opportunity to hear in the famed synagogues of Berlin, Amsterdam, London and New York.

However, religious life in the Argentine colonies slowly, but steadily, declined. The remoteness of these settlements from the main centers of Jewish life was a primary factor; lack of deeply-felt religious zeal and motivation was another. Beyond this, the colonists were influenced by the attitudes which developed among the Argentine-Jewish city dwellers. Among these, a secularized kind of Jewishness prevailed, based on the Yiddish language and culture.

THE COLONIES TODAY

But, today, new hope is to be found for a renascence of religious life among the Jews of Argentina. No longer do the community leaders, though still largely secularist, look upon religion as an "opiate." They are warm, national-minded Jews with a positive attitude toward their religion. The new trend is reflected in the Jewish agricultural communities too. On my last visit to Moiseville I found the "Yahadut" Hebrew Teachers Seminary, organized and subsidized by the Vaad Hakehillot of Buenos Aires, a Beth Midrash Hagadol, a Baron Hirsch Congregation, a Beth Knesseth Ashkenazi (also called the Litvishe Shul), and even a Synagogue of Baaley Melochah (artisan's and workmen's shul).

What are the Jewish colonies in Argentina like today? What has become of the noble idea of Baron de Hirsch to change Jews from city dwellers to farm people, and to show the world that Jews too can undertake productive labor?

I happened to be in Argentina on the 75th anniversary of the founding of the colonies, and I attended a conference of the Jewish colonists. The delegates to this conference were the sons and grandsons of the pioneers of the Argentine settlements.

For one who remembers the farm colonists of the old days, this conference was somewhat of a disappointment. It lacked the broadboned Jewish farm proletarians with their gnarled, peasant hands, that once would give you a hearty *sholom aleichem!* accompanied by an equally hearty smack on the back. The broad Bessarabian-accented Yiddish was also lacking; the speakers and the resolutions were all in the Spanish language. The sessions were conducted in formal, parliamentary fashion, far more reminiscent of the city than of the farm.

Nonetheless, these Jews were still villagers and farmers even though they were wearing starched shirts with ties, instead of the primitive kerchiefs of their grandfathers and fathers. There was still the feel and the smell of the farm about them. Though they used another language, the content of their speeches was still akin to that of former years. They spoke about Jewish fields, about Jews making sure that they work and occupy these fields, not permitting them to fall into the hands of others. They discussed the strengthening and improvement of the Jewish cooperatives. They talked about preparing and producing a film that would tell the story of Jewish colonization in Argentina.

Many settlers have been unable to endure the sufferings and difficulties of pioneering on the *pampas,* and the number of colonists has continually dwindled as the Jews moved to the cities. Some of the historians of the Argentine Jewish colonies attribute this trend to the fact that a number of the ICA officials, who were assimilated Jews, did not understand the mentality of Jews from Eastern Europe and having neither sympathy nor appreciation for the idealistic goal of the ICA, they treated the colonies in a purely materialistic and commercial manner. Another reason given is that the ICA purposely set up the colonies at distances from each other, in order to avoid the creation of Jewish towns and cities which, it was feared, might tempt the colonists to revert to urban occupations and livelihoods. Paradoxically, this had the opposite effect, for some colonists could not bear the loneliness, and escaped back to the city. But the blame for the move to the city cannot be laid exclusively at the door of ICA personnel. One ICA administrator of Eastern European background, Benjamin Zion Mezibowski, has indicated that it was when the colonists began to prosper that the movement to the city began. It was at the very moment when the prices for their farm produce began to rise that the urge to go to the city became greater. This urge, therefore, had nothing to do with the pressure of poverty or with the attitude of the ICA bureaucrats. When the young people left the colonies to seek their fortunes in the cities, and the cultural and community life in the settlements dried up, the parents felt their loneliness more keenly, and some of them left the colonies.

Thus, Jewish colonization in Argentina did not attract the masses. But despite the movement into the cities the Jewish colonies to this day have remained the special pride of the Argentine Jewish community. It can be said that the majority of the cultural and community leaders of Argentina's Jewish communities are sons and grandsons of the colonists. The education and training they received in the environment of the colonies imbued them with a sound and healthy spirit. They brought new blood to the cities and made valuable contributions to Jewish community life. They occupy important and creditable roles in the liberal professions, in Argentine literature and the press, and in the leadership of Jewish communal and cultural institutions. The cooperatives still occupy an important place in Argentina. Sixty years ago the first Jewish cooperative was established; it was called the Sociedad Agricola Lucienville. The initiative came from two pioneers, the finest figures of Jewish colonization in Argentina: Dr. Noah Jarchi and his brother-in-law, Miguel Sacharow, who was crowned with the title "the grandfather of the Jewish colonies." This cooperative movement grew and expanded until it embraced most of the colonies. Its aim is more than selling the products of the colonies and purchasing materials and goods for its members. It occupies itself as well with the cultural and community needs of its members, by organizing libraries, schools and hospitals. The Argentine press has often cited, with approval, the achievements of the Jewish agricultural cooperatives and their vital contributions to the cooperative movement in Argentina.

These cooperatives publish their own journal, *The Colonist Cooperator*, printed in Spanish and Yiddish. They have their own agrarian bank which gives loans to the colonists. Its main purpose is to preserve the integrity of Jewish colonization, to see that Jewish colonies and farms do not fall into the hands of others, and to encourage everyone in the colonies to stay on the farm and not to seek urban livelihoods.

On my last visit to Moiseville, I went to the cemetery, a living memorial of the sufferings and martyrdom of Jewish colonization in Argentina. There stand many of the graves of the pioneers of Moisesville who were murdered by the halfsavage natives years

199

ago. On every tombstone appeared the line, *shenirtzach biyedei achzarim*—"murdered at the hands of the marauders." Here is a group of graves of an entire family "murdered in Palacios—the Wiseman family: Mordecai-Joseph ben Ephraim-Zalman Levy, his wife Pessil, and son Baruch." Here is the grave of "the maiden Miriam, daughter of Zalman," who was violated and murdered in the year 1897, and here I stand before an odd-looking tombstone marking the grave of a martyr, and bearing the date 1894. The name on it was, "Ben-Zion Zalman ben Meir, born in the city of Kros in Austria," probably Krosno near Rzeszow in Galicia. (One wonders what sort of fate impelled a Jew from Galicia to come here more than seventy years ago.) So, one tombstone follows another, and they all stand as mute witness to the suffering and death of these pioneer Jews.

Further along are the tombstones reflecting the golden age of Moiseville, from the period when it merited the appelation, "the Jerusalem of Argentina." Here is the grave of Noah Katzovitch, one of the builders of Moiseville. The inscription on his tombstone begins with the words, *Noach ish haadamah*—"Noah a man of the soil." Here lie the scholars and rationalists, I.B. Fleischer, H. Rinsky, Jacob Langer, Baruch Rechovitzki (who died young) —all writers and bearers of enlightenment whom I knew when I visited Moiseville, and who were, at the time, leaders of the turbulent, active Jewish community.

Now you can understand why Moiseville is no longer what it was. There are no others to take the places of those idealists.

Moiseville is the oldest Jewish colony in Argentina. In addition to the well-merited reputation it acquired in the heyday of Argentine Jewish colonization, it was also the crowning glory of Argentine Jewish colonization. The Jewish community organization in Buenos Aires, the Va'ad Hakehilloth, has been doing all within its power to see that Moiseville does not lose its essential Jewish identity.

✸   ✸   ✸

Formosa is the last large town on the road from Argentina to Paraguay. From it a primitive road leads to Clorinda, which is the last border village between the two countries. In Formosa one has to count on being lucky with the weather. If the sky is clear and cloudless one can hire a taxi or a "sulky" (a small vehicle for two) and drive over to Clorinda. If there is the slightest bit of cloud visible to the eye, you must take a room in the hotel, and wait for the rain to fall and for the road to dry before you make a further move.

Rain in that remote tropical corner is not merely a shower. Nature indulges in her full share of caprice, and a downpour for three solid days without interruption is not unusual. The primitive roads all turn to mud, and one risks being buried alive if he sets out on these roads when they are in this state. Fatal mishaps have occurred where passengers, driver and car or wagon have sunk forever out of sight in the slippery quicksands.

Ten Jewish families live in Formosa. They have a small synagogue that serves as a community center, and they brought in a teacher from Buenos Aires to give their children a Jewish education. This was due not so much to conscious idealism on their part, but because of the fact that even children of mixed marriages here are considered *Judios* (Jews), and do not have a place in gentile society.

On the edge of the river separating Argentina and Paraguay is the primitive settlement of Clorinda, the last border town between the two countries. From there you cross the river on a quaint, old fashioned raft-ferry which looks like my grandmother's kneading trough. After this you mount a high farm wagon where the passengers are tossed among bundles of hay, until you come to another river which looks like a canal. Here a Paraguayan boat equipped with an ancient motor takes you over the river and brings you to Asuncion, the capital city.

Clorinda has a few hotels which look like pauper's shelters. The streets are narrow, unpaved and muddy. With few exceptions all the houses are wooden hovels. In Buenos Aires I was given the name and address of one Zalman Kishka who lived here. I found him in an earthen-floored store in a low-built clapboard cottage. Zalman Kishka gave me his hand with a cordial, "*Sholom aleichem*. Where does the Jew come from?" Then he added quickly:

201

"Which night do you want to choose to 'become a rabbit'?" When I replied that my papers were in order and that I planned to travel in broad daylight and in full legal status, he shrugged his shoulders saying, "Then why did you come to me?"

I explained that I was interested in meeting him and other Jews in this faraway corner. When he learned where I had come from, his eyes opened wide. "You came all the way from New York to this God-forsaken corner?"

He offered me a wooden bench, and asked if I wanted a glass of the best Paraguayan liquor or whether would prefer a Coca-Cola? Then he sat down to tell me about the Jews thereabouts.

There were six Jewish families living in Clorinda. The large, fashionable shops, on the only decent looking *avenida*, were all Jewish-owned, and the Jews were the town's main businessmen. A Jew from Lithuania is the president of the local Jockey Club, the city's only approximation to a big city "club." Jews are the exporters and importers between Argentina and Paraguay, and business had been quite good. There had been a larger community, but a number of Jewish families had left for Buenos Aires—their children were growing up and they feared they might lose them.

By the light of an old-fashioned oil lamp, among the shelves of dried tropical fruits, Paraguayan liquors, and colored, cloth fabrics for women, Zalman Kishka began to tell me of his wanderings and tribulations, and how he had arrived at this remote corner of Argentina.

"Believe me," he assured me, "for the few *pesos* I have put away I could establish myself quite well in Buenos Aires, but how can I abandon the Jews whose safety and salvation lies through Clorinda, who need to get into Argentina from God knows where, and sometimes," here he paused seriously, "even from Argentina to Paraguay." And he told me of scores of such cases where he had led a whole crew across the border, guiding them in his Yiddish dialect which he brought from the Polish town of Ostrowce.

Before I took my leave of Zalman Kishka, I lent him a film on Israel that I was taking with me to Paraguay. He assured me I would have the film back in time. Quite early in the morning, when the sky was beginning to turn blue, an Indian carried my luggage to the boat that was to take me across the Pilcomayo River, the river across which Zalman Kishka had led so many hundreds of homeless Jews to safety in the dead of night.

CHAPTER XV.

Paraguay: A Small But Lively Jewish Community

The Paraguayan is remarkable among South Americans for his cheerfulness, his good humor, his sense of fun. This keeps him going through all the difficulties his country has been experiencing for years. He is, as a rule, a short, brisk, little person with bright eyes that seem to see right through you, and though you are an *Americano*, which means a very important person, he is not a bit overawed. He has his own pride, his *"dignidad."* The Paraguayan is not depressed by his poverty. He accepts it as his way of life, and manages to be quite cheerful despite it.

Paraguay, the smallest country in South America, has an area slightly larger than that of California, but its population is little more than a million and a half. Cut off from the sea, it must depend for its limited import and export trade on the Paraguay River. This accounts for Paraguay's slow economic growth.

For more than 150 years Paraguay has been engaged in a struggle between anarchy and dictatorship. Within 27 years it had 22 presidents. One lasted only 22 days; another 53 days. But for 26 years it was ruled with an iron hand by the dictator, Francisco Solano Lopez. He had refused to accept the fact that Paraguay was deprived of access to the sea and in 1865 he went to war against Argentina, Uruguay and Brazil. It was a five-year war, in which Paraguay put up an astonishing fight against the triple enemy, twenty times its size and twenty times as strong. It was David and Goliath all over again—only this time Goliath won. Half the Paraguayan army was killed, but Lopez would not yield.

He mobilized boys and went on fighting, until he himself was slain in battle.

Between 1929 and 1935 Paraguay was again at war, this time with Bolivia, over the disputed Chaco territory. Paraguay won this war, but only at the price of immense bloodshed.

The Paraguayans make light even of their wars and revolutions. In one of the revolutions Paraguay was left without a president. Under the Constitution, the Chief Justice takes over the presidency, but when the generals came to the Chief Justice, Dr. Juan Priches, he said, "Gentlemen, you are mistaken; an honorable family lives here." It is related that after his inaguration, he kept asking the Guard of Honor every day, "Am I still President? You are the ones who will know."

Paraguay may be described as a woman's country. So many men were killed in their wars that men are very much in the minority now. Consequently, the women are accustomed to the idea that they must do the heavy work, and they also take the initiative in their approaches to the men. The Paraguayan woman is very beautiful, perhaps because she is a mixture of several strains: Guarani Indian, Spaniard, and other Europeans. She matures early in that tropical land, and is a ripe woman when she is little more than a child. But she also ages quickly. At 30 she is an old woman. The Paraguayan woman acts very much like a man. She smokes a pipe. She wears a man's hat. She does the physical work. She is the breadwinner. She is both father and mother. Children in Paraguay need not be registered under the father's name. They are usually registered in the name of the mother, and no one asks who the father is.

Paraguay has a small but lively Jewish community of about three hundred and fifty families. Their only communication with other Jews is by way of the Paraguay and Parana Rivers, with the Jews of the Argentine.

There are traces of Jews who lived in Paraguay at the time of the Inquisition in Spain and Portugal, when some Marranos saved themselves in the "New World." After the Inquisition was abolished, in 1811, and the dictator of Paraguay, Jose Gaspar Rodriguez Francia, "El Supremo" as he was known, proclaimed his own state, he called in Jewish engineers and technicians from Austria to help develop the country. However, not many traces of these Jews have remained.

Officially, Jewish settlement in Paraguay may be reckoned from 1908, when a number of Sephardim from the Old Yishuv in Palestine came there. Among them were the families of Joseph and Elijah Levi, Solomon Bachut, the brothers Hadari, and Moses and Elijah Raphael. Elijah Raphael brought with him a *Sefer Torah* from Jerusalem, and started the first *minyan* in Paraguay. He acted as the *hazan* until his death in 1942. The formation of the first *minyan* was, as usual, soon followed by the acquisition of a Jewish cemetery. Joseph Levi took the initiative by buying a piece of land adjoining the general cemetery. Eight years later, in 1916, the first Jewish institution in Paraguay, the Alianza Israelita del Paraguay, was organized, and three years after that, the Sephardic community founded the Sociedad del Templo Israelita Latina del Paraguay, and built the first synagogue in Asuncion.

By 1917 there were about six hundred Jews in Paraguay, and an attempt was made to begin Jewish colonization in the country. An agricultural colony was established, named Colonia Franco, but the experiment was not successful because of the unfavorable climatic conditions and the limited market for agricultural produce.

Other Jews came to join the community from Argentina, and in 1921 the Jews of Asuncion decided to build a larger place for Jewish religious and cultural activity. They organized the Union Hebraica del Paraguay, with a membership of two hundred. There was considerable Jewish immigration to Paraguay after the Second World War, but most of these immigrants later went on to other destinations, mainly Argentina.

The Jewish community today embraces a Zionist Organization, B'nai B'rith, the Chaverim Youth Club, which publishes its own bulletin, *Chaverim*, WIZO, Hanoar Hazioni (which has sent a group of *chalutzim* to Israel), the Sociedad Israelitas Alemanes (an aid society for German Jews), and the pride of this small community, the Estado de Israel School, which is recognized by the Minister of Education. It has an enrollment of three hundred Jewish children, 100% of the Jewish child population of the country. Recently, they have also established a Jewish Students' Society, Centro Universitarios Sionistas, to which all the university students and some professionals belong. The Jewish Consejo Representativo Israelitas de Paraguay (CRIP) is a central representative body uniting the Sephardic, East European and German Jews. The Union Israelita also has a synagogue in Asuncion.

The Jews in Paraguay are engaged mostly in the import trade, and some are shopkeepers, tailors, cabinet makers, and the like. They have not grown wealthy in this country that is always on the brink of revolution, and whose foreign trade is restricted by the difficulties of communication. They have nevertheless, established a number of small factories, producing textiles, ready-to-wear clothing, and furniture.

The small Jewish population of Paraguay is not very conspicuous, but, as in the rest of Latin America, there is some anti-Semitic feeling—not so much among the indigenous population, as among the Germans and white Russians, who came there in large numbers between the two World Wars. The number of German immigrants was so large that in one town, San Bernardino, German flags were flown outside the school. When Hitler ruled in Germany anti-Semitic propaganda was intensified, and as a result seventeen Jewish families were deported in 1937. The following year all immigration was stopped.

The Jews in Paraguay sometimes find themselves in an awkward position, as for example, after the Chaco war with Bolivia. When the Paraguayan army came marching back victorious, all the immigrant groups went to meet it with banners flying. The Jews were in a dilemma. They were afraid to display the Jewish flag, because that might harm the Jews living in defeated Bolivia. But in the end, the Jews participated, flying the blue-and-white flag, and there were no difficulties. When the Jews of Paraguay planted a Herzl Forest in Israel in memory of the fallen heroes of

Paraguay, the Government sent a representative to attend the inauguration of the forest.

Paraguay played a decisive role in the United Nations at the time of Israel's creation. Vasconles Cezar was Paraguay's representative at the United Nations at that time.

In recent years, a new synagogue in memory of the 6,000,000 martyrs was established by the Union Israelita in Asuncion. After the ceremony, in which all the Jews took part, a service memorializing the victims murdered by the Nazis was conducted.

CHAPTER XVI.

Bolivia — The Roof of the World

When you take your seat in the plane that is to bring you from Buenos Aires to La Paz, the capital of Bolivia, you find, beside the usual safety-belt at your seat, a rubber tube marked "Oxygen." As soon as the plane flies out of Salta, the last frontier town in the Argentine, it climbs higher and higher, above the great mountains, over the clouds. The engines are all "out," like when an automobile is making its way up a steep hill. Your eyes begin to swim. Your head turns dizzy. You are short of breath. Like the other passengers, you have to use the oxygen tube to inhale.

You are too much taken up, far too much, with your own breathing difficulties to pay much attention to the other passengers. But you notice that your neighbor to the right who was so jolly and talkative until now is oblivious to everything, except the oxygen tube which he holds to his mouth. There is a trickle of blood from his nose. The stewardess passes him a bottle of medicine. She asks me how I feel. And I, smiling bravely, answer, "Fine." But it isn't true. I feel as though somebody was playing ball inside of me. We climb still higher, and it's like a hammer beating at my brain.

The sign in front of us lights up at last: "Fasten your safety belt." The engines roar. The plane descends. We have landed at the airfield of the Bolivian capital, La Paz, the roof of the world. When you leave the plane you feel as if you are groping your way along a roof from which you might topple at any moment.

La Paz is four thousand meters above sea level. To the new arrival, it seems to be suspended in the air. The streets look

209

as though they were stuck to the tops of the mountains that wind upward. Your breath fails you when you start climbing those steep streets. Your heart thumps and your feet drag. You feel as though you are walking over empty space. Passersby keep stopping to catch their breath. They lay their hand to their chest, and then continue on their way.

Everywhere in South America it is hot both in summer and in winter, but in La Paz it is cold and windy all the year round, and the rain is always lashing at your face, reminding you of autumn in Eastern Europe.

La Paz looks wonderful at night, with thousands of lights shimmering over a dozen mountain heights, along the tortuous winding streets that keep climbing higher and higher. A cluster of houses from a distance looks like a pillar of fire. More than half of the population of three million are Indians, and one quarter are half-breeds, mestizos, a mixture of Indian and Spanish, known as Cholos. Fifteen percent of the population are whites of European descent, and about three percent are Europeans. Although the official language is Spanish, not all Bolivians know Spanish.

In Latin America, Bolivia is referred to as "the beggar who sits on a pile of gold." For many years the country was ruled by a privileged class of "zinc barons," who exploited the miners living in a sub-human state and working for hunger wages. Bolivia, Paraguay and Haiti are the three poorest countries in Latin America. They have the highest birth rate, the highest illiteracy rate and the highest mortality rate. The per capita income in these countries is less than $100 a year.

To dull his hunger and his woes, the Bolivian often chews coca leaves. This is the plant from which cocaine is manufactured. It is a drug forbidden in other countries, except for medicinal use. The Bolivian chews it as the North American chews his gum.

The extreme poverty is, undoubtedly, one cause for Bolivia's many revolutions. Since it became an independent state in 1825, it has had over a hundred revolutions. Not more than a dozen times in all its history has a new president taken office without

210

bloodshed. To the Bolivian, yesterday is sad and woeful, the present is still worse, so bad that there is nothing to lose. "How can things be any worse than they are?" they say. "Maybe a revolution will change things!"

It is an axiom in South America that the poorer a country is, the more emphasis it places on its pride—*"dignidad,"* as it is called here. The various wars in which its neighbors—Chile, Argentina and Peru—were involved have carved away large slices of its territory. Chile took Bolivia's only port and cut her off from the outside world. Paraguay took her entire Gran Chaco territory. All this has left the Bolivian in a state of super-sensitivity. One needs only step on his foot, and he will immediately shout: *Viva la revolucion!*

✓ ✓ ✓

The Jewish community of Bolivia is actually the youngest of all the Latin American countries. Due to its capricious climate and its unsettled economic conditions, Bolivia did not attract Jews for settlement. The first Jewish immigrants who arrived in this century came with the hope that from Bolivia it would be easier to cross over to the neighboring countries where larger Jewish communities and better economic opportunities exist.

But there are unofficial dates which go back much earlier. According to these, Jews appeared in Bolivia soon after the Spanish conquest. They settled in Potosi, where Bolivia's most celebrated silver mines are situated. There is a church in Potosi whose windows bear pictures of the Prophets: Isaiah, Jeremiah, Amos and others. At that time, the area was part of Peru, and when the Inquisition was established in Lima, with its jurisdiction extending to La Paz, the Jews fled into the mountains. The Argentine-Jewish historian, Boleslao Lewin, in his book, *La Inquisicion en Hispanoamerica,* states that the first action of the Inquisition in Bolivia occurred in 1545. In 1737 there was an Inquisition Commissioner in Potosi, and one in Oruro. They came into conflict with the Church, necessitating the intervention of the Holy Tribunal of the Inquisition and of the Viceroy of Lima.

One still comes across Jewish names among the best families

in Bolivia. There was a Senator in the province of Ruba Alta who believed himself to be of Jewish descent and who had an old *siddur* which had been handed down in his family for generations.

In the 1800's a Jewish officer from the Austrian-Hungarian army, Eduardo Posnanski, whose adventures brought him to the New World, built a museum in La Paz where one can see remnants of the past Inca civilization. In 1890 a group of Jews arrived in Bolivia, but it appears that they were in transit, and did not stay very long.

Again, in 1905, after the Russian Revolution and the pogroms which followed, a group of Jews came to Bolivia. The "Columbus" of the Polish-Jewish immigrants in La Paz was a Jew from the Polish city Zaklikow, who "discovered" Bolivia, brought over his family, and was followed by other residents of that city. A large part of the Polish-Jewish immigrants in La Paz are Zaklikower *landsleit*.

A more extensive Jewish immigration to Bolivia began in 1938-39, when Hitler came to power. Bolivia then had a young liberal President, German Bosh, who did not make it difficult for the Jewish immigrants. It is estimated that about ten thousand German Jews fled to Bolivia, but the great majority later left for the United States, Argentina or Brazil.

During the period of Hitler's victories, the Nazis tried to gain a foothold in Bolivia, but with the aid of the German-Jewish mining magnate, Mauricio Hochschild, who discovered the plan, the American secret service was able to prevent a Nazi takeover. But German anti-Semitic propaganda was effective in Bolivia. In May 1940, an official circular went out to all Bolivian Consulates abroad not to issue visas for Bolivia to "elements of the Semitic race."

The anti-Semites also, succeeded in convincing the President of Bolivia to expel the Jews from the country and confiscate their wealth. Jews received an order that by a specific date they must leave the country. Then a strange incident occurred which recalls the story of the Book of Esther. The famous Argentinian dramatic artist, Bertha Singerman, idolized throughout Latin America as the "Ambassadora de la Poesia" (Ambassador of Poetry), went to the President of Bolivia who, was one of her staunch admirers, and explained that he was committing a grave injustice against innocent people.

He asked her, "My God-blessed artist, what interest do you have in the Jews? I see that you even have tears in your eyes."

"I, too, am a Jewish daughter," she answered.

The decree was revoked.

To counteract Nazi agitation, an exhibit was arranged with the aid of the Joint Distribution Committee, illustrating what the Jews had done in Bolivia in the short time they lived there. Thousands of people, including the President, General Panaranda, visited the exhibition and saw how Jews had started dress factories, were making carpets, lamps, mirrors, even microscopes and other scientific instruments. What little there was of industry in Bolivia was largely the achievement of Jewish refugees, who were a civilizing agent in the country. The newspapers printed appreciative reports and articles about the impressive contribution made to Bolivia's development by a handful of Jewish immigrants.

The present Jewish community is engaged mainly in the export trade and in the manufacture of shirts, raincoats, knitted goods and furniture. The largest silk factory in Bolivia belongs to a Jew named Glicksberg. Jews have opened the first modern shops in the country, and operate hotels on the European model.

There are two Jewish cultural and social institutions in La Paz: the Circulo Israelita and the Beth Am. Most Jews in Bolivia came from Germany and Austria, so there is a good deal of Viennese *"gemuetlichkeit"* about them. There is also a central representative Jewish body comprising all the different sectors of Jewish life, composed of the Jewish religious community, the B'nai B'rith, the Zionist Federation, and the Circulo Israelita.

Jews from Poland, Galicia, Lithuania and Bessarabia, who are a minority in Bolivia, wanted something more like the Jewish life they had known in their old home, and have erected a Jewish Center (Centro Israelita).

With all that the Jews have done for the development of Bolivian trade and industry, they are not liked, as is evidenced by the experience of the Danish author and traveller, Carl Eskelund. He writes in his book, *Head Hunters*, that he had an interview with the head of the Department of Immigration in Bolivia.

"You want to know our attitude to the Jews, Señor Ecken-stein?"

"My name is Eskelund. I am a Dane."

"I see! You're a Dane! And I was under the impression you were a Jew. You live in the Pension Neimann, and all those who live there are. . . No, Señor, we in Bolivia don't like the Jews. We've had bad experiences with them. In the old days we had Jews here from Spain, but they merged with our people. The Jews who are here now came in as farmers, or on some other pretext. Forty thousand Jews came to Bolivia. There are ten thousand in La Paz alone. They came with empty pockets, and today they own the best shops on the main streets and they run our small industry. They insult our national honor. Rarely does one of them marry a Bolivian girl."

Carl Eskelund says he heard similar objections about the Jews in Ecuador, Peru and Colombia. He then comments in his book that a fellow-Dane he met in La Paz had told him that when he had first arrived there it was the dullest city he had ever known. There wasn't a decent restaurant; there wasn't a decent shop in the place. When he wanted to buy anything good he had to go to Peru to get it. But today the Jews run first class restaurants and hotels in La Paz, and provide fine shopping facilities. The Jews have done marvels, for the development of Bolivia!

Carl Eskelund is full of admiration for the Jewish refugees he met in Bolivia. He cites, as a typical case, the story of a man named Goldberg who had owned a factory in Germany. He came to Bolivia in 1940, and became a dishwasher in a restaurant. His hours were 8 p.m. to 3 a.m. From 6 a.m. to 1 p.m. he worked as a mechanic in a garage. (He had owned a car in Germany and had done his own repairs.) When he had saved a little money he bought an old washing machine and a pressing iron, rented a shack, and started a laundry. He did well. Then he opened a shoe shop which grew into a large shoe business.

The present government has a liberal platform, and the Jews find conditions much easier than under the previous regime.

When the agreement was signed between Bolivia and Israel, under which Israel gives technical aid to Bolivia, there was a military parade, the band played *Hatikvah,* and the Israeli flag flew alongside the Bolivian flag. The Israeli instructors in the kibbutz-patterned agricultural communal settlement established by the Bolivian Government were received by the settlers with *"vivos!"* Bolivian children have been enrolled in the Jewish school in La Paz. And when the Jews commemorated the Warsaw Ghetto uprising a number of leading Bolivian politicians attended, including the Foreign Minister and the President of the Senate.

ᚱ ᚱ ᚱ

Cochabamba has the second largest Jewish community in Bolivia. Unlike La Paz, Cochabamba has a mild and pleasant climate, which may explain why the people there are more easy-going. The city panorama is like the dream of a great painter-flat terrain with tall mountains surrounding it on every side. Everywhere the streets end where the great mountains begin to tower. It is impossible to go any further. It is like the end of the world. You must go back.

There, cut off from the world, lives a small, but very active and vital Jewish community, Jews from Polish and Galician townships, who have brought their old Jewish folkways with them. Every evening when the mild breezes blow through the tall trees in the Plaza, you can find them all together on the Jewish benches. They sit there discussing the latest news from Israel, sharing a newspaper that has reached them after many days' delay. They argue about world politics and about local politics. And there is a lot of gossip.

One bench belongs to the Jews who have lived for years in Cochabamba, and consider themselves almost natives. The bench next to it is that of the new immigrants, the greenhorns, people saved from death in the camps. They had a very hard time before they managed, after much wandering, to get into Bolivia. You don't have to listen to them long to discover that they feel cramped, hemmed in here, and that they are trying to get away to Israel. Sometimes, in the dark of the night they still see the

215

fires of the crematoria ovens. Then one of them starts humming Hirsh Glick's, Song of the Partisans: "Never say this is the last road that you walk!" And the others take up the song.

The Jewish cafe faces the Plaza. Any time you enter it you will find members of the community having a coffee or discussing business deals. But it is not only business that brings them there; each of them wants to see the others every day. The community is so small that they huddle closely together. If one misses coming to the cafe one day, everybody gets anxious and wonders what has happened.

In this remote town, hemmed in by mountains, I found a Jew from my own hometown. Berl Fisher had managed to get out of Poland with his family a few days before the Hitler invasion, and found his way to Bolivia. The wealth that he had salvaged from Poland and brought with him consisted of his books of Jewish learning, his big Hebrew tomes, his *tallith* and *tefillin,* his sable *shtreimel,* his silk *caftan,* and his wife and three small children. Berl started peddling with a pack on his back, climbing the steep mountain roads, five thousand feet high, in all kinds of weather, burned by the hot sun, drenched by the rains, choking in the stifling heat. He sold trousers, shirts and shoes to the mine workers, and like an observant Jew he carried his own food and utensils, so as not to have to violate the dietary laws.

He managed to save some money and opened his own shop. He keeps it closed on Saturday, although it is the best shopping day. Of course, he must keep his shop closed on Sundays as well.

On Friday evening, when the shadows of night began to creep over the Cordillera mountains, I was Berl Fisher's Sabbath guest in his home in Cochabamba. The table was laid with a fresh white Sabbath cloth, the candlesticks he had brought from the old home gleamed, and when the candles were lit the room was filled with nostalgic memories. Berl Fisher said *Kiddush,* to the tune of the Roptchitzer Chassidim. He and his children sang *"Shalom Aleichem"* with true Chassidic fervor.

The Bolivian may be poor, but he puts on a cheerful face. No sooner does he get his salary than he has spent it. He is generous, open-handed, and will promise you anything you ask. He hates to haggle about prices when buying something for himself, and particularly for his wife. The Bolivian woman loves rich colors and is fond of finery. In that respect she is like all women, whether they do their shopping on Fifth Avenue or in a town several thousand feet high in the Cordilleras. The Jews have learned to understand the Bolivian *cholo*, so the *cholo* is a good customer in Jewish shops. Thus it is that a small Jewish community has grown up around the town of Oruro, near the copper, zinc and lead mines. As the Jews began to prosper economically, they sought to organize a Jewish community.

These days Jewish social activity centers around Israel, so it is a great thing for this small group of Jews in Oruro that one of them, Israel Fogel, is an old Zionist worker, a veteran of the Zionist movement in Galicia and Bukovina. He was a delegate at several Zionist Congresses, and worked at the side of famous Zionist leaders. He is active in Zionist affairs not only in Oruro but all over Bolivia, and was one of the founders of the Bolivian Zionist Federation.

Arrangements were made for me to speak about Israel and to show a film that I had brought along. The entire community came—children and adults. They took their seats in the comfortable hall of the Circulo Israelita, and listened attentively, to my message from Israel. I have spoken in many different places all over the South American continent, but never have I known an audience to hang on my every word the way this small group of Jews did in Oruro. I felt smothered in warmth and love. When I finished, the entire gathering rose spontaneously and sang Hatikvah. As I stood on the platform, singing with them, I repeated to myself the words of the Zionist hymn, "Our hope is not lost." No, indeed, not when there are people like these, in this remote spot, who feel so intensely about the Jewish future.

CHAPTER XVII.

Jews in Uruguay: The Democratic Model

The relationship between Argentina and Uruguay is similar, in many superficial respects, to the relationship between the United States and Canada. The language in these two neighboring Latin American countries is the same, the culture is the same, even in the *kiosks* of Uruguay you see newspapers from Argentina. The temperature is the same, and the cafes, with their habitues, are duplicates of each other.

However, the visitor very quickly becomes aware of a difference between Montevideo and Buenos Aires. The democracy in Uruguay is so tangible that it can almost be touched. In no other country in Latin America does one find so much criticism and satire of the government.

Uruguay is the most advanced welfare state in Latin America, with cradle-to-grave social benefits, retirement on full pay at the age of fifty five or earlier, a low birth rate, and a record of democracy that goes back two generations.

It was with good reason that the late President, John F. Kennedy, chose Punta del Este, the beautiful seashore area near Montevideo, as the locale for the historic conference of the Alliance for Progress, attended by delegates from all Latin American lands. The city of Montevideo is encircled on three sides by seacoast, and cool breezes waft in from the ocean to moderate the tropical climate. The area draws tourists from all over the world.

Uruguay is a small country hemmed in between two massive neighbors, Argentina and Brazil, upon whom her economy is dependent. Her frontier with Brazil is a land border; she is separated from Argentina by the La Plata River which, in some spots, is shallow enough to wade across. She must, therefore, stay on good terms with both. Her area of 72,173 square miles supports a population of 2,550,000, of whom 89% are of the white race.

Uruguay was discovered in 1516 by Diaz de Solis, a Spaniard. The Portuguese, who had an established colony nearby, conquered it, but after a long conflict Spain regained it. In 1811, the people revolted against Spain, and a few years later the Portuguese invading from Brazil retook it. With help from her other neighbor, Argentina, Uruguay won her independence back in 1825, and in 1830 she became a republic. In South America she is known as "the crimson country," because of the blood that was shed for her freedom in wars and internal fighting.

The country, now a model for democracy well beyond the boundaries of Latin America, has had two heroic figures in its history, Jose Gervasio Artigas and Jose Batlle y Ordoñez, who introduced social reforms long before the era of Roosevelt's New Deal. Batlle was a journalist and editor of the daily newspaper *El Dia.* He decided to eliminate poverty in Uruguay under the slogan, "Bread and Work," and introduced women's suffrage, an eight-hour working day, and early retirement with full wages.

Uruguay is called the Switzerland of South America, and this name is no exaggeration. It bears similarities to Switzerland in its natural beauties, and in its former governmental structure. Until 1966, the government was composed of a Colegiada (council) of nine members: six from the majority party, the party which drew the most votes, and three from the minority. It has a basic two party system. The more conservative *Blancos* (Whites), and the more liberal *Colorados* (Reds) who were in power for 93 years, until 1959. Although each of them had their internal frictions, they were considered as single parties. Each year a member of the majority party was named chairman of council. Recently, a referendum was held. The council system was abolished, and a president was elected.

But it is no easy matter to maintain a democratic system in the midst of the political chaos and ferment of Latin America where a revolution is not an unusual occurrence. Soviet Russia has sought to exploit the democracy of Uruguay, and to use it as a center from which to spread Communist propaganda throughout the other Latin American countries. This has now been supplemented by Castroite propaganda which works hand in glove with the Communists. Soviet Russia has flooded Uruguay with spies, for this democracy has no restriction on those entering the country. While the Uruguay embassy in Moscow had six officials, 60 Soviet families were installed in the Soviet Embassy in Montevideo. On one of my visits to Montevideo it was possible to buy Soviet-published books at less than half price. Newspapermen, union leaders and students were given free trips to Soviet Russia on the pretext of cultural exchange. When the American invasion of Cuba misfired, anti-U.S.A, propaganda was stepped up, and the Uruguayans were threatened in the conflict between the leftists and the liberal element. In addition a flood occurred which seriously damaged the Uruguayan economy. Moreover, her products which she exports, such as wool and meat, slumped badly on the world market because of the competition of larger countries. Uruguay is not capable of competing with her larger neighbors, Brazil and Argentina, in the export of meat. This makes it difficult for her to maintain her ongoing social welfare reforms. In recent years, Uruguay has become highly industrialized, and to protect herself has had to impose high tariffs.

This situation undermined the country externally and internally, and has brought it to its present severe monetary crisis. The Uruguayan peso, which used to be on par with the U.S. dollar, has fallen badly. The Castroist and Communist elements are exploiting the critical situation and, of course, lay the blame for it squarely on "Yankee imperialism."

During my second visit to Montevideo, when I was spending the summer months on a beautiful seashore, I travelled one day from Montevideo to Las Toscas with two Uruguayan students. The highway was a broad, American-type, asphalt road. The students mentioned that it had been built by Americans, but one of them repeated the same complaints one hears so frequently in these countries, that American imperialism has undertaken to "submerge the world." The second student complained about an

American film company which had shot a motion picture in Uruguay. It had chosen an impoverished district and told the dwellers whom they had engaged as extras to dress as Indians. "What do they think of us in the U.S.A.?" he protested, "that we are wild Indians living in a jungle? Why didn't they film the beautiful seashore?"

✓ ✓ ✓

Uruguay's Jewish community today totals over 40,000. For many years it was a sort of annex to the much larger Jewry of adjacent Argentina, but now Uruguay's Jews possess their own diversified communal and cultural structure, their own school system, their own press in Yiddish and Spanish, and three Jewish radio programs which provide daily news from Israel in addition to local reports.

The Uruguayan Jewish community began officially in 1907. A Sephardi named David Maran, and an Ashkenazi named Abraham Bressler were the founders. Some Jews had come earlier, but they had concealed their Jewish identity. There are also traces of Jews that go back to the tragic epoch when the Inquisition hounded the Jewish fugitives in the New World.

The Argentine Jewish historian, Boleslao Lewin, discovered a facsimile of an order issued in Montevideo barring Moors and Jews (the word *Judios* is used) from holding public office. A second document, dated 1801, sent by the Inquisition Tribunal to the governor, states that the heretical books confiscated at the customs office should be burnt in the public square. When the Portuguese captured the city of Colonia near Montevideo in 1778, a number of Marranos were among them, and there is no doubt that many of these settled in Montevideo. The Inquisition was abolished in Uruguay in 1813 by decree of the liberator, Jose Artigas.

The beginning of the community was marked by the establishment of a burial ground. Before this the Jews had buried their dead in a specially rented area which was owned by local English Protestants. When the First World War broke out, the English no longer wanted *Alemanes* on their cemetery (in the early years many Jews were known as "Germans"), whereupon the Jews

221

purchased a lot and opened their own burial ground. Soon an association named *Ezra* was formed, whose function it was to assist newcomers. Later on, a number of communal and cultural institutions developed.

As in Argentina, after a while, the radically-oriented among the immigrants dominated the Jewish scene. They were assisted, in part, by their control of a bank. Most of the immigrants were then *clientelchiks* (peddlers), and banks served as a means of drawing the newcomers into radical circles, for credit was extended preferentially to their own followers.

As a counter-effort, and after a hard-fought struggle, an all-community Jewish bank was formed called, the Banco Uruguayo Palestino. Thus, gradually, the radicals lost their hegemony in Jewish society. Today, the radical element among Uruguayan Jewry has shrunk to a negligible number, and has no influence beyond its own circle.

The Jews of Uruguay can be divided as follows: 26,000 are of East European origin; 8,000 are Sephardim; and about 7,000 are German and West European Jews. There are four communal organizations *(kehillot)* in Montevideo: East European Ashkenazic, Sephardic, German and Hungarian. The German Jewish *Nueva Congregacion Israelita* has its own building, a rabbi, various social clubs, welfare agencies, a religious school and even its own publication, *Das Gemeinde Blatt*. The Sephardic community has a rabbi and a building for its communal needs. The Hungarian group also has its own rabbi and synagogue building which incorporates a Hanna Senecz Club. The East European sector is the largest, and carries on broad educational and cultural activities. Most of the synagogues are affiliated with it. It is considered to be the leading communal body.

Some time ago an ultra-Orthodox group organized its own "Kehilla Torah V'yerah." They built a yeshiva, imported teachers from Israel, and attempted to transplant traditional Jewish life from Europe to Uruguay. In addition to these ultra-Orthodox, in recent years a sizable number of Orthodox Jews have come to Uruguay, and religious Jewish life is there now on a higher level than in the larger community of nearby Argentina. New religious educational institutions have arisen, although the percentage of Jewish children attending the Jewish schools is no higher than in Argentina.

Jewish youth organizations carry on their activities in Spanish, and concern themselves with Jewish interests and problems. There has been substantial *aliya* from Uruguay to Israel, consisting of young people who have been trained in the *hachsharot* in Uruguay. A recent youth symposium arrived at the conclusion that the survival of Jewish culture can only be conceived of in a place where there is a vital and continuing Jewish life: in Israel.

The official address of the Uruguayan Jewish community is the Central Committee. It is the roof organization of all four major communities, patterned after the Argentine Daia, and affiliated with the World Jewish Congress. Each year, in rotation, a representative of the various communal groups serves as President of the Central Committee.

The attitude of Government and populace to the Jewish community is quite friendly. Jews will never forget the part played by democratic Uruguay at the time of the establishment of Israel. Uruguay's delegate to the United Nations, Enrique Rodriguez Fabregat, was a member of the Hook Commission which visited Palestine and made a report favorable to Jewish aspirations. He was among the first to vote for a Jewish state. His interest in Jews, he once explained, dates back to his earliest childhood. His father, an immigrant from Spain, once discussed with his mother a book about the Dreyfus case, and he would often hear his father repeat the word *antisemitismo*. When he asked what this meant, his father replied, "It is a disgrace to humanity. We discriminate against people because of their race or religion." From that point on he decided to fight for equal rights for all, regardless of race or religion. On another occasion he indicated he was writing a book about a Jewish girl from Montevideo named Dvora Epstein. Dvora Epstein left a comfortable home in Montevideo to fight in Israel with the Haganah at the time of the war with the Arab countries. She fell in the fighting near Ein Hashlosha before the liberation of the Jewish state.

Uruguay was the first Latin American state to recognize Is-

223

rael officially, the first to receive an ambassador from the new state, and the first to open an Embassy in Jerusalem. When Israel's fate was being dealt with at the U.N., President Luis Batlle Herrera, nephew of the statesman Jose Batlle, convened a special session of the parliament upon his instructions, and the Uruguayan U.N. delegate, Enrique Rodriguez Fabregat, voted in favor of a Jewish state.

Thousands of Jews thronged outside the palace, their faces beaming with pride, when the first Israeli Ambassador Yaacov Tzur, handed over his credentials to the President of the Uruguayan republic. The latter said, "We too are a small country hemmed in between two larger and much stronger neighbors, and we cannot rely on our military strength. Small states exist only thanks to international justice. Their fate is always the same. Let us then receive and protect a second small state with sympathy and understanding."

President Daniel Fernando Crespo, who held office in 1963, after being mayor of Montevideo, visited Israel and returned with high praise. A third, high ranking statesman, Senator Adolfo Tejera, a member of Uruguay's U.N. delegation and an energetic anti-Nazi fighter, wrote a sympathetic book on his impressions and observations of the Jewish state.

Nevertheless, Uruguay has not remained totally immune to the anti-Semitic infection of the Argentine Tacuara. Two Uruguayan political leaders, both connected with the *Colorado* party, have made anti-Jewish pronouncements. One was Benito Nardoni. He was a member of the nine-member governing council. While serving as President, during the period of the Eichmann trial in Jerusalem, he made a public attack on the Jewish people, employing the familiar cliches about their having undertaken to control the world.

A second member of the government council, Cesar Pacheco, a son of the founder of Uruguay's democratic system and its liberal and social reforms, also made a public attack against the Jews. An anti-Jewish propaganda campaign got under way in Uruguay. Swastikas began to appear on Jewish homes and institutions, and there were physical attacks on Jews. A Jewish doctor was summoned late at night on a sick-call and was then attacked and brutally beaten by hoodlums. Onslaughts also took place on Uruguayan democratic institutions. The Colorado party denied that those two leaders spoke for the party.

The Uruguayan parliament was immediately called into extraordinary session and issued a condemnation of the statement. Students at the universities and high schools carried out mass demonstrations in opposition to this anti-Semitic expression. Declarations by parliament, syndicates and labor organizations, as well as groups of intellectuals and professionals condemned anti-Semitism. The rector of the university sharply condemned the acts of vandalism. "Uruguay," he said, "will never tolerate that kind of discrimination against any race, color or religion."

The effect of the anti-Jewish incitement on Uruguayan public opinion can be gauged by an important brochure written by Moises Gerber, editor of a Spanish-language daily. The title reads: "El Uruguay Contra la Barbarie Antisemita—Documentos para la Historia." The brochure contains excerpts from dozens of articles which reacted against the anti-Jewish incidents. Radio broadcasts, pronouncements of statesmen and intellectuals, professors, patriotic groups, leaders of labor unions, interviews with leading political figures, parliamentary resolutions—all of these emphasize the tragic experience the Jewish people underwent with its loss of six million who were brutally murdered by the Nazis. Without exception, all stressed that Uruguay makes no distinction because of race or religion, and all citizens are equal.

During one of my visits to Montevideo, when Victor Haedo was president of the Colegiada, I interviewed him in the presidential palace. Señor Haedo, a thickset, heavily built man, received me without the slightest ceremony. I immediately broached the subject of anti-Semitism, and recalled certain events that had occurred in Uruguay. "I want you to know," said the president, "that such attacks are not only aimed at the Jews, but against all democratic institutions. They are a product of persons who want to destroy our democratic fundamentals."

"Do you know," I asked the president, "what the Jewish people went through in recent years? What is your general view on anti-semitism?"

He replied: "I am familiar with the violence committed in the last war against the Jewish people. This is a product of fanatics who were infected with pride and arrogance. Our democracy is based on justice and equality for all. This is one of the fundamentals of our constitution. The prestige of our democracy is at stake." Then he added, "who knows whether there were no Jews among my own ancestors?"

One can be sure that once a government authority takes a firm position, any campaign of incitement is bound to fail. It should be stressed that within both political parties—the Blancos and the Colorados—small "deviationist" factions exist. Among the Blancos there is a grouping called, the Herreristas, who have been inspired by their leader, Luis Alberto Herrera. They are extreme nationalists who are much closer to the Mussolini type of Fascism than to other Western political ideologies. The Colorados also have an extreme leftist faction. It is not entirely to be discounted that these two factions, both of which have expressed anti-Jewish views, might be considered a political unit.

Interestingly, the Uruguayan national anthem, which is much older than the country's Jewish community, proclaims: "Let us honor our legislature, and keep it as pure as Israel keeps her Holy Ark."

✓   ✓   ✓

The story is told of a Jewish traveller who was hurrying to get home for the Sabbath, and who lost his way in the forest just a few hours before sunset. He saw that candle-lighting time was fast approaching and he was perturbed. Suddenly, a beautiful palace sprung up from the ground before his eyes. On entering, he found himself in a room where the Sabbath candles were shining, and where a table was spread with Sabbath foods and *kiddush* wine.

In a second large room, which had the appearance of a *beth medrash*, people were receiving the Sabbath with prayer and rejoicing. Following the prayers, *kiddush* was recited, *Sholom*

Aleichem and other Sabbath songs were sung, and all enjoyed a delicious meal. So it went for the entire Sabbath. After *havdalah*, the palace vanished, and the wanderer found himself again in the forest, making his way homeward.

When I arrived at the La Boya Hotel at Las Toscas, in the Uruguayan forests, I was reminded of this tale. Here too, in the midst of the woods, with tall trees diffusing their sweet fragrance, was a palace, and devout worshippers. Sparkling white tablecloths graced the tables which were set in honor of the Sabbath; Sabbath candles glowed; and I participated in Friday evening services replete with holy devotion. The difference was solely that there the palace and the worshippers did not disappear after *havdalah*.

As the flames of the Sabbath candles twinkled at me in the Hotel La Boya, the sweet melody of *Lechu Neranena* was intoned in a chassidic style, and I was immersed in memories of tranquil days long since past, of a world that had met its destruction, the nostalgic memories of a Sabbath in my small Galician home-town.

Sabbath, during the services, the *baalei tefilla* avail themselves of a blend of chassidic styles. Now it seems to be the Ropshitzer style which is being used, then the Belzer, then the Strettiner.

Little boys, scarcely weaned, shake with devotion in their prayers. I approach one of the boys and ask him, *"Psok li psukach* —what is the *sidrah* of the week?" Like a sound of silver bells comes the quick response: *"Bo."* He rushes to tell me the entire content of the *sidrah* in a juicy Yiddish.

An older youth reports that he is learning Gemara and *Yoreh Deah* at the Yeshiva on Maldonado.

I ask him: "Do you envisage ever going to Israel?"

"Certainly," is his quick response.

"Are you a Satmarer chasid?"

He hesitates, then answers—a Vishnitzer.

Who are these children? What brings them here, to this gray region whose inhabitants have never seen Vishnitz, Belz or Satmar?

I was told that pious Jews hailing from pre-war Hungary had

established a community of their own in the Uruguayan capital of Montevideo, and that these were the children of those parents, who stood up with rocklike fortitude against the deluge raging outside, which was constantly severing pieces of our Jewish body.

✓   ✓   ✓

The lively and noisy streets of Montevideo recede as one travels through the broad stretches of land reaching out into the horizon—wide fields shining in the sun with ripe golden ears of corn. Then the fields are replaced by orchards laden with fruits. On each side of a road appear small whitewashed houses with red-tiled roofs, hedged around with gardens. Those who live here raise vegetables and dairy products for the city population. They have taken the place of the *peon* of old who so many years toiled for the wealthy *estancieros* (landowners).

The bus moves quickly over the asphalt roads. I look out the window and my mind summons up memories of forty years ago when I was the first Jewish teacher in the Jewish colony named "The Nineteenth of April," the town for which I am now headed.

I was then taking a trip through the Jewish colonies in the province of Entre Rios in Argentina, and soon I had reached the Uruguay River. My *wanderlust* impelled me to ignore the boundary, and one day at twilight when the sun hugged the horizon on the Uruguay side, I slipped across the river to the other bank. On a sunny morning I found myself in the Uruguayan town of Paysandu. The sun pounded down mercilessly, roasting my white European skin, and I sought a shady spot to escape the blazing heat. Bathed in sweat I went over to a park area and then realized that I had walked into a cemetery whose trees shaded elegant tombstones and family mausoleums of marble and platinum adorned with paintings.

Impelled by curiosity I walked about from one family grave to another and read the names which were inscribed in expensive carvings and colors. My eye suddenly lit on a small flat stone which stood between two larger granite memorials, and to my astonishment I read on this small stone three simple words: *Ha-ishah Klastornik Libe.*

The caretaker of the burial ground looked at me rather oddly when I asked for information about the three words which were inscribed in this most unlikely place. After looking through the register of graves he gave me the name of the *Ruso* (Russian) who had put up the tombstone: Isaac Klastornik, a member of the Nineteenth of April colony which was not far from Paysandu.

Late that night I came to the colony and saw a light shining in the window of a *rancho* near the road. It was surrounded by barbed wire, and I slapped my hands a few times—a signal that there was a stranger at the door. A broad-shouldered Jew came out, greeted me with a *"Buenas noche, Señor!"* but looking at me more closely he stretched out his calloused hand and exclaimed: *"Sholom Aleichem!* Where is a Jew from?"

Very early the next morning before the day began to break, I went out to the fields with Isaac Klastornik. Behind us lay the fields wrapped in a smoky fog. He held the plow firmly in his hand as long strips of earth were tossed up on each side. His broad beard which was sprinkled with pearly dew drops was blown to and fro by the small breezes. In the hazy atmosphere of that early dawn I observed his hardened, parchment-like face. As the first rays of daylight broke through to the fields, a small speck on the horizon approached. It was Kalstornik's 11-year-old daughter, on horseback, wearing a white *guarda polvo* (dust jacket), her hair hanging in braids, bringing us food. We sat down on some fresh grass under a clump of trees, and Klastornik started his story:

"There were ten Jewish families who first pioneered Jewish settlement in the fields of Uruguay. The story really began in the Ukraine which they had left at the call of Baron de Hirsch (may his memory be a blessing) to be productive Jewish farmers in a distant land. After vicissitudes and wanderings they came to a Jewish colony in Brazil called Quatro Irmaos. There they suffered for years in the mud and swampland. The weaker ones left for the nearby towns and took to the usual city livelihoods. But a group of twenty families remained stubborn, not wanting to divorce themselves from Mother Earth. Quite by accident they learned that the government of Uruguay was granting land to the colonists on good terms. They came here, worked the land and

229

built homes. Drenched by the rains, roasted by the tropical sun, and without a roof over our heads in the early day, we were attacked by animals and bitten by snakes. Not all of us were able to bear it. My life's companion was among those who succumbed. I could not even give her a proper Jewish burial. "Now," he ended sadly, "she lies there on the Christian graveyard, surrounded by crucifixes. . . ."

On my last visit to Montevideo I met some of the descendants of these colonists: Leibel Klastornik, the son of the colonist to whom I had spoken, and his daughter who by then was a mother of children. The report I got was a sad one. In 1930 when the colonists had trouble meeting the mortgage payment they sent a delegation to the Jewish community in Montevideo seeking aid. At that time however, the economic situation of the local Jews was not too good and help was not forthcoming. Gradually the farmers were compelled to abandon their venture.

By 1935 only five colonists survived. In 1949 the last member came to Montevideo with the request that the bodies of all the dead farmers be re-buried in one place on the grounds of the colony. This was the end of the pioneers of Jewish farm-settlement in Uruguay, the end of those who tilled the Uruguayan soil.

CHAPTER XVIII.

Brazil: The Oldest Jewish Community in the New World

The first time I saw Brazil was 40 years ago. I arrived on board the Regia. She slid silently into the harbor of Rio de Janeiro, a harbor which at night looks like an illuminated, enchanted palace, with thousands of lights shimmering and sparkling in the darkness. When I revisited Brazil some years later, the capital, once again, revealed itself to me in all its glitter and splendor: a light blue sky was spread above the picturesque houses which extend outward in long rows from the point you leave the port. When you go for your first walk on the Avenida de Rio Branco, the outlook is even more breathtaking: a broad sweep of avenues lined on either side with statuesque palm trees. The sidewalks are of mosaic tile, and one feels as though Persian carpets had been laid out for the feet of the pedestrian. And then ... historic monuments come into focus—for as far as the eye can reach.

The Brazilian will tell you that when the first king entered Brazil and planted the first palm tree, he gave orders that any seed that might fall from the tree be destroyed. But there were daring souls who disobeyed the order, and thus it was that palm trees grew up through the length and breadth of the city.

On my third and fourth trips, I saw Rio from the sky. The plane descended along the endless chain of mountains and streams which surround the city like a garland of flowers. When I left Rio de Janeiro at daybreak, the city appeared like a bride at her wedding. As the aircraft ascended, my eyes began to distinguish row upon row of mountains, and upon them castles strewn about like toys on a table top.

From the plane they all look like separate towns. The mountains seem to trace out a human profile—a giant nose carved by a gifted sculptor, an outstretched figure that looked like a giant at sleep. Through the airplane window you see the giant Sugar Mountain (Paŏ de Azucar), and the Ganabara Bay which cuts deep into the land for some miles, and then narrows as it approaches the Pao de Azucar.

Brazil is a nation of 80 million inhabitants, with an area of more than three million square miles. It has great mineral wealth, but like other Latin American countries, Brazil still suffers from the legacy of the Portuguese *conquistadores*. A great part of the soil and the mineral wealth belongs to a small group of the descendants of these *conquistadores* who have contributed to the ruination of the country's economy. They have accumulated millions, and they sit in their luxurious villas in Madrid or Lisbon and invest large portions of their income abroad. This has created the recurring crises and the galloping inflation from which Brazil has been suffering.

The vast inequities in land ownership, and other injustices, create increasing bitterness among the millions of poor, ignorant and submerged Indians, *Mestizos*, Negroes and Mulatos who face a daily struggle to remain alive. Between the two extremes of great wealth and abject poverty is a relatively small middle class —among whom the Jewish community is usually numbered—that is growing wherever industrial progress exists, but is just beginning to be really significant in economic and political circles. In the meantime, the population mounts at a fantastic rate, outstripping food production.

Poverty also provides a striking contrast with the naturally endowed beauty of Rio de Janeiro. The poorest sections of Rio are located on the slopes of the beautiful mountain on which the city is built; the higher one ascends the more shocking is the poverty. I visited the *favelas*, as the huts are called, in the company of a Brazilian colleague, who is a well-received, regular visitor. The *favelas* are made of tin crates put together with lime and brick. The sewage runs through the lanes in an open stream. The dwellings contain neither table nor bed. Sometimes, in a heavy rainfall, the shanties are washed away with their occupants. Caroline Mario de Jesus, a resident of the *favelas*, kept a diary describing the dismal life of the poor souls who live in this misery and squalor, and who lack even a crust of bread to ease their hunger. *Diary of a Hungry Woman* appeared in a newspaper and later in book form. It is a powerful protest, and a cry of pain and distress against the injustices suffered by those whom life has aggrieved and dealt with so shamefully. The author mentions Jews in her book. "It is September now," she writes, "and the Jews are observing Easter (she meant Succoth). Moses saw that his people were barefoot and unclad, and he asked the God of the Jews to give them riches. This is why they are now wealthy. The Blacks," she continues, "have no prophet to pray for them."

To the visitor, the *favelas* stand in stark contrast to the modern structures in the heart of the handsome city. This painful situation is not peculiar to Brazil, but applies to most of Latin America. In each country the slums have a different name. In Argentina they are called *villas miserias* (misery towns) ; in Chile, *callampas* (mushrooms), since they spring up overnight. In Peru they have acquired a romantic title by way of irony: *perlas del sol* (pearls of the sun). In Lima a whole suburb exists called, *El Monton* (the pile), where more than 5,000 people live next to a garbage dump, in houses of cardboard, tarpaper, tin and cement. In Venezuela and Colombia they are called *ranchos,* and are located on the mountaintop looking down over the luxury palaces of Caracas.

What are the reasons for this unhappy phenomenon, and why does it appear in the very center of the metropoles and so close to their most modern buildings? In the first place it should be noted that more than 50% of the fertile soil of Latin America is the property of 1½% of the population who are the *latifundistas* (landowners). The *campesinos*—the farm laborers, whose status approaches peonage, receive a slave-wage amounting to less than $100 a year. After World War II, the *campesino* was drawn to the cities where industrial growth was proceeding at a rapid pace. Here, he had an opportunity to find employment, and however inadequate the payment, it was still much higher than the pittance received for farm labor. Housing was difficult to find because of the rapid rise of industry, but the *campesino* was not accustomed to any luxury—so he built a simple shelter over his head out of scap materials.

The very poor people do not practice birth control and produce the largest families. In Mexico City, where these dwellers are spread around the city in a so-called "belt of misery," the city's population in the last fifteen years has more than doubled, and has now passed the six million mark. Of this number about a million and a half occupy the "belt of misery." Ten years ago Santiago, the capital of Chile had 32,000 *callampas;* recently the number was ascertained to be 200,000. In Caracas, one of the most beautiful cities in South America, the misery towns house almost a million paupers adjacent to the breathtaking mountains and the streamlined skyscrapers. Of the 200 million population of South America, about 40 million people are to be found in such slum dwellings, usually in the capital cities.

The governments of the various states do what they can to solve this painful problem. With the aid of the Alliance for Progress a number of housing projects were created for the inhabitants of the *favelas*. However, it is not an easy matter to eliminate them for in many cases the occupants refuse to abandon them. They wish to live close to the heart of the city where jobs are available. Usually, the new housing projects are built on the city's outskirts, and getting to work involves transportation costs and loss of time. The nearby luxury hotels and restaurants which cater to tourists also provide sources of food for the slum-dwellers, who scavenge their garbage pails.

Villa Kennedy, for example, built by the Alliance for Progress on the outskirts of Rio, cost millions of dollars, but is far from successful.

Slums are by no means peculiar to Latin America. They occur even in such wealthy countries as the United States and Canada, but there they lack the utter squalor of the *favelas*. Certain distinctions must be kept in mind. The farm laborer in North America is not exploited so much, because a wage scale exists.

Moreover, if he wants to change his mode of work he can, with relative ease, reach a nearby city where employment can be obtained in industry. The city slums of the United States are generally populated by Negroes. Sometimes one finds a primitive church constructed of crudely hammered boards and bearing the inscription of a religious sect. Here, the inhabitants of the slums assemble on Sundays to pour out their embittered hearts. It is remarkable how similar those melodies are to those I had heard in the *favelas* of Latin America. Both are lyric outpourings of the poorest of the poor.

The Brazilian is the most hospitable of the Latin Americans. As the saying goes, he carries his heart on a tray. He very rarely loses his temper. He does not wait for you to start the conversation, but takes the initiative and begins a friendly chat. However, once you wound his national pride he won't overlook it, for this affects his *dignidad*. Sometime ago, an American reporter looking for a good story took a photograph in the *favelas* of Rio de Janeiro. *Life* magazine carried the picture of a child, one of a large family, lying on a soiled, torn mattress infested by bedbugs. The article produced a negative reaction in Brazil. The popular Brazilian journal *Cruzeiro* sent a camera-man to New York. He took a similar picture of squalor and poverty on the East Side of New York, five minutes from Wall Street and its mighty financial institutions. The picture was of a Puerto Rican family named Gonzales with eight children. The background was also—a soiled mattress.

The Brazilian, in general, has no aggressive ambitions for himself. He accepts his poverty and distress as a normal condition that he has inherited from past generations. The expression *Calma Brasil!*—"Don't rush, take it easy, you won't be late!" is appropriate to the country's mood and mentality. Despite the galloping inflation, the Brazilian is a kind of merry pauper. This is best seen at the time of the annual carnival. The *carioca*, (as the inhabitant of Rio de Janeiro is called), for all his poverty, is a romantic. For months prior to the carnival he saves his pennies to buy the best possible costume. He parades in the finest districts of the city and revels at the aristocratic Capacabana Beach. The carnival lasts eight days and during this time he is released from his troubles and sorrows. He lets himself go, frees himself from all controls and self-discipline. After the carnival the birth rate increases tenfold.

✓   ✓   ✓

The oldest Jewish community in the Western Hemisphere is that of Brazil. Jews played an important role in its discovery and later in its growth and development. When Brazil's discoverer, Pedro Alvarez Cabral, landed there in 1505, among his most trusted advisors was the Marrano, Gaspar de Gama of Granada. A year later a large group of Marranos arrived in Brazil under the leadership of Fernando do Noronha. He had signed a contract with King Manuel I of Portugal granting his group full exemption from taxes for one year, and a parcel of land of more than 1,000 quintales which they could cultivate. In the second year they would be liable for only one-sixth of the normal tax.

Brazilian history is rich in documentary material on the influx of the Marranos. Dozens of books have been written on that period and more material continues to be uncovered. The Inquisition pursued the Marranos from Portugal, and they showed true courage and heroism in maintaining their Judaism in secret, even after they were discovered by the bloodhounds of the Inquisition and deported to Portugal to face the *auto da fe.*

At that time, Spain and Portugal were in active competition to gain new territories, and for this effort they both needed not only money, but men of initiative and daring to devolp new territories. The Marranos seized these opportunities for distant travel and settlement, in order to get as far away as possible from the watchful eyes of the Inquisition, and be able to carry on, unmolested, as Jews.

Abraham Zacuto, a Jew, had developed a system of navigation which made possible transoceanic trips; the Jewish mathematician, Pedro Nuñez, helped considerably in the plans of the expedition. All the cosmographers and geographers at the Portuguese court were Jews. Jufurda Cresques, a Jew, was the first to propose a marine school in Portugal, an institution which was to assist greatly in the discovery and exploration of new continents.

According to Moshe Cohen, the Brazilian Jewish historian, the founder of Sao Paulo, Joao Ramalho, was a crypto-Jew. The personal signature of this semi-legendary figure was always written in the shape of a horse-shoe, revealing the two Hebrew letters *kaf* and *tzadeh,* the initials of the Hebrew words: *kohen tzedek,* one of the appellations of Jews of priestly descent.

In 1902, the Historic and Geographic Institute of Sao Paulo conducted an investigation, and came to the conclusion that Joao Ramalho was a Jew who had fled from Portugal for fear of the Inquisition, or who, with other capable and high placed Marranos, had been commissioned by the King of Portugal to carry out a project in the newly discovered territories of the western hemisphere. Dr. Horacio de Carvalho wrote a monograph for the *Revista do Instituto* wherein he comes to the conclusion that Ramalho's signature is a secret clue to his Jewishness.

The same historian has shown that the first Governor General of Brazil, Some de Souza, whose mission it was to found the town of Salvador (now Bahia), had a Jewish mother and, on his father's side, had a Jewish grandmother.

Santos Licurgo Philo, in *The History of Medicine in Brazil,* demonstrates that all physicians, surgeons, and pharmacists whom the Portuguese Crown contracted to send to Brazil in the 16th century, were Marranos. This is certainly true of the first two physicians who were sent by the Portuguse King to Brazil, and were later arrested by the Inquisition for practicing Judaism. Arthur Hehl Neiva, the former advisor on immigration to the Brazilian government, is of the firm conviction that all Brazilians of Portuguese origin have some Jewish ancestry. Between 1573-1576 the influx of Marranos to Brazil was so great that the churches were filled with Marrano priests, since for Marranos to have a priest in the family was the best way to avert the persecution of the Inquisition. In 1602, the Bishop of Brazil warned against admitting any more Marranos to the priesthood. The Brazilian historian Rudolpho Garcia writes that Bento Teixeria

Pinto, the father of Brazilian poetry, was a Marrano from Oporto.

The following historical note is of interest: The late Oswaldo Aranha of Brazil was President of the Security Council in the United Nations at the time of the historic vote for the establishment of the State of Israel. When he saw that the motion was still short of four votes, he postponed the session for the next day, until the Jewish representatives succeeded in getting the necessary votes.

Ten years later, when Abba Eban, now the Israeli Minister of Foreign Affairs, gave a party in honor of Oswaldo Aranha, among the Brazilian guests were Freitas Valle and Professor Hermes Lima, now a judge on the Brazilian Supreme Court. At this gathering, Freitas suddenly asked: "Who among us, in your opinion, has the most specifically Jewish features?" Then he pointed to Oswaldo Aranha, and said: "We both are cousins, and would like you to know that we are descendants of Marranos who escaped from Portugal to Brazil at the time of Inquisition." Oswaldo Aranha was silent. This story was revealed by Yizhar Harari, a member of the Israeli delegation at that time, on the occasion of the dedication of a Cultural Center in Aranha's memory in Kibbutz Bror-Chail, where many Brazilian *chalutzim* live.

The New Christians in Brazil maintained secret synagogues, and were in close touch with the Jews of Holland who would send them prayerbooks and other religious necessities. According to a tradition related by Felipe Cavelcanti, the Florentine traveler, the Marranos had secret worship places in various towns. He tells of coming across such a secret synagogue in Camaragibi, which was conducted by Benito Diaz de Santiago, a royal tax official, and an owner of a sugar factory. The clandestine synagogue was actually inside the sugar factory. On certain days, the sexton of the synagogue would tie a rag to his foot and walk through the town. This was the signal for the Jews to assemble and worship. Though the synagogues were secret, in some cases the authorities knew of their existence, and took bribes to look the other way.

In 1624, when the Dutch seized northern Brazil a new era

began for the Jews of this area. A Jewish community flourished in Pernambuco; communities sprang up in Tamarica, Itmarca and Paraiba. In one year, 600 Jews came to Recife from Amsterdam, accompanied by Isaac Aboab de Fonseca, who organized the community under the name, Kehilla Kedosha Tsur Yisrael. Moises Rafael de Aguilar acted as reader or *hazan.* The community had a Talmud Torah, a yeshiva called *Etz Hayim,* for the older students, and a number of functionaries. The community was so well regarded that the famed scholar Menashe ben Israel of Amsterdam, who visited it, dedicated one of his books to its leaders.

After Portugal regained northern Brazil in 1654, persecution of the Jews was renewed. Retaliatory measures were taken against the "New Christians" for their collaboration with the enemy and for their "impudence" in publicly returning to Judaism. The Marranos sought to flee the country using all possible avenues of escape. Not all were successful, for the Inquisition, newly indignant and enraged, made every effort to cut off their escape by spreading its net throughout all the nearby countries.

Some, however, succeeded in reaching other lands, and many were dispersed throughout the Caribbean islands. A group of twenty-four Jews fleeing Brazil landed in New Amsterdam. Others fled deeper into the interior where, in the course of time, they mixed with, and were absorbed by, the surrounding population. The sugar industry, which Jews had introduced in Brazil, was ruined.

Only in 1822, when Brazil achieved independence and persecution stopped, did Jews begin to re-enter the country. This was the country's second period of Jewish settlement. The first inhabitants were Sephardim who occupied the most remote areas of northern Brazil and founded communities on the banks of the Amazon. The first synagogue, *Shaarei Shamayim,* was in Manaus and the second in Belem.

It was not until 1901 that a synagogue was erected in Rio de Janeiro. Its members were probably English and German Jews who had come as technicians in the service of foreign firms. Later, as a result of the Czarist pogroms, the Baron de Hirsch fund in addition to its colonization schemes in Argentina and Canada, also started two Jewish farm colonies in Brazil: the first (1903) is named Philipson, and the second, Quatro Irmaos (Four Brothers). Both were located in the Province of Rio Grande do Sul.

The third period of Jewish settlement in Brazil took place between the two World Wars. The first to come in this period were Bessarabian Jews who emigrated with the idea of staying for a few years, saving some money, and returning home. But as the political situation in Europe became more tense, the emigrants began to think of settling down in Brazil.

Over the course of years, men who were carpenters in their homes in the Ukraine or Bessarabia became furniture manufacturers; former tailors became textile industrialists; the *clientelchiks* opened stores. The erstwhile immigrants are also well represented in the paper, leather and diamond industries. Because of their connections, they also serve as representatives of important American enterprises, are active in import and export trade.

The Jewish population of Brazil can be estimated at 160,000. Of these, 65,000 are in Sao Paulo and 50,000 in Rio de Janeiro. There are 12,000 in Porto Alegre and in smaller communities such as Curitiba, Bella Horizonte, Recife (Pernambuco), Bahia and other settlements scattered throughout the country.

Brazil's Jewry has undergone the same testing and trials that other Jewish communities on the continent have experienced. From a tiny relief committee called, Achi Ezer (Brother in Aid), and a small prayer house called, Beth Ya'acov Tifereth Zion, an entire community apparatus with all the appropriate and necessary institutions has developed. The credit cooperative established in a modest office by the Jews of Sao Paulo for the purpose of assisting immigrants with small loans, has now grown into an institution with a large staff who service Jewish manufacturers and importers.

I have visited Brazil five times, and each time have noticed changes in Jewish life in general, and particularly in the economic sphere. The sons and grandsons of the peddlers, and of my former pupils in the Jewish school at Santa Maria (near the old Jewish farm colony of Philipson), Curitiba and Porto Alegre, are now physicians, lawyers, engineers, architects and army officers. As I was talking to an audience in a Jewish center in a small town, the door opened and the chief of police walked in. I was apprehensive, as one never knows what to expect in these countries. But the chief walked over to me and extended his hand to me with a, *"Sholem aleichem, professor."* It was one of my former pupils who even recalled my name (teachers are addressed as professor in these countries). He hugged me with a true Brazilian *abrazo.*

The second and third generations of Brazilian Jews are assuming prominent positions in the country's public and political life. One of the leading Brazilian playwrights is Pedro Bloch, who is also head of the Cultural Department of the *Hebraica.* Professor Fritz Feigl, former President of the Jewish Confederation, is an internationally renowned chemist, and was honored by the Brazilian Government with the highest award of the country: the Officer's Orden of Rio Branco, for his achievements and contributions to the country that adopted him after coming as a refugee from Nazi Germany. Professor Arthur Moses is President of the Brazilian Academy of Art. Jews are well represented in journalism, in films, and in television.

The Brazilian Parliament has a number of Jewish members. Prominent among them is Senator Mauricio Steinbruch, son of one of the early Jewish farm settlers in the Province of Rio Grande do Sul. For a long time Horacio Lafer was Finance Minister and Secretary of State. There are fifteen Jewish colonels, and four Jewish generals in the Army. One of these, Levi Cardozo, was an intimate adviser of the late Brazilian President, Marshall Castello Branco. A second general, Rafael Zipin of Porto Alegre, is active in Jewish community life.

In Rio de Janeiro, there are streets named after Theodor Herzl and Ludwig Zamenhoff, the inventor of Esperanto. Two squares in the finest part of the city are named after Ben-Gurion and Chaim Weizmann. One public school is named, Estado do Israel, and another Anne Frank. A fashionable street in Sao Paulo, the Imperial Avenue, is named after the late Brazilian Jewish leader, Horacio Lafer, the former Minister of External

Affairs and Finance. A street was also named after the heroes of the Warsaw Ghetto.

Through the intervention of the United Hias Service, Brazilian immigration authorities have authorized, lately, nearly 8,500 visas for Egyptian and North African Jews. This represents the most liberal immigration policy toward Jewish immigrants in Latin America. United Hias activities in Rio de Janeiro and Sao Paulo cover premigration services, the obtaining of visas, port reception and post-migration services, including financial assistance, technical schooling, etc.

When I pass through Rio de Janeiro, my heart beats faster at the memory of the days, forty years ago, when I was an *habitué* of Praza Once, the Jewish literary cafe. Other regulars of that day were Eduard Horovitz, the poet Jacob Nachbin, who died in the Spanish Civil War, the writer J.L. Karkushansky, Nathan Becker who was a devoté of the doctrines of Chaim Zhitlovsky, and Naftali Yaffe. At that time, writers' gossip and malice were not yet in style, and we were content to read each other our songs, stories and poems, and dream of seeing them in print some day. When I am in Rio I always hail a taxi to take me to Praza Once, and each time, I leave it with a feeling of sadness, for Praza Once is no longer what it was. On my last visit I found, instead of the old cafe, Schneider's restaurant, where Jews from the richer suburbs come in their automobiles to enjoy the taste of *knishes* and *gelfilte* fish.

However, in the metropolis of Sao Paulo, the Jewish quarter on Retiro has retained its old Jewish character. There, too, Jews have moved away to roomier and more comfortable quarters, but in the main they continue to maintain their businesses in the Jewish area. In Sao Paulo, Jewish life is more concentrated than in Rio, and for that reason it is better organized, and the best organized element are the German Jews. These brought with them the talent for organization and efficiency, and possess a *kehilla* with all the necessary functionaries.

A confederation of Brazilian Jewish bodies has been formed which is affiliated with the World Jewish Congress. There is a network of schools, a home for the aged, and all the other institutions required in a community, but the essential—an organized central body—is missing.

The absence of a central communal body is the result of the influence exerted by the radicals on local Jewish life. When I lived in Brazil, from 1926 to 1928, the late Rabbi Isaiah Rafalovitch, of Liverpool, was assigned to Brazil. His task was to establish a central *kehilla*, but the radicals who then were influential in Jewish circles initiated a campaign against it, complaining that a *kehilla* meant fanaticism. Because of this concerted opposition, Rabbi Rafalovitch left Brazil, and the plan for a central community organization was abandoned. However, with the influx of West European Jews, a sort of confederation of Brazilian Jewish bodies has been formed.

Most Jewish schools in Brazil are all-day institutions where the child is instructed in both general and Jewish studies. There are thirty such day schools in Brazil, of which thirteen are in Rio de Janeiro, ten in Sao Paulo, and the others in provincial communities such as Porto Alegre, Curitiba, etc. Brazil has two teachers' seminaries and youth clubs with names like Hebraica, Mount Sinai, Maccabee, etc. Despite this, the results are not impressive. Only 7,000 children attend the Jewish day schools. Out of a total Jewish population of 160,000, this is a tragically small proportion!

Part of the cause is due to the fact that like Argentina, Brazil concentrated its efforts on Yiddish-secular education, a form of training which was alien to the second and third generations. At a conference of Jewish youth in Jerusalem, Abraham Hamavi, delegate of the United Jewish Youth organization of Brazil, stated that no less than 75% of Jewish students in Brazil were quite ready to marry non-Jews.

Because of this condition, the Jewish Agency took steps to provide teachers from Israel for the Jewish schools of Brazil, and has arranged to bring young Brazilians to Israel in order to expand their Jewish knowledge. They will return to Brazil to act as youth leaders and teachers.

With the assistance of the American Jewish Committee, an "Instituto Brasileiro Judaico e Devulgacao," was organized in

1957, whose purpose it is to encourage Jewish culture and education among the second generation. Efforts are being made to acquaint Jewish youth with Jewish values, and to create a bridge between the young generation and their immigrant parents.

Special attention is given to Jewish students. A study of Jewish university students and their attitudes towards Jewish problems was conducted in Sao Paulo. Assistance was given to a group of Jewish students in Rio de Janeiro who organized seminars for Jewish leadership. In addition, support has been given to special libraries, such as the Interfaith Library of the Christian-Jewish Brotherhood of Rio de Janeiro, the Library of Judaica of the University of Sao Paulo. A Chair in Hebrew studies at the University in Rio has been established. A Brazilian publication, *Comentario*, was begun in 1964, and its contributors are well known among Brazilian Jewish and non-Jewish authors.

The Instituto Brasileiro Judaico is an adviser to the local bodies which conduct their own activities. A well-planned program of research was created. A bibliography of the Instituto shows that from 1948 to 1961 over 110 books and brochures on Jewish themes were published in Portuguese.

Recently, with the influx of more traditional-minded immigrants, Jewish religious life has deepened its roots in Brazil, as in other Latin American countries. Jewish education also has begun to place more stress on Jewish content.

A leader of the Agudath Yisrael, the late Benjamin Citron, took the initiative in establishing a Beth Hayeled which now has an enrollment of over 500 children, and a staff of teachers brought in from Israel. A Beth Yaakov religious school for girls was recently established. While this has not yet assumed the proportion of a mass trend, it is a satisfying and significant start. In addition, the Lubavitcher Rebbe has begun to interest himself in Jewish education in Brazil. He has organized a yeshiva and Talmud Torah staffed with Brazilian-born teachers who were trained in the Lubavitcher Yeshiva in Brooklyn.

The Brazilian makes no distinction between brown, yellow, black or white skin. However, there is a certain amount of anti-Jewish feeling in the country. There are certain provinces, such as Rio Grande and Santa Catharina, where entire districts are populated by Germans. German is the spoken language. School is conducted in German and newspapers are printed in German. For a while, after World War I, the rumor spread that Kaiser Wilhelm II would be coming to Blumenau—a German colony in Brazil. A joke used to make the rounds among these Germans: "We have been here almost a century, and the Brazilians have not yet learned to speak German!" When Nazism emerged and began its anti-Jewish campaign, the Germans in Brazil acclaimed the new philosophy, and spread Jew-hatred among the friendly Brazilians.

Although there is no "official" anti-Semitism in Brazil at present, latent anti-Semitism is beneath the surface and could swiftly be triggered in the event of a severe economic crisis, political upheaval or drastic social change. It would be encouraged by reactionaries, backed by Arab League emissaries (Brazil has a large Arab population—mostly Syrians), influenced by ex-Nazi war criminals and by the German population. However, the decisive role will remain in the hands of the ruling regime.

CHAPTER XIX.

Remnants of a Jewish Colony in Brazil

While visiting the town of Porto Alegre, in the province of Rio Grande do Sul, I picked up a newspaper which carried a front page story about hundreds of *intrusos* (intruders) who had invaded the Jewish colony of Quatro Irmaos (in the same province) and had seized the fields. Government troops were expected. My journalistic instinct was aroused, and I decided on the spot to travel there and find out what was happening. This was easier said than done.

The only airplanes flying there are very small six-passenger aircraft which shake and quiver. But my nose for news got the better of me, and soon I was flying through the sunny, blue sky of Brazil. We landed in Paso Fundo, where I boarded a bus to Eroshim, and there transferred to a second bus which was to bring me to the Jewish colony of Quatro Irmaos—a trip which should last about six hours, but which became a day's battle with the elements, as a wild and capricious semi-tropical storm broke out, flooding the primitive road. The bus finally ground to a halt in the ever-rising water, which slowly spread over its floorboards. The passengers were contemplating the encroaching darkness and the swirling waters with dread, when tiny shimmering points of light began to approach the bus. They turned out to be Brazilian peasants armed with ropes and axes, who leaped down from their swimming horses and started the rescue work. Eventually, the bus was back on the mudcaked road and, finally, the bus station of Quatro Irmaos came into view. There I was met by the administrator of the colony, Mr. Schall, a warm, Jewish man of German origin, who brought me a pair of dry boots and took me to his house to warm up.

My first walk through the colony left a dismal impression of long enduring poverty. Little shops reeked of pauperdom, and were reminiscent of those in Poland in the days of Grabski, when Jews walked about with cotton-stuffed vests. The houses were clapboard, woven and hammered together, and in a state of utter disrepair. Here and there an old man or woman peered out. The youth had all left for the towns.

"Anyone with strength has gone from here," said an old Jew clothed in an ancient and ragged coat. "The others lost their strength here—and some their lives." He looked at me curiously. "You know it's not so easy to abandon this place. You give your years to the soil, invest your sweat and blood—how can you suddenly leave it all? Some of us were stubborn and stayed. Here is where we'll end our days."

The sexton of the synagogue, who performs a dozen other jobs for his livelihood in addition to his official post, took me to the synagogue, the only brick structure in the area. *Yahrzeit* lamps were flickering, and a partly damaged pulpit was held together with boards. A Hebrew passage was painted on the Holy Ark: "A prayer without devotion is like a body without a soul." A faded, worn-looking Torah mantle bore the Hebrew inscription: "A gift of David Feinglas and his family, in memory of the soul of his wife."

Torn prayer books were lying helter skelter on the seats. On the east-wall hung a placard of the Unificado (the United Zionist Organization of Brazil) calling for aid to the United Israel Appeal. On the opposite wall was a replica of the Declaration of Independence of the State of Israel and in a small ante-room hung portraits of Herzl, Weizmann and Ben-Gurion. The sexton saw me looking at the portraits, and explained: "We would have hung these portraits in the synagogue proper, on the east-wall, but there are some pious members who say we must not, as the portraits are bar-headed, and after all this is a holy place."

The sexton, a talkative type, went on: "Do you see these

yahrzeit lamps? They are in memory of people who died right here in Quatro Irmaos—but not of natural causes. One died of a snake bite, another of malaria, a third of some tropical sickness. I'm one of the earliest to have come here," he said. "You have to be Samson to withstand the suffering, the climate, and all the other plagues."

The Jews of the village found out that there was a Jewish visitor from abroad who was neither an ICA official nor a fundraiser, and gradually began to file uncertainly into the synagogue, to shake my hand and offer *sholom aleichem*. I felt hands hardened with callouses and blisters. Whiskered faces, burned and hardened by hot winds and rain, looked at me with curiosity. Perhaps, they thought, I have some good news from afar? A Jew with a broad, full beard asked: "Will salvation ever come to the Jewish people? We're in great trouble here. *Malchus* (i.e. the government) is on our side, but . . ." and here he was interrupted by a companion who said: "We'll be able to handle the mob of shirtless beggars."

I spent the night at the home of Mr. Schall, and learned the details of the attack by the *intrusos*. It was nothing new—an old phenomenon. The landless, Brazilian natives ride about the country on their horses with their supply of *asada* (roasted meat) and *mate* (a type of tea made of herbs) in their pack. This is all they own. Several thousand of them fell upon the colony and simply took possession of the unused portions of the land. The government sent in troops and expelled them. Dr. Schall assured me that this was not a question of anti-Semitism. It was quite simple: the presence of the untilled land attracted the *intrusos*. The provincial government had made several efforts to enact a law to take the land belonging to the "Yevish" (a Brazilian distortion of the English word "Jewish," meaning the ICA—Jewish Colonization Association), and divide it among the landless, rather than let it go uncultivated. So far this has not succeeded.

The next day I was invited to ride on "the Jewish railway" which belongs to the ICA. It consists of 40 cars and a locomotive, clearly labelled ICA. The engine driver, Abiezer Mozhalib, a Jew from the ancient town of Safed in *Eretz Israel* drove me through the length of the colony, and the locomotive issued a few blasts in honor of the distinguished guest—a special token of homage only for visitors from the outside. Mozhalib speaks Hebrew, and as he drives his locomotive sings Israeli folk songs.

The colonization project which started over sixty years ago has not been a success. This applies both to the first colony, *Philipson,* founded in 1903 near Santa Maria, and *Quatro Irmaos,* established a few years later. The Jews who came found it hard to adjust to the tropical climate and the heavy labor. Most of those who came were without any previous experience in agriculture. They struggled for years in the bare fields, surrounded by swamps. Most of them ruined their health and became debilitated, after which they left for nearby Brazilian towns where they took to the common Jewish livelihood of South America—carrying a pack and knocking on doors. Later they opened stores.

The colonization was halted for a decade, until 1921, when the well-known Palestinian agronomist, Akiba Ettinger, was brought in. He recommended that in addition to straight crop-raising, livestock should be bred, agricultural industry be developed on a small scale, and each colonist be given more land. His recommendations were about to be implemented when another revolution broke out in Rio Grande province, and the plans had to be set aside. The uprising and resulting unrest caused many of the remaining colonists to leave.

When things became quiet, the ICA made another effort to reorganize the colony. New farming candidates were brought in. Each was to receive 50 hectares of forest land, and was to install sawmills. But again the experiment failed. The Jewish immigrant was a product of the East European *shtetl* where there was a long established and clearly defined social and religious pattern of life. Suddenly, with no transition, they found themselves in the midst of giant primeval forests, rarely penetrated by the light of day, jungles teeming with reptiles and lizards, cut off from the world outside. Adjusting to life in this environment and in these circumstances was extremely difficult, although there were many who persevered, and who tried with all their strength to accept and live with these conditions.

249

The German colonists who lived nearby proved to be an aggravating factor in the situation. There was a heavy concentration of them in Rio Grande province, and they infected the primitive Brazilians with the poison of Jew-hatred. Soon, anti-Jewish incitement became a daily occurrence—at first in mild forms, and later it was quite open and brutal in its manifestation. There were even cases of people being killed, and the Brazilian government was forced to dispatch troops from neighboring army posts to maintain order.

After a few days in Quatro Irmaos an American jeep took me through the muddy and dangerous road to the station of Eribango, the nearest town. The road led over large uninhabited stretches of land and thick forest. Late at night, as I waited for the train which was to take me to Pasa Fundo, I heard a weird song sung to jarring music coming out of a bar which was lit by a kerosene lamp. Through the open door I could see the customers: half civilized men with unkempt hair and beards, wrapped in ponchos, some barefoot; and women dressed in rags. The whole scene was one of stark primitive backwardness. Even the railroad official who sold me the ticket to Pasa Fundo had on a well-worn poncho with a broad sombrero-like hat.

That night, in the darkness, I had the opportunity of making an analysis of my observations of the facts and of the complaints I had heard. It is true that the former ICA officials bear a large share of the blame in the failure of the colonization scheme. Many of these officials were without knowledge of Jewish life, and had no understanding or appreciation of the Jewish common man, his characteristics or his needs. But, it must be admitted, this was not the only factor that led to the present fiasco.

More than twenty five years ago, I saw the same process in effect in the Argentine colonies. Even then the younger generation was fleeing from the farm colonies. And at the very time when the prices of their products were rising in the market, many colonists were leaving the farms. One is forced to the conclusion that Jews can only do work of a pioneer nature in a country which is their own, where the environment and the social and communal background is compatible and, above all, where there is an ideal to spur them on.

✓   ✓   ✓

The town of Belem is located in a distant corner of Brazil, in the province of Para, in the tropical Amazon delta region. Only 200 miles away live tribes of Indians who have never laid eyes on a white man. The distance from modern Rio de Janeiro to this tropical outpost was covered in a six-hour, non-stop flight. Among the passengers aboard the plane was a man with an odd gait, a sunburned face, and restless eyes that kept returning to watch me.

"Are you a Jew?" I asked him uncertainly.

"What else?" he replied quickly. "And where are you going?" he asked.

"To Belem," I answered.

He moved over to the adjoining seat.

"My name," he said, "is Chaim-Zalman Leibov. But in Brazil I'm known as Zalman of Belem."

He had been in Brazil many years, and had lived in all its provinces. His business was now crocodile hides. Belem is the main source of this product. As his voice was drowned out by the roar of the engines, he drew closer and whispered confidentially, "You know it's not good for us Jews here—that is, in these small, far-off communities. Cut off and isolated from other Jews, what can one do? You make a living, such as it is, as much as one needs . . ."

I sensed a yearning and a deep longing in his voice.

"What do you think I was just doing in Rio de Janeiro? A couple took a child from a poor family and raised her. Later the poor family decided to move to Israel and wanted the child back. The girl had become attached to her foster parents, and wouldn't leave them; they, too, loved the child as their own." He had been asked to come to Rio and be the intermediary.

"What became of the child?" I asked.

"Don't ask," he replied. "It was a tragedy."

When we landed at Belem, Zalman Leibov advised me to

come and stay where he stopped, the Hotel Avenida. There was another hotel more fashionable and luxurious, but this hotel had a coffee shop where the local Jews congregated. I took his advice and registered at the Avenida.

Stepping out of the hotel in the morning, I was gripped by vast waves of heat which tugged at my throat, threatening to choke me. Though this was the winter season, my clothes were drenched in sweat. In the few intervening hours since the plane had landed, Zalman Leibov had assembled all ten Jewish families, mostly refugees from East Europe, and introduced me. Wearing suits of light fabric and summer shirts, they sat at the tables drinking their demi-tasses, eager to hear from me. The traditional greetings and exchanges were followed by their complaints.

"What will become of us here?" asked a middle aged Jew with a complexion that was a blend of blotched pale and sun yellowed skin.

"It takes a week to get here by boat from Rio," said another. "We're utterly isolated from other Jewish communities. Why do we always get emissaries and fundraisers, but never a teacher or a rabbi?"

"Why don't we Jews follow the example of the Catholic Church which sends missionaries here? You'll meet them at every step. When our children grow up they become strangers to us. What will happen to them?"

As their spokesman said this, they all turned to me to see if I had the answer, or perhaps at least some advice. Most of them were *klappers* (door knockers, i.e. peddlers)—no easy trade. All day long they knock at doors offering goods on credit. Often they get what they call *"tzvekis"* i.e. deadbeats, customers who won't pay up. These peddlers have a folklore of their own, witticisms and tales of their trade that should be collected. This is a chapter in Latin American Jewish history equal in suffering and sorrow to the North American sweat shops of long ago.

Not all *klappers* succeed in striking it rich, particularly in the province of Para, the hottest in all Brazil, where it is possible to work only a few hours each day, when the sun does not burn quite so fiercely.

Remnants of a Jewish Colony in Brazil

As in many other remote parts of Latin America, I found traces of a Jewish past in Belem. I was led to an old cemetery in the center of town, with crumbling tombstones surrounded by an iron railing. In Manaus, in the Amazon area, I saw such old vestiges. Today there is an old Sephardic community there as well as in Belem since 1822, when Jews began to reenter the country. Shaarei Shamayim, in Manaus, was the first synagogue established after the reentry. Its members are well-to-do traders in tropical products.

Late at night, when the flagstones were cooling off in the evening air and the Panamerican plane was to take me to Surinam, the hotel porter woke me. As I walked out into the light of the hotel lantern, I saw standing in front of me Zalman of Belem. His wide-brimmed sombrero was pushed back behind his ears. He had arisen in the middle of the night to escort me.

"Goodbye," he said, offering me his hand," and do not forget to bring the great Jewish world outside a greeting from this forgotten group of Jewish wanderers."

CHAPTER XX.

B'nai B'rith: Unifying Force of Latin American Jewry

B'nai B'rith is carrying out a vital role among the Jews of Latin America. It performs, as it were, the function of a melting pot, bringing together Sephardim and Ashkenazim, East European and West European Jews—in a non-partisan manner. The task is not an easy one, for it must be realized that the patterns of immigration, and the economic and political circumstances are quite different in Latin America from those of the United States and Canada.

In some of these countries Jewish communal affairs are still being directed by immigrants. In others, communal Jewish life has just begun to crystallize, and traditions are still in their initial stages. Although, to this day, there are vestigial traces of Jewish life that go back to the period of the Spanish Inquisition, most of the present day communities began to take root in the days after the first World War. When the survivors of Hitler's destruction in Europe arrived on the scene the roots began to spread.

Almost all these countries had old, small settlements of Sephardic Jews—in some countries *kehillot*—which carried out activities of a purely religious nature on a limited scale without any kind of communal or cultural program or apparatus. The Jews who arrived from the European countries were a minority in the beginning, and many of them, possibly the majority, were not religiously inclined, with the result that there was little contact between them and the previously settled Sephardim. The Jewish

254

melting pot was not as effective as in the United States, for there had been no mass wave of immigration large enough to wipe out the demarcation lines between the various Jewish groups.

There can, therefore, be no comparison with the communities in the United States which by now include third and even fourth generations of Jews, and where a certain amount of internal "assimilation" has taken place between Litvaks, Galicians, Polish and Rumanian Jews. In many of the Latin American countries until quite recently, the demarcation between Jews who hailed from different countries was quite distinct, and their special peculiarities and distinctions were clearly defined. Their languages, outlook, and way of life varied considerably from each other. Each followed different paths, and each "tribal" community had little contact with the other.

With the establishment of B'nai B'rith in Latin America, an impartial platform, a sort of union of *kol Yisrael chaverim* (all Israel are fellows) was created, in which Jews of differing origins could find a common meeting place from which to carry on communal and cultural activities in all areas of Jewish life. B'nai B'rith, which was recently recognized by the Organization of American States for its useful and idealistic work, conducts an admirable program in Latin America's Jewish life.

In the ranks of B'nai B'rith, the non-Zionist becomes interested in Israel and the assimilationist begins to develop a taste for fostering Jewish education; the Jew who has been totally oriented toward the State of Israel sees the need for local cultural and communal work; the women's chapters and youth groups of B'nai B'rith create a common basis for Jews who stem from different countries and thus, keep the younger generation from estrangement. Quite frequently "mixed marriages" occur between Litvaks and Galicians, and even between German Jews and Sephardim. The "enabling" factor here has been the B'nai B'rith youth groups.

Recently, I made a tour of the continent, and had the opportunity of becoming acquainted with B'nai B'rith lodges in various countries, their activities, and the role they play.

In Chile, for instance, where the Jewish community recently

marked its fiftieth anniversary, B'nai B'rith was organized on the initiative of a former member from Germany, who arrived in Santiago in the newest immigrant stream, and suggested to the Washington, D.C. office that a B'nai B'rith unit be established in Santiago. The Argentine B'nai B'rith, which has numerous lodges, assisted in the founding of the Chilean unit, with the result that the Santiago B'nai B'rith is the result of the efforts of members in three countries—a threefold expression of Jewish solidarity. Today there are five lodges in Chile. On the initiative of the Chilean B'nai B'rith, a sister lodge was organized in Bolivia.

In Montevideo, Uruguay, I was invited to a special meeting of B'nai B'rith, and met its leaders in the elegant, lodge headquarters. The lodge president described its varied program, which includes Hebrew courses for adults, and support for the State of Israel. Montevideo has four separate Jewish *kehillot:* Sephardi-Hungarian, German and East European. The leaders and members of the separate communities meet and mix.

Throughout the Jewish communities in Latin America, "ethnic" lines are still clear and visible. Each group has its own structure. In Lima, Peru, too, the communities were functioning separately. However, though each one, as the Yiddish saying goes, *"hot gemacht Shabbes far zich,"* they all considered B'nai B'rith an impartial platform where they can meet on a common basis and do mutually useful work.

B'nai B'rith fulfills a unifying function in Brazil, too. Brazil's vast area presents a major difficulty. Because of the great distances between one city and its nearest neighbor, Jewish life suffers from a gap in communication. Since the establishment of Brazil's first lodge in 1953 in Rio de Janeiro, this problem has been overcome. Today there are twelve B'nai B'rith lodges in Brazil located in the following centers: Rio de Janeiro, Sao Paulo, Porto Alegre, Curitiba, Belo Horizonte, Salvador (Bahia), Recife (Pernambuco), as well as Belem and Manaus, the most remote communities on the Amazon River.

In the smaller centers in the hinterland of Brazil, the Jewish communities clearly reflect the origin of the early comers who generally form the majority, as later immigration from overseas did not, as a rule, come directly to these towns. In Curitiba-Parana, the first to come were Galicians who still are the dominating group. Porto Alegre is a mixed community of Polish and Bessarabian Jews. The first Ashkenazim to arrive in Belo Horizonte were Jews from the old *yishuv* of Palestine. Belem has a Sephardic community, and the same applies to Manaus.

This is the situation in other communities on the South American continent: Bolivia received predominately German refugees, beginning with the 1930's, and it is the German Jews who set the tone there. In Ecuador, as well, the Polish Jews are a small minority among German Jews. The Jews of Guatemala and nearby San Salvador are from the province of Posen (in what was Prussian Poland). Nicaragua has Bessarabian Jews with a small admixture of Hungarians. Costa Rica, on the other hand, has only Polish Jews. As a result, when one meets the B'nai B'rith leadership of the various countries, it is clear that they differ widely in their origins.

Through these scattered lodges B'nai B'rith has created a link between the far flung Jewish settlements dotted over the vast continent of Latin America. When one realizes that in the short space of fourteen years, B'nai B'rith has succeeded in penetrating the most isolated Jewish settlements, what better proof is there of the order's success? The *kibbutz galuyot*—the fusion of the many Jewish "diasporas"—being effected by B'nai B'rith in bringing together Jews of varying origins can best be seen in the composition of the order's executive committee, comprised of members of all the Jewish "ethnic' groups: Sephardi, East European and German Jews.

The Argentine Jewish community is known for its secularist outlook on Judaism, and at the time of one of my visits to Buenos Aires, where the majority of the country's Jews live, there was not a single kosher restaurant. B'nai B'rith then took the initiative and opened a kosher eating place.

B'nai B'rith in Argentina was also among the initiators of the "Confraternidad Judeo Christiana," modeled after the Conference of Christians and Jews in the United States, which is fighting anti-Semitism. The organization has chapters in other countries, such as Brazil, Uruguay and Costa Rica. The Anti-Defamation League of B'nai B'rith, in cooperation with other national Jewish organizations and local communities is fighting anti-Semitism wherever it occurs.

CHAPTER XXI.

How Jews Fight Anti-Semitism in Latin America

What are the reasons for anti-Semitism in the countries of Latin America, and how deep does the current run, and how do the Jews combat it?

Basically, it must be borne in mind that envy directed at any foreigner is easily transformed into hate. As a rule the foreigner in Latin America is envied for his competence and his vitality. The difference between the foreigner, in general, and the Jew is that the Italian, the Englishman or the German attends the same or similar church as the indigenous population, and he or his children assimilate fairly quickly, though their communities are still known as Colonia Italiana, Colonia Alemana, etc. With Jews the situation is different: they do not assimilate as rapidly, have their own religion and place of worship, and build their own distinctive cultural and social institutions. Thanks to their energy and resourcefulness, they rise rapidly on the economic scale. Moreover, Nazism, on the one hand, and Arab propaganda on the other, have in recent years spread anti-Jewish defamation into this area.

The economic background of Latin America also is a contributory factor to anti-Jewish feeling. Though the countries of the southern continent differ from one another in their rate of growth and level of development, they all share the same tragic legacy which goes back to the time of the Spanish *conquistadores*. The explorer-conquerors divided the wealth of the new lands among themselves and created a situation where the

259

privileged class flaunts its wealth and lives in luxurious villas in close proximity to the masses who dwell in squalor and want, sheltered by tin huts, patched and pasted together with lime. The land and natural resources of the Latin American countries still lie in the hands of a small privileged group whose wealth is constantly growing at the expense of the poor. This leads to discontent and constant political unrest and instability. If, after a revolution (a far from uncommon occurrence), a new government seriously wishes to do something for the masses, it has to contend with the privileged class which uses the army as its instrument.

The continent of South America cannot be compared to its northern neighbor which welcomed political and religious refugees from a variety of countries, and whose new citizens were imbued with the concept of building a better and more just society. As Lleras Camargo, a statesman and journalist who served as President of Colombia and as President of the Organization of American States noted: "The Latin American countries were originally Spanish colonies under the control of Spanish law and religion; they were in effect isolated geographically from the rest of the world and even from each other, since travel from one country to another was forbidden; trade was permitted only with the mother country; immigration was strictly controlled by Spain; all government administrative offices were staffed by Spaniards who imposed censorship modelled on Spanish policy. It is only recently, since the world has opened up through television and other mass media, and through ease of travel, that the Latin American has become aware of the unhealthy conditions in his own home, where he has no food for his belly, though his fellow-citizens may live in opulent luxury."

At a United Nations Food and Agriculture Organization conference held at Viña del Mar in Chile, it was pointed out that there are twenty million people in South America who do not get enough to eat and are constantly on the verge of hunger. The backwardness of farming methods conspires with the explosive growth of population, a growth based on the highest birthrate in the world. The conference came to the conclusion that by the end of the century the continent will have 300 million inhabitants more than it does now, and that in order to avoid tragic consequences the countries must carry out basic land reform. Tens of millions of workers must be given land, for in almost all of South and Central America the soil is in the hands of the latifundists— in the feudal pattern of the Middle Ages—and the largest part of the land remains untilled.

While vast stretches of soil remain uncultivated, many Latin American states purchase food from the U.S.A. totalling millions of dollars. The Alliance for Progress program expressly states that the countries must create some domestic order, carry out land reform, and collect taxes in full. In some of these countries the non-payment of taxes is not considered a criminal offense, and millionaires find it easy to evade the payment of taxes to which the government would normally look for its budget. In addition many wealthy people transfer much of their wealth abroad, and "live it up" in their luxury-villas and hotels in Madrid, while the worker in the Brazilian coffee plantation gets a starvation wage for his daily toil. In many countries the weekly wage of a worker is less than the daily wage received by an unskilled worker in the United States or Canada.

Some time ago, Eugenio Chang Rodriguez, a Peruvian, and professor of Latin American Civilization at New York University, spoke to the Overseas Press Club on the subject of "The Hemisphere's Eleventh Hour." He issued a warning in anticipation of the peril awaiting the continent now that Castroism has come to Cuba. Quite aside from his Communism, Castro is regarded by the hungry masses as a second liberator of Latin America. The regimes in power also welcome his presence, for they use it as a lever to press further millions from Uncle Sam. As the deposed parlor-Communist President of Brazil, Joao Goulart, put it: "Castro's confiscation of American property is no serious offense." Goulart's own brother-in-law, the Governor of the Rio Grande do Sul province, made a start in expropriating American installations.

It is somewhat easier to understand the reasons for anti-Semitism in South America, when one realizes that it bears a relationship to the envy of the foreigner who achieves quick success. The indigenous inhabitant of South America is not a man of great ambition; moreover, the continent greatly suffers from illiteracy. In addition there is the factor of the tropical climate which robs one of initiative. The foreigner, on the other hand, is often educated and generally motivated. He is not affected by the climate in his early years as much as are those who have been there for generations.

As it happens, with the exception of those countries with a large German population, anti-Semitism has declined in South America. This is due mainly to the counter-attack and the educational campaign carried out by the Jews against the anti-Jewish poison. The envy of the foreigner dates back to the beginning of European immigration, when the Jewish settlements consisted of raw, green immigrants who did not know the language of the new land, and who did not have the means or opportunity to refute the accusations and libels. In one country, the Jews hired a Spanish writer to reply to the anti-Semitic accusations that began to appear daily in the press, only to discover later that the accuser and the defender had made a partnership between themselves: they divided the payment that the defender received from the Jews.

Today the matter is entirely different. There is not a single Jewish settlement in Latin America that does not possess a Jewish intelligentsia. Among the sons and daughters of former immigrants there are professionals who occupy important positions in public life, and second and third generation Jews head the Jewish organizations in some countries today.

The current generation of Latin American Jewry does not permit intimidation, and reacts with pride and dignity against any attack on Jews. Moreover, this generation possesses the intelligence and education to deal properly with the defamations that are circulated.

The American Jewish Committee maintains close contact with the national Jewish organizations in these countries and has been concerned with anti-Semitic manifestations there since its program was launched 20 years ago when two sister organizations were established in Latin America: the Instituto Argentino de Cultura e Informacion in 1948, and the Instituto Brasileiro de Cultura e Devulgacao, in 1958. The bonds of friendship and cooperation which had been developed during the previous decade were strengthened by the first visit of an AJC delegation to Argentina, Brazil, Chile and Peru, at the invitation of the leading Jewish institutions.

In 1964 it was clear that the time was ripe for further commitments. Many major changes had taken place in the Jewish communities and in the general situation, especially in Argentina, which became a center of anti-Jewish propaganda, terror tactics, and outright violence provoked by neo-Fascists, former Nazis and Arab League agents. Large quantities of anti-Semitic literature, published in Argentina, were destributed throughout the continent. The AJC created a Latin American Community Service Program, conducted jointly with local groups to combat anti-Semitic propaganda. It has pioneered research projects on anti-Semitism, self-studies within the Jewish community, and other sociological research. It has also promoted Christian-Jewish organizations, similar to those in the United States. After gathering data on the activities of anti-Semitic individuals and organizations, determining the origin, contents, appeal, and impact of anti-Semitic literature, it has intervened with appropriate officials in the U.S. and Latin American Governments, as well as with church leaders and intellectuals.

In addition, the AJC offices in Latin America have helped organize, and have worked closely with Christian-Jewish Brotherhoods in Argentina, Brazil, Chile, Peru, Uruguay and Mexico and with other interfaith organizations in those countries. Useful relationships have been developed with church officials to promote revision of their religious textbooks by eliminating invidious references to Jews and Judaism. Printed material has been produced in order to create better understanding and to encourage increased study of Jewish history and Jewish life today, especially among the clergy.

When a committee initiated the building of an "Argentine House" in Israel, Cardinal Antonio Caggiano received a Jewish deputation, and warmly commended the step with the comment that this would help bring about better understanding between Catholic, Protestant and Jew. "We live," he said "in a new era, and must seek a common understanding between men, forgetting the difference that separates them. I am well informed of the accomplishments that Israel has to her credit, and I hope to be there shortly." He expressed the wish to be the first member named to the committee.

In the middle of the heated Eichmann trial, when an anti-Semitic wave swept through the land under the pretext that Jews violated Argentinian sovereignty by the capture of the Jewish mass-murderer on Argentinian soil, and by taking him to Israel, Cardinal Caggiano received a Jewish delegation that came to award him a certificate of the Golden Book of the Jewish National Fund. After thanking the Jewish representatives for the honor bestowed upon him, the cardinal declared: "More than once have I let my voice be heard against any appearance of Jew hatred. Unfortunately there remains in our country roots of a dangerous growth that is foreign to us, the Argentinian nation, and which was planted by strangers. Jews and Christians," the cardinal continued, "should stand today united against the common danger. Hitler annihilated six million Jews, and the Communists have now taken over their methods. May God protect us from seeing among us the disgrace of Jewish persecution. Our Argentinian history is clear of race persecution and suppression."

When the Buenos Aires Friends of the Hebrew University celebrated the fortieth anniversary of that institution, Dr. Adolfo Lanus, one of the editors of *La Nacion,* the largest and most influential newspaper in Latin America, quoted Disraeli in his speech: "The vineyards of the Jews have been destroyed but the Jews continue to observe the celebrations of all the festivities that are rooted in the soil of Israel in order to be able to enjoy their vineyards once more. The Jews, dispersed and spread throughout the world, have maintained their link with their ancestral land. Fifty years after Disraeli made this prophecy the Hebrew University was founded in Jerusalem. The hope of the Jews became a reality, which in time becomes more and more attractive. All this is a result of the perseverance and determination of the Jewish people which has succeeded in casting off destruction and attack in the long path of exile."

The democratic Republic of Uruguay has distinguished itself in its action against the spread of the anti-Jewish bacilli by the Argentine Tacuarists. It is appropriate to report something that appeared in a Montevideo newspaper, *La Accion*, in commemoration of the Warsaw Ghetto uprising. The caption read: "The Jewish People Raise the Banner of Hope on the Martyrdom of Warsaw Ghetto." Under this was a three-column picture of a Nazi trooper aiming his gun from behind into the neck of a Jewish mother with a child in her arms. The caption to this read: "Murder—A Soldier of Nazism Against a Family." A second article bore the title, "The Immortal Epic of Despair and Heroism," and tells the story of the ghetto revolt, including the number of Jews killed by the Nazis. Another column called "Symbol of the Ghetto," recounts the messages and telegrams sent abroad by the ghetto fighters which went unanswered. In another section, across a whole page, there is a montage with a figure in the background of a pregnant Jewish woman standing on the ruins of the Ghetto of Warsaw and a line beneath: "On the Ruins of the Ghetto Hear the Beat of a New Life in the Womb."

During the visit of the President of Israel, Zalman Shazar, to Uruguay, the Catholic newspaper *El Bien Publico* had the following headline on its first page: "Under the Rainy Sky—the Sun of Sympathy." Also, in Uruguay, a technical school was named "Israel;" an Albert Einstein monument was erected in the finest park in Montevideo; and a street in the capital city was given the name "Estado de Israel."

Immediately after an anti-Israel resolution was passed at the Tricontinental Conference in Havana calling for the breaking off of relations with Israel, her exclusion from all international organizations, and condemnation of the Zionist movement and the state of Israel as tools of the imperialistas, Uruguay—true to its democratic spirit—issued a sharp protest, stating that she recognized the right of the Jewish people to its homeland, that Israel is not a tool of imperialism; denounced the Havana resolution as deceitful propaganda.

In Santiago de Chile representatives of the Senate and Chamber of Commerce attended the celebration of Israel Independence Day. In Rio de Janeiro the former President, Joselino Kubitchek, attended the memorial service for the heroes of the Warsaw Ghetto. In Chile, Cardinal Silva Henriquez, who is also Archbishop of Santiago, visited the B'nai Israel Synagogue and delivered a speech on religious tolerance and respect for the individual.

The Chilean delegation to the Tricontinental Conference in Havana was led by Senator Salvador Allende, a well known leader of the leftist, Communist Socialist Popular Front Alliance called, *Frente Revolucionario de Accion Popular*. He has twice been candidate for the Chilean presidency. On his return to Santiago, Senator Allende denied that the Chilean delegation had voted for the anti-Israel resolution, and in a letter to the Jewish Representative Committee he noted that although his movement was not always in agreement with the policy of the Israel government, it was in full sympathy with the State of Israel and with the Jewish people. The socialist newspaper, *Ultima Hora,* came out sharply against the Havana resolution as a measure aimed against a people who had been the chief victims of the greatest, most murderous brutality in all history.

Chile, it should be noted, is an important Arab center in Latin America. Its Arab colony controls important business enterprises and spends large sums in political activity. In Santiago the first Arab Congress in South America was held, and it was there that an Arab Central Bureau for the Liberation of Palestine was set up.

The Bolivian Foreign Minister, Colonel Joaquin Amaya, on a visit to Israel, expressed his opposition to any religious or racial discrimination, and stressed that all international conflicts should be resolved by direct negotiation which should fully respect the independence and sovereignty of all states. "Bolivia," he said, "is a land without access to the sea. She, therefore, is keenly appreciative of the struggle Israel is carrying on for her historic recognition." He also mentioned the important work of the Israeli *Nahal* groups in Bolivia.

A Bolivian poetess, Yolanda Bedregal, has written a poem entitled, "Jerusalem" which has the warm longing and nostalgia one would associate with a Jewish poetess.

Brazil recently was host to a conference of Latin American intellectuals protesting the discrimination against Jews in the Soviet Union. The delegates accepted a resolution demanding that the USSR give its Jews the same cultural and religious rights it accords other minorities.

This great improvement in Jewish-Christian relations does not mean that there are no anti-Semitic incidents from time to time. These unsavory episodes are incited by the most benighted reactionaries, egged on by anti-Jewish, pro-Arab and neo-Nazi propaganda, and by a malcontent element which is envious of Jewish property. It must also be borne in mind that the inhabitants bear no special affection for foreigners, in general, and that many of these countries suffer from an inferiority complex which explodes into violence when it is subjected to propaganda and incitement. This tactic is exploited by both sides, the chauvinist-nationalists, and the Communists, who on Moscow's order are now cooperating with the former.

JEWISH CONTRIBUTIONS TO LATIN AMERICA

The contribution made by the Jews to the development of the countries of South America dates back to the discovery of the New World, when the Marranos played an important role in the development of new areas. It was they who discovered and exploited the hidden wealth in minerals, developed sugar plantations, constructed ships and railways.

Again, after the demise of the Inquisition, when the Jews began to return to South America, they participated in the struggles for liberation of the Latin American states. The Marquis Alejandro Maria Aguado (1784-1842), a Jewish financier and military man, assisted the liberator San Martin in his struggle against the tyranny of Spain. A second Jew, Mordecai Ricardo, was a close friend of Simon Bolivar. Luis Brie took part in an expedition against the despot General Rossas in Argentina. Alejandro Bernheim was an aide to the Argentine liberal, Domingo Faustino Sarmiento.

Later, when Jewish immigration increased, the Jewish contribution to the develpoment of commerce, industry, finance, science and other fields rose correspondingly. From time to time leading statesmen have expressed praise and admiration for the Jewish contribution to their countries. It is worth noting some of these statements:

When the late Salomon Zack, a Jewish millionaire of Santiago, established a Zack Foundation for higher education in Chile, a special session was held of the Chamber of Deputies and Senate. Warm words of appreciation were expressed on the contribution made by the man who started as an impoverished boy from Czarist Russia, acquired his fortune through his own energy and initiative and showed his appreciation to the country which enabled him to do so.

In Santiago there is a Council of Jewish Women which is concerned with the welfare of the needy working population and undernourished children. These women are called by the children *Las Mamasitas Judias* (the Jewish Mothers), and in performing their humanitarian task they wear a yellow Star of David on their sleeves. The Hitlerite badge of shame had been transformed into a sign of Jewish pride and virtue. The president of the Republic conveyed his gratitude to the women's group, and thereby paid tribute to the entire Jewish community. The women visit the slum areas, register the names of the underfed children, and give them supplementary food and vitamins. They also provide spiritual food, distributing books and journals among the people at no charge.

The members of a Jewish youth group known as Maccabee, erected a school to aid the local government in its campaign against illiteracy. This move was greeted with praise and appreciation in Chilean circles.

In Sao Paulo an organization of Jewish women volunteers called Ofidas has as its main function the care of underpriviledged children. Its efficient administration, and the competence and devotion of its medical, technical and social workers earned it such respect that several Catholic organizations requested Ofidas to take the lead in establishing the first Council of Social Agencies in Brazil. This is now in successful operation. As with other Jewish organizations in Sao Paulo, Ofidas does not confine its services to Jewish children and their families, nor does it keep records of the races and faiths of its clients, but the percentage of non-Jews being serviced is believed to be at least half.

In Montevideo the Jewish community built a school for the general community which bears the name Estado Israel.

In the tiny community of Costa Rica the Jews saved a school which had to close. In recognition of this, the school's name, which for forty years had been called *Escuela Labrador de San Antonio de Coronado,* was changed to *Estado de Israel.*

In Panama the Jews organized a special blood bank for the local hospital.

In Mexico the Jews erected a magnificent school, named it after Albert Einstein, and donated it to the city of Guadalajara.

In the Mexican capital a second Albert Einstein school was erected for the general public by the Jewish community at a cost of four million pesos. This institution is a vocational high school with an enrollment of 3,000 Mexican pupils. The Jewish community contributes an annual subsidy for its maintenance.

A Jewish immigrant, Elias Sourasky, a native of Bialystok, who has had a successful career in finance and is now the owner of important financial institutions, contributed ten million pesos for scientific research in response to the call of the Mexican government to aid the country's educational system. Only one other bank followed his example. The Mexican press featured the news prominently, but only one newspaper commented on his being a Jewish financier. Sourasky also endowed Jewish education in Mexico by building a home for the Tarbut school in the name of his late father, Yaakov. He has also established a Literary Prize in the amount of 150,000 pesos, given each year to outstanding Mexican poets, writers, artists and historians who have distinguished themselves in their fields. The Mexican President, Ordez

Diaz, has recently awarded the highest order of the "Aztec Eagle" to Mr. Sourasky in recognition of his contribution to Mexican culture and education.

In the small community of Bolivia, where Jews had suffered greatly from anti-Semitic incitement and baiting, the Jewish community built a pavilion in Ciudad del Nino (Boy's Town). The chief of the military junta appeared at the dedication with his cabinet and expressed the gratification of the Bolivian people. He and the Minister of Labor stressed the Jewish contribution to the development of Bolivia.

On Israel's Independence Day, the Jewish community of Ecuador gave a donation of $30,000 to the *Patronato del Nino* (Child Welfare). A delegation headed by the Israeli Consul, and the president of the *Asociacion de Beneficencia Israelita*, were welcomed by the members of the Junta Militar and the Ladies Committee of the Patronate in the presence of the Chief of Protocol.

San Marcos, the oldest university in the Americas (in Peru), honored Marcos Perlman, a Jewish immigrant from Bessarabia, by awarding him a doctorate, *honoris causa,* for his achievements and service to his adopted country. Like all immigrants Marcos Perelman started with nothing, except the labor of his hands. Today he is president of *Banco del Progreso,* has founded an insurance company *La Universal,* and has organized a firm which, with the help of the Alliance for Progress, has built hundreds of dwellings for junior officials, middle class persons and civil servants. He is one of Peru's wealthiest millionaires. He has served several times as chairman of the United Jewish Appeal and has built an assembly hall for the Jewish school.

A second Jewish immigrant, Michael Rodzinsky from Semiaticz near Bialystok, has constructed a large woolen goods factory in Lima which employs thousands of Peruvians. He was president of the Lima Jewish community, and a member of the World Council of the Mapai party. He erected a woolen goods factory in Afula in Israel.

There is no doubt that the rise of Israel, and the heroic victories of the Haganah have had a favorable effect on the Latin American attitude towards the Jews. The groundwork was well prepared by two men who might be called "missionaries." These men undertook to explain to the South American public that the Israelis and the Judios were one and the same. Moshe Tov created the Pro-Palestine Committee, prior to the United Nations vote, and Benno Weiser, now the Israeli Consul in Santo Domingo, continued the task. Israel Friendship committees now exist in almost every country in Latin America, and comprise intellectuals and government personnel, including some cabinet ministers. The local press rarely lets an event involving Israel pass without some sympathetic comment. A whole series of articles in the South American press have conveyed positive comments about Israel.

Israeli specialists are now found in numerous countries, assisting the governments in executing various projects. Young men and women are sent to Israel where they learn to be agronomists and technicians. A Shalom Club in Lima was founded by young Peruvians who had been trained in Israel in various aspects of reconstruction for underdeveloped countries. A correspondent of an Israeli newspaper, while in Peru, attended the club's opening and wrote that the speeches were reminiscent of the old days of pioneer Zionism! The founders of the club declared that their experiences in the Jewish state, and the atmosphere which they had absorbed had given them new inspiration and new insight into how to go about the reconstruction of their own land.

In Mexico, Israeli specialists are instructing the natives how to double the fish catch in the lakes by using certain new methods. In Venezuela, Israeli agronomists are teaching peasants the newest methods of agriculture. In the remote areas of Brazil, Israelis are demonstrating to the peasants how to transform neglected and arid wastes into flourishing fields. The area bordering Chile and Peru, which suffers from permanent drought, was visited by Israeli technicians who taught the peasants how to irrigate the land according to the latest techniques. Similar instruction was given to Ecuador. Israel is sending agricultural scientists to Argentina to give assistance to the farmers in the northern province adjoining the border of Chile.

Israel also carries on a cultural exchange with these countries. Cabinet ministers, university professors, writers and intellectuals

271

visit Israel from time to time and return expressing admiration for the many great achievements in the brief period of Israel's existence. In appreciation the Peruvian navy despatched the ship *La Independencia* to Israel. The sailors themselves planted trees on Jewish National Fund land and the naval chaplain blessed the soil of Israel, and implored the Almighty to lend strength to the hands that till the sacred earth and turn it into blossoming fields and gardens. The scroll, presented to the sailors by the State of Israel, has been given a place of honor in the ship.

Andreas Townsend Escurra, editor of the daily *La Tribuna* in Lima, author of a book about the Chilean historian, Jose Toribio Medina who wrote volumes on the Inquisition in the New World, visited Israel and wrote *Shalom Israel* on his impressions and observations. He had high praise for the Jewish State.

CHAPTER XXII.

Encounters with Descendants of the Marranos in Latin America

My first personal contact with the descendants of the Marranos was in the remote townships of Brazil. One of them was characteristically named Santa Maria. According to various sources, all the different "Santos" and "Mesias" are indications of Jewish origin. The Jews there told me that in the homes of the most primitive inhabitants they found traces of Judaism. Sometimes it was an old Mizrach, with half-obliterated Hebrew lettering; other times, a Menorah.

An old Brazilian woman, in a tiny village in the province of Rio Grande do Sul, told me that once a year—at the end of the summer—her father would wrap himself for an entire day in a white sheet with black stripes, would not touch food all day, and would read various prayers out of an old book. Another family had inherited the tradition of spreading a white tablecloth on the table every Friday night, and they would light candles, though they did not know why they did this. A professor in a town in the province of Parana would often come to Jewish gatherings and talk about Jewish customs and prayers. Once, he whispered to me secretly that he came from Jewish ancestry.

In Lima, I was told that when Dr. Michael Simon was the Israeli Ambassador, he received a letter from a women's committee raising funds for the Church of the Holy Virgin in Sedelen, asking him for a contribution. The women wrote that they were descendants of Portuguese Jews who had fled to Peru when the Portuguese conquered Pernambuco from the Dutch. Sedelen, a town with seven thousand inhabitants, about a hundred miles from Lima, has among its present residents some who bear the names of their Marrano ancestors: Perez, Espinoza, Castro, Prado, Medina, Alcalay and Dagon.

There is a hamlet in Peru named Todos Santos (All Saints). The women there light candles on Friday night in the cellar. They are devout Catholics, and don't know why they do it, but it is a custom passed on from generation to generation.

In Montero I was told the Mayor's name is Roca-Sela, the same word, (stone) in Spanish and Hebrew. The name of the Mayor of Iquitos, the last town near the Brazilian border by the River Amazon, was Ben-Zakon.

In a suburb of Mexico City, I met a community of the descendants of Marranos. They have their own community called, Kehilla Kedosha B'nai Elokim (The Holy Congregation of the Sons of God). It is situated in Calle Caruso, a poor slum street in a working-class district. Both sides of the street are lined with stalls from which fruit, vegetables, and other things are sold. The stallholders shout their wares noisily. At the Sabbath service in the synagogue, there were about thirty men and women bearing definite Indian features.

Sabbath service was conducted in Spanish by the leader of the community, Señor Baltazar Laureano Ramirez, a lawyer. The worshippers were attentive and devout. Every now and then I heard a Hebrew word interposed in the Spanish service. When the Scrolls were taken from the Ark, the congregation sang a prayer, and I distinctly heard the words, *Shema Yisroel*. One of the tourists was given the honor of reading the Torah, and each of us was called up to recite the Torah blessings.

After the service I had a talk with Señor Ramirez. He told me: "Our congregation is not the only one. There are about three thousand of our people, Judios-Mexicanos, in Mexico, scattered throughout the country. There are many who openly declare themselves Jews, and a large number who have not embraced the Jewish faith officially, though they know they are Jews. Most of them are intermarried with the Mexican population."

I asked how they know they are Jews. In reply Señor Ramirez

related to me the history of these Judios-Mexicanos. When Hernando Cortes discovered Mexico there were Marranos in his expedition, among them Hernando Alonso. He was afterwards condemned by the Inquisition to be burned at the stake, when it was found that he was practicing Judaism secretly. In 1579, King Ferdinand ordered Luis de Carvajal to proceed to Mexico with a fleet to put down a revolt of the natives in the Tampico area. Luis de Carvajal jumped at the chance. Himself a secret Jew, it gave him the opportunity of taking a number of secret Jews with him in his expedition. The king appointed him Governor of the Province and granted him the privilege of colonizing a stretch of 138 square kilometers in the region of Nuevo Leon.

The ground was fertile. It produced a rich crop, and the settlers were optimistic. But the agents of the Inquisition became suspicious. They spied on the Governor and discovered that he was secretly practicing Judaism. He was arrested and accused of keeping the Sabbath, eating *matzoth* during Passover, and fasting on Yom Kippur. He was released when he promised to do penance: to fast every Friday and to say the *Ave Maria* fifty times a day. He was arrested a second time on the same accusation as before. In February 1590, the Inquisition Tribunal condemned him and his family to be burned at the stake, and all their possessions confiscated.

After this incident, the secret Jews fled from Pachuca, Tampico, and other places, to Monterrey, where they settled among the Indians and changed their names. But the Inquisition followed them. Out of fear, many secret Jews attended mass, and some joined the Catholic Church, though they still practiced Judaism in secret.

"You must have noticed," said Señor Ramirez," that some of our members in the congregation have Indian features. Many Indian slaves adopted the religion of their Jewish masters, and intermarried."

Even after the Inquisition was abolished, in 1821, when Mexico gained her independence, they were still afraid to say they were Jews. It was only in later years that some who had preserved their Jewish customs from generation to generation, began to practice Judaism openly. "Our community," said Señor Ramirez, "was organized in 1917."

In Venta Prieta, a typical Mexican village, sixty miles from the capital, in the Province of Hidalgo, I visited another community of descendants of the Marranos. When I got out of my car I found a crowd of children playing under the hot Mexican sun. It was during the school holidays. As soon as the children saw the American with his camera, they stopped playing. The shouting stopped; all eyes were turned on me.

"*Muchachos,*" I began in Spanish, "can anyone of you show me where Señor Enrique Tellez lives?"

Some friends in Mexico City had given me his name and told me that he was the head of the Jewish Community.

"*Yo, Yo!*" Hands shot up all round me, and the children cried, "I know! I know!" And the whole crowd conducted me along the primitive road to Señor Enrique Tellez's house.

"Are you a *Judio?*" I asked one of the children.

"*Si, Señor!*" he answered.

"And you?" I asked another.

All around me the children were trying to outshout each other. "I am a *Judio!*"

"When I grow up," one of the children nearest to me said, "I shall go to Israel."

"And I'm going to New York," cried another, "to study in the Seminary, and become a *Rabino.*"

Señor Tellez's little house was neat and clean, with a pleasant garden around it. He was expecting me. The news had reached him that an American had come to the village and wanted to see him. He took me into a nicely furnished sitting room. A girl of about 18 welcomed me with "*Shalom.*" A neighbor came in soon after, and Señor Tellez said, "He is also a *Judio.*"

I explained who I was and what I had come about. When Señor Tellez heard that I was a journalist he said that many *periodistas* (journalists) and rabbis had been there before. He still remembered some of their names.

I stood looking at an old *Mizrach* on the wall—it showed

Moses with the Tablets of the Law. Another daughter came in, and offered me a cold drink.

"How many *Judios* live here?" I asked Señor Tellez.

"A hundred," he answered.

About seventy years ago, he said, a group of Mexican *Judios* had lived in Zamora. It infuriated the Catholic population, and there was a pogrom. His grandfather was ordered to become a Catholic. When he refused they put him into the skin of a cow and set it on fire. He died in great agony. Then all the *Judios* fled and came to this place, which was then uninhabited, and built this village.

An old woman who came to Señor Tellez's house to see the guest said to me: "We are *Judios*. My father took over his Judaism from his father, and my grandfather from his father, and so back for generations." They gave me a list of names of people who had at various times visited their village, among them Egon Edwin Kisch, the Czechoslovakian novelist and journalist, and the historian Dr. Raphael Patai, who had conducted a number of psychological tests among the inhabitants of Venta Prieta.

"We don't need any help from our brother Jews," I was told. "We only want to have contact with them. Not to be isolated."

Señor Enrique Tellez told me an interesting story how he met a Jew in Pachuca, not far from Venta Prieto. An immigrant had settled in Pachuca, and opened a store. Many Indians from the neighboring villages were among his customers. One day an Indian who owed him money brought him a young pig to settle the debt.

Then one day Señor Tellez came from Venta Prieto to Pachuca, and walked into Factor's shop to buy some food. Factor offered him the pig, and when he refused to take it as a gift Factor wanted to know why.

"Because my religion forbids it."

"Your religion? What is your religion?"

"I am a *Judio*."

"I am also a *Judio*," Señor Factor cried, surprised and delighted.

And thus, in the remote Mexican town of Pachuca, in the year

1910, the two Jews, Factor and Tellez, exchanged a Jewish greeting: *Sholom aleichem.*

Their Scrolls of the Law and their Hebrew prayer books were provided by Reform Rabbis who had been taking a great deal of interest in them. They had even sent a Reform Rabbi to the town. The Mitzvah Corps, the Youth Movement of the Union of Hebrew Congregations in U. S., recently built a new Community Center in Venta Prieta, and repainted the adjoining old synagogue.

They observe Yom Kippur (the Day of Atonement) and fast the whole day, the same on Tishah B'av (nine days in the month of Av). Rosh Hashanah is to them the most important holiday. Kashruth is strongly observed. On Pesach they eat *matzot,* and slaughter is carried out strictly according to Jewish ritual law. Their children and grandchildren are given Hebrew names.

Herschl Filler, the *mohel* of the ultra-Orthodox congregation, Etz Chaim Synagogue, told me that he circumcized in Venta Prieta over thirty children and adults. Three of the boys settled in Israel, one studies in a Yeshiva in the United States, and one of them married a Jewish girl from Mexico City.

The most difficut problem they have is in observing the Sabbath rest. Most of them are unskilled workers or government employees and must work on Saturdays, the same as all Mexicans do. Every Saturday morning services are conducted by their rabbi, an immigrant from Guatemala, who came there a few years ago and is employed on weekdays in the nearby town, Pachuca. After the services they go to work.

Their synagogue, built several years ago, is a small, modest structure, externally and internally decorated with a seven candle menora, a candelabra, a Holy Ark with a Sefer Torah, and a pulpit with a large Star of David.

In answer to my question if there are mixed marriages, the answer was that there are also mixed marriages among Jews in Mexico, whom they accuse of refusing to intermarry with them.

When Rabbi Shlomo Goren, Chief Rabbi of the Israeli Army, visited Venta Prieta with Mr. Seymour Liebman, he was given a royal reception. The Rabbi handed down a decision that in order to be fully committed as Jews they must first go through the process of formal admission to Judaism. Mr. Seymour Liebman, a historian who wrote a book about the Mexican Inquisition, does not believe that the Judios Mexicanos are descendants of the Marranos. He came to the conclusion that they are a religious sect practising Christianity and Judaism. He proves that even some of their spiritual leaders are former leaders of another sect called, Iglesia de Dios.

From my personal experience with the present day Marranos in Portugal and in a number of Latin American countries, I must say that their method of observance, and the content of their prayers, though obviously based on some sort of Jewish foundation, results in a strange blend of Christianity and Judaism. Time and lack of contact with other Jews has eroded or erased all Jewish distinctiveness.

There are some Indian tribes in Latin America today where the women go to church on Friday evenings, and light candles before the images of the saints. Their Catholic sisters do not practice this custom on Friday evenings. The custom arose when Marrano women, in fear of the Inquisition, chose to light their Sabbath candles in the security of the church, where it would appear to be an act of devotion to the saints. As they lighted the candles the women would whisper the Jewish blessing over the candles. After many centuries they still light their saints' candles on Friday night, but have entirely forgotten the original motive.

The late Professor Nahum Slouzsch has written about this in connection with his own experiences among Marranos in a remote part of Portugal. He observed that on a certain day in the fall, the women assemble out-of-doors, holding pieces of pork in their hands. This custom also arose as a means of misleading the Inquisition agents. While these "good Catholics" were out-of-doors the men were able to recite the *Kol Nidre* down in the cellars. Here, too, the purpose was forgotten, after many years, and the pork was no longer symbolic, but was eaten as food.

In Arica, a small out of the way port in Chile, a Jewish factory owner told me that some of the women refuse to work on the Sabbath; they stop work on Friday afternoon. I spoke to these women, and found that they come from an Indian township called, Chimpay, in the Patagonian Andes, where there are many descendants of the Marranos. They have openly declared themselves Jews, and have left the Catholic Church in a body. Some of them make the journey to Santiago, the Chilean capital, to live among Jews and learn more about Judaism from them.

In a nearby township, the head of the Marrano community married a Jewish woman whose husband had divorced her. She came from an Ashkenazic family. The community referred to Jewish law and argued that the leader of the community was a Priest—a *kohen;* and a *kohen* must not marry a divorced woman. They brought down a Jewish authority from Santiago, but he explained that a man does not become a *kohen* through his position; that a *kohen* must be (born) a descendant of the Sons of Aaron— and that their leader was not a real *kohen.* Many among the Marrano community were still dissastified, and a split developed. The group which was not reconciled and refused to accept the leader, were more Jewishly oriented, while the section that accepted him more nationalistically inclined. Some of its young people have emigrated to Israel.

In Argentina, I visited a Marrano group near Carlos Speggazene, who also came from the Indian township, Chimpay. The head of this group, Luis Bravo, told me that they keep the Sabbath and observe Jewish customs. He concluded that they are descended from a group of Jews who had lived in Lima, and had fled from there in the 16th century, to escape the Inquisition. He pointed out that they have also passed on some Jewish customs to the Indians who worked for them.

After the establishment of the Jewish State in Israel, Señor Bravo reported that his group has had a great desire to settle in the Jewish land. They went to Buenos Aires, visited the Israeli Consul, and asked to be sent to Israel. He said it wasn't such an easy matter. Then they visited the Rabbinate in Buenos Aires, and the rabbis explained that a mass conversion to Judaism was not practical for several reasons. They didn't want to return home, so they established themselves near the township of Carlos Speggazene, and started a farm there. The Rabbinate told them that before they could have a mass conversion to Judaism they must learn more about the Jewish religion. And that is difficult, because few of them can read.

The Israel-Argentine Cultural Institute engaged a Hebrew teacher for them. For two years the teacher taught them to read Hebrew, and all about Jewish customs. When the Rabbinate finally agreed to accept them as proselytes, they received the news with joy and thanksgiving. They hope to settle in Israel.

One of the most interesting groups of Marrano descendants I met lived in the district of Camino de Las Flores (Road of Flowers), about sixty kilometres from Buenos Aires, Argentina. I spent Passover with them.

They, too, had come to Buenos Aires hoping to emigrate to Israel. When their plans were delayed, they bought some land cheaply from the Argentine Government, built rough dwellings, and live a kind of collective *kibbutz* life there.

This group, which calls itself, Hijos de Sion (Sons of Zion), has been in contact with the mainstream of Jewry for more than forty years. Originally from south Chile, the group appeared at a Chilean Zionist Conference in Santiago in 1919, and asked for recognition as Jews. They spoke about *Eretz Yisrael* with love and enthusiasm, and since then they have paid their *shekel*, raised funds for the Jewish National Fund, and been represented at Zionist conferences.

Their main center is in Temuco, and Cuenco, in Southern Chile, but they are also to be found in other places throughout the country. When Chile granted recognition to other religions beside Catholicism, they established contact with other Jewish groups. In Cuenco their community is called, Iglesia Israelita (Israelite Church). They live apart from the rest of the population, marry among themselves, and follow certain Jewish practices and rites which, like other crypto-Jewish sects, are distorted forms, mixed with Catholic concept and ceremony.

I was welcomed upon my arrival at Camino de las Flores by a middle-aged man with a short, trim beard. He wore a small Star of David in his lapel. He said, *"Shalom hermanos,"* and explained that he had been sent to take me and my wife to the settlement. He took our bags, and after we had walked for about an hour we reached the village of Hijos de Sion. It was the afternoon of the eve of Passover.

The settlement with its low barracks looked like an Israeli *ma'abara*. We were met by the community's spiritual mentor, Ruperto Cordova, with a *"shalom hermanos!"* We were taken straight to the synagogue over which flew a blue-white flag with the words, *"B'ruchim Habaim,"* in Hebrew letters.

Ruperto Cordova, a young man with an olive-skin complexion and a pitch-black beard, pointed to the synagogue, "This is where we will have our *Seder* to-night." Then he took us to the house where we were to stay, with Matias Seguro, the wealthiest member of the community. It was the only brick house in the settlement, all the others being roughly built shacks. Our host turned out to be the "scholar" of the group. He used Hebrew phrases in his conversation, and told us that he had led the community's delegates to Zionist conferences. He was a "wealthy" man, because being a mechanic, he earned more than the others.

Both he and his wife were friendly and hospitable, and served us food which had been brought in all the way from Buenos Aires. Two lovely girls, Sulamith and Esther, sang Hebrew songs: *Havenu Shalom Aleichem* (shalom was pronounced, *tchalom,* because Spanish has no "sh" sound), *The Song of the Partisans, Hayom Yom Shabbat, Yehudim Anachnu* and *David Melech Yisrael.*

The synagogue, the biggest and most imposing building in the settlement, had been built by the members themselves. A picture of Herzl, with his words in Hebrew: "If you will it, it is no dream," hung in front. There were also portraits of Weizmann, Ben Zvi and Ben-Gurion, and the words, *"Mo'adim L'Simcha."* The Hebrew School, which bears the name Ben Zvi, is also here, and on the wall is a copy of the letter from the Israeli Ambassador in Buenos Aires which he had sent on behalf of Ben Zvi, the late past President of Israel, expressing appreciation for having the school named after him.

The men are all laborers, employed only in those factories nearby where they do not have to work on the Sabbath. They keep all the Jewish feasts and fasts, and refrain from work all through the Passover week and the Succoth week, doing no work in the intermediate days, *Chol Hamo'ed.* On Shavuoth they observe the festival of the first fruits in the biblical manner. They conduct the Passover *Seder* by acting out the Exodus from Egypt, carrying their packs on their backs, and symbolically "dividing the Red Sea."

I chatted with some of the people. "How do you know you are *Judios*," I asked.

"Our fathers passed it down to us, and they in turn had it from our grandparents. They had received it from our great grandparents, and so it came down from one generation to another. We recognized each other by noting who it was fasted on Yom Kippur or rested on the Sabbath or carried out other Jewish customs."

When I returned to my lodging, my hostess had already lighted her candles before going to the synagogue, where everybody would attend the communal *Seder.* Noticing that there was only one bedroom and one bed, I asked where we would sleep. Señor Seguro's answer was: "No one sleeps on *Seder* night." The prayers and the songs go on all night.

We walked to the *synagogue* in the growing darkness. The glow of many paraffin lamps shone out from the small *ranchos.* A strange feeling came over me; I felt as though I were suddenly back in my *shtetl,* with Jews walking in the dusk to the synagogue.

When we arrived, everybody was already in the synagogue—even women with babies in their arms. Before long, more people came in from outside the settlement, from the neighboring community of Monte Grande, where they have no synagogue. They greeted each other with a kiss on the forehead, saying, *"hermano."* This custom dates back to the Inquisition, when those condemned to death would pass each other on the way to execution and kiss on the brow. The women wore black dresses and white veils. The men and the children were in their best clothes, ready for the festival.

Ruperto Cordova went to the pulpit and recited some prayers in Spanish. I caught the two Hebrew words: *Shema Yisrael.*

Their prayers make mention of belief in Christ, citing the seventh chapter of Isaiah, verse 14: "Therefore the Lord himself shall give you a sign; Behold, a virgin shall conceive, and bear a son, and shall call his name Immanuel."

Another verse is from Micah (5:2): "But thou, Bethlehem Ephratah, though thou be the littlest among the thousands of Judah, yet out of thee shall he come forth unto me that is to be ruler in Israel."

They believe that Jerusalem was destroyed and the Jews were dispersed over the earth for not following Jesus and for asking for his death. This brought about the Exile which lasted until 1917, the year of the Balfour Declaration.

They observe the Sabbath and other Jewish festivals, and have different prayers for each holiday. They refrain from eating pork, and marry only among themselves. In my honor they recited their *Seder* prayers standing, rather than seated.

Here are the words of one of their prayers:

We thank Thee, God, who hast given us the holy Pesach day to rest. Give us a week of prosperity, peace and blessing, fear of Heaven, forgiveness for the sins of the bygone week, peace for the Jewish people, and especially for the Israeli Jews who suffer so much now. May God bring the Redemption closer. May He summon the Jews from all corners of the earth.

When the cantor mentioned the words, "the sins," and asked for forgiveness, the worshippers with their heads bowed, all shouted: "Forgive us! forgive us!" Then the congregation rose and continued to pray with great emotion.

One song consisting of four verses mentions Jesus four times.

(The name Emanuel in Christian terminology is synonymous with Jesus.) Here are some of their songs in translation:

COMFORT MY PEOPLE!

Comfort my people,
Says our God.
For their punishment
Was over long ago.
Unite thyself my people,
Says our God,
Forward without fear!

Chorus

Forward without fear,
    Forward,
March forward, O Israel!
His Ruler is to lead him,
To his fatherland.

Blow the trumpets,
O Daughters of Zion,
The land is free
Free of the tyrant.

Forward—no fear!
Adonai!
He calls us
From Mount Zion.

Hear, O Israel!
Free the aged,
And the child
Of every land.
Go forth and shout:
Forward, without fear!

At the end of the prayer they add this: "If, God, you cannot do it for our sake, do it for the pure and holy blood which Christ shed for our sake."

In response to my later questions, it emerged that there were among them those who were more inclined to Christianity, while others gravitated toward Judaism.

Index

290

* Was lately awarded a governmental citation for his contribution to education in Venezuela.

299

Index